THE POLITICS OF THE EARTH

THE POLITICS OF THE EARTH

Environmental Discourses

Third Edition

....

John S. Dryzek

OXFORD
UNIVERSITY PRESS

OXFORD

UNIVERSITY PRESS

Great Clarendon Street, Oxford, OX2 6DP,
United Kingdom

Oxford University Press is a department of the University of Oxford.
It furthers the University's objective of excellence in research, scholarship,
and education by publishing worldwide. Oxford is a registered trade mark of
Oxford University Press in the UK and in certain other countries

First edition 1997

Second edition 2005

Impression: 2

British Library Cataloguing in Publication Data

Data available

ISBN 978–0–19–969600–0

Printed in Great Britain by Ashford Colour Press Ltd

PREFACE

A lot has happened in the last five decades of environmental affairs. Environmental crisis arrived in the late 1960s, along with dire warnings about global shortages and ecological collapse. Since then, the Earth's population has almost doubled. There have been spectacular nuclear accidents at Chernobyl and Fukushima, and spectacular nonnuclear accidents at Bhopal in India, Prince William Sound in Alaska, and the Gulf of Mexico. Extreme weather events, as predicted by most models of climate change, have become more common, putting New Orleans under water. Green parties have emerged as a significant electoral force, and joined governing coalitions in several countries. Mainstream environmental groups have developed massive memberships. Populist backlashes against environmentalism have flared. Global environmental issues relating to climate change, biodiversity, and ozone layer depletion have come to the fore. We have had World Summits, Earth Days, environmental presidents, ecological sabotage, civil disobedience, legislation and regulation by the bookful, and movements for environmental justice, sustainable development, deep ecology, antiglobalization, "wise use," and climate change denial.

The idea of this book is to make sense of all these developments. I do so by deploying the notion of environmental discourses. A discourse is a shared way of looking at the world. Its adherents will therefore use a particular kind of language when talking about events, which in turn rests on some common definitions, judgments, assumptions, and contentions. There turns out to be rather little in common between (say) partisans of a discourse believing in the unproblematic nature of uncontrolled economic growth and a radical green discourse seeking renewed harmony among humans and between humans and nature. The history of environmental affairs is largely a matter of the history of the discourses I survey, their rise and fall, their interactions and impacts. All these discourses are still with us, and none has fallen by the wayside (which itself says a lot about the increasing complexity of environmental affairs). I will recount their history, and assess their impact, strengths, and weaknesses as ways of dealing with environmental issues.

I have tried to approach these questions from a position of critical detachment, but at the end of the day I do have some strong positions of my own.

I have left an explicit statement of these to the conclusion, under the heading of ecological democracy, though they do put in occasional earlier appearances.

This book began life on September 9, 1994 at 12.45 pm, when Tim Barton of Oxford University Press suggested I write it. Ruth Anderson of Oxford University Press helped guide the second edition, Catherine Page and Martha Bailes this third edition. The world changes. While the basic classification of discourses remains the same as in the second edition, the content of each has undergone significant change.

The deeper life of this project exists in years of environmental discourse with students, scholars, and activists. In Oregon I learned much from Joseph Boland, David Carruthers, Irene Diamond, Dan Goldrich, Jeff Land, Gerry Mackie, Michael McGinnis, Ronald Mitchell, Alan Moore, David Schlosberg, Stuart Shulman, Paul Thiers, and Michael Welsh. In Australia, ecopolitical interlocutors have included Mani Banjade, Mike Bennell, Mark Carden, Peter Christoff, Louise Clery, Weng Dano, Steve Dovers, David Downes, Charlotte Epstein, Robyn Eckersley, Simon Grant, Carolyn Hendriks, Kersty Hobson, Peter Kanowski, Kathryn Kelly, Janette Lindesay, Alex Lo, Nicholas Low, Freya Mathews, Simon Niemeyer, Val Plumwood, Adrianna Semmens, Cassandra Star, Will Steffen, Richard Sylvan, Janna Thompson, Ken Walker, and David Yencken. Elsewhere, correspondents and conversationalists have included Laurie Adkin, Terence Ball, Brendan Barrett, John Barry, Walter Baber, Robert Bartlett, Gary Bryner, Margaret Clark, Tim Clark, Andrew Dobson, Frank Fischer, George González, Robert Goodin, Adolf Gundersen, Garrett Hardin, Bronwyn Hayward, Tim Hayward, Hans-Kristian Hernes, Qingzhi Huan, Christian Hunold, Susan Hunter, Michael Jacobs, Sheila Jasanoff, William Lafferty, Oluf Langhelle, Sang-Hun Lee, James Lester, Hemant Ojha, Stig Toft Madsen, Masatsugu Maruyama, Hiro Matsuno, James Meadowcroft, John Meyer, Soon-Hong Moon, Arne Naess, Richard Norgaard, James O'Connor, Catherine Oelofse, Claus Offe, Robert Paehlke, Thomas Princen, Craig Rimmerman, Dianne Scott, Graham Smith, Clive Spash, Paul Wapner, Albert Weale, Douglas Wilson, Edward Woodhouse, Iris Young, and Oran Young. It has been a pleasure to work with members of the Earth System Governance community, especially Karin Bäckstrand, Frank Biermann, Aarti Gupta, and Ruben Zondervan. I have also learned a lot through my membership of the Science Committee of the International Human Dimensions Program on Global Environmental

Change. The particular shape taken by this book depends a lot on advice from Douglas Torgerson and Maarten Hajer (Maarten once insisted in jest that every book should end with a chapter in which democracy comes to the rescue). I have worked with David Schlosberg on co-editing editions of the companion reader to this book, *Debating the Earth,* and benefited a great deal from his insights and advice. More recently, David and I co-edited *The Oxford Handbook of Climate Change and Society* with Richard Norgaard, I have worked extensively on the global governance of climate change, and especially its discourses, with Hayley Stevenson. Thanks to people such as these, the environmental field is today alive, growing, and the site of some of the most interesting thinking in social science, philosophy, public policy, and practical politics, making a book like this so much easier to write. I would also like to thank readers from around the world who have given me feedback on the previous two editions (even when they didn't get some of the jokes) and suggestions for this one. For research assistance I thank Elaine dos Santos.

In the preface to his classic *Risk Society,* Ulrich Beck says that he wrote most of it overlooking a picturesque lake, and that readers should imagine a lake in the background. I wrote most of the first edition overlooking a garbage dump that is now a park. The second edition was completed in the pleasant surroundings of a dry sclerophyll forest. I suggested that readers should imagine tall eucalyptus trees and the call of parrots in the background—but watch out for bush fires. This third edition is completed in that same forest, which it turns out had much more to fear from bulldozers than fire. One day they will have to go.

J.S.D.
Aranda, Australian Capital Territory, July 2012

NEW TO THIS EDITION

- Expanded and up-to-date coverage of climate change, planetary boundaries, and green growth.
- Reworked material on innovative forms of governance and new kinds of policy instruments.
- Analysis of changing forms of activism, including movements for climate justice, transition towns, and radical summits.
- More extensive discussion of ecological democracy and deliberative systems for achieving it.

CONTENTS

DETAILED CONTENTS

LIST OF BOXES AND FIGURES

Boxes

Figures

PART I

INTRODUCTION

1

Making Sense of Earth's Politics: A Discourse Approach

The changing terms of environmental politics

Over the decades, the politics of the Earth has featured a large and ever-growing range of issues. The early concerns were with pollution, wilderness preservation, population growth, and depletion of natural resources. Over time, these concerns have been joined by worries about energy supply, biodiversity, species extinction, climate change and other disruptions of the Earth system, depletion of the ozone layer in the upper atmosphere, toxic wastes, the protection of whole ecosystems, environmental justice, food safety, and genetically modified organisms. All these issues are interlaced with a range of questions about human livelihood, public attitudes, and our proper relation to other entities on the planet (occasionally even off it). Thus the whole environmental area is home to heated debates and disputes, ranging from the details of the implementation of policy choices in particular localities, to the appropriate construction of responses to global environmental change.

The terms of these debates have changed substantially over time. Consider the following illustrations:

• Once areas of marshy land were called swamps. The only sensible thing to do with swamps was to drain them, so the land could be put to useful purpose. Governments subsidized landowners to drain swamps. Today, we call these same areas wetlands, and governments have passed laws to protect their value in providing habitat for wildlife, stabilization of ecosystems, and absorption of pollutants.

- In the nineteenth century, European colonization moved gradually west-wards in North America. The United States government provided all kinds of incentives to tame the frontier. Today, the land at the edge of European settlement, which used to be called frontier and was there only to be subdued, is now called wilderness, to be treasured and protected.

- Meanwhile, in Australia and New Zealand, European colonization was followed by the establishment of Acclimatisation Societies to introduce European flora and fauna. These societies approached their task in a spirit of altruism and concern for the public good. Today, governments and citizens in these two countries devote massive effort to the protection of native plants, animals, and ecosystems, and to the extermination of exotic imported species that threaten these ecosystems—imports once culti-vated so lovingly by the Acclimatisation Societies.

- After the attacks on the World Trade Center and Pentagon on September 11, 2001, "terrorists" were confirmed hate figures. Radical environmen-talists associated with the Earth Liberation Front were attacked as terror-ists by the US Federal Bureau of Investigation (especially in its 2005–2006 "Operation Backfire"), and received much longer jail sentences than if they had been classified as "vandals" in the eyes of the law. Even before 9/11, activist Jeff Luers was in 2001 sentenced to twenty-two years in prison merely for burning three sports utility vehicles at a dealership in Eugene, Oregon (he was released in 2009). What exactly is "ecoterrorism" if the description apples to someone who wants only to destroy ecologi-cally harmful objects, and not hurt people, still less terrorize them?

- What is a whale? Once whales were regarded as sources of food and other useful products such as oil and baleen. The idea that whales were sentient creatures with a right to flourish free from human interference would have been laughable. Yet this view is now globally dominant to the point whalers can act like an oppressed minority resisting the weight of world opinion.

- What are people? The idea that there is such a thing as "population" is no more than two hundred years old. Population as an aggregate is some-thing to be controlled and managed: that is, it is more than just "peo-ple." Given that once there was no such thing as population, the idea of population as a problem, still less population explosion, could not be con-ceptualized. The Pope, Islamic fundamentalists, and some contemporary anti-environmentalists still resist conceptualizing population in these terms.

- What is the environment? The environment did not exist as a concept anywhere until the 1960s (though concerns with aspects of what we now call the environment, such as open spaces, resource shortages, and pollution do of course predate the 1960s). Today, most countries have environmental legislation and government departments with environmental missions, and environmental problems are at the forefront of public attention.

- What is nature? Some radical environmentalists believe that any area modified by human activity is no longer worth caring about. In Edward Abbey's novel *The Monkey Wrench Gang,* one of the environmental heroes measures road distances in terms of six-packs of beer, and having finished a can throws it out of the window. The litter is irrelevant, as it ends up in places that have already been destroyed by the construction of a road. But then how can nonhuman nature be conceptualized if, as some scientists now claim, we have entered an "Anthropocene" era whose defining feature is that humans shape the entire Earth system? It is fashionable in some circles to speak of "the end of nature."

- What is wilderness? One widely held definition is that wilderness consists of land that remains untouched by human extractive activity. But what about the indigenous peoples who have long populated such areas, and in many cases shaped the landscape? And can there be such a thing as wilderness restoration in lands damaged by industrial and agricultural activity?

- What is climate? Once climate was thought of as average weather. More recently it has been conceptualized as an integrated biogeophysical system highly vulnerable to human interference. Climate change as a concept became so powerful that it looked for a few years in the 2000s to be capable of subsuming just about all environmental concerns.

- What is the Earth? We have long known it is a planet, but the idea that it might be a finite planet with limited capacities to support human life has only received attention since the late 1960s. Not coincidentally, this was when the Earth was first photographed from space. Since the early 1980s, there has also been a sustained attack on the idea that the Earth is in any sense finite.

The moral of these examples is that contests over meaning are ubiquitous, and the way we think about basic concepts concerning the environment can change dramatically over time. The consequences for politics and policies are major. The most basic consequence (to which the last example of the finite Earth points) is that we now have a politics of the Earth, whereas once we did not. If the environment itself were not conceptualized—and it was not, prior to the 1960s—then a book about environmental politics could not be written. Today, of course, we not only have an environment, but most of the important things that happen to it are the subject of politics, and the target of public policy.

Some of the examples I have adduced might seem to suggest we have a clear trajectory pointing to environmental enlightenment; it is just a matter of humanity becoming more sensitive or aware as time goes on, and escaping from past misconceptions and ignorance. Even if one believes in progress (as I do), it would be a mistake to think of the history of environmental affairs in these terms. What we see instead is that these matters are subject to continuing dispute between people who think in sharply different ways. Some people deny that environmental issues matter at all (how else could President Ronald Reagan have once said that "90 per cent of pollution is caused by trees"?), that they are just cover for insidious political agendas (curiously, this claim can be found on the cultural left as well as the more obvious hard right wing of politics). Consider the following examples of environmental conflicts:

- Citizen-activists in the United States and elsewhere have mobilized in protest against toxic pollutants, responding to seemingly obvious damage to the health of residents and workers. But when scientists employed by government agencies investigate these cases, they typically cannot prove by their own standards that pollution caused death and illness. Activists are rarely persuaded by these results, and continue their campaigns, sometimes winning, sometimes losing. Why is there no consensus on what evidence counts, and what constitutes proof? How should risks be approached in the absence of public confidence in scientific standards?

- Though recognized as a possibility since the 1890s, the idea that human activity could cause significant and damaging climate change took a long time to take hold. In 1992 the United Nations Framework Convention on Climate Change was established to seek global agreement. But even governments who agree on the problem seem unable to craft a solution. With time the major negotiators came increasingly to emphasize their national economic interests at the expense of global social-ecological concerns, and to fight for those interests. Why did this shift happen? Was it inevitable? Why does an organized climate change denial movement flourish in the United States, Canada, and Australia, but fail to register just about everywhere else? Why does the main conservative party in the UK proclaim its zeal to reduce greenhouse gas emissions, while the main conservative party in the United States sees any action to reduce emissions as close to communism? Why do some corporations see climate change as providing another opportunity for capitalism to flourish, while others (often in the same industry) see it as a threat to the very idea of capitalism?

· The initial growth of the nuclear industry in the 1950s and 1960s took place in secret. By the 1980s, proposals for new nuclear installations were typically the subject of extensive public inquiries. In Austria, Sweden, and the Netherlands broad national discussions took place in the late 1970s about the whole future of nuclear power, and the kind of society it helped construct. In Britain, inquiries focused narrowly on safety. It was assumed that the economic benefits of any proposal were positive. Objectors were not allowed to introduce economic evidence against the proposal, still less arguments about whether nuclear power belongs in a free society, or is consistent with environmental values. The most notorious British nuclear plant is at Windscale/Sellafield on the Irish Sea. A pipeline carries nuclear waste material into the Irish Sea. In 1990 a team of Greenpeace divers placed a symbolic plug in the end of the pipeline. Greenpeace was fined £50,000, and admonished by the judge for being so arrogant as to put their special interests above the law. Why did "the law" in Britain consistently serve the interests of the nuclear-industrial complex, and fail to accommodate ecological concerns that motivate a group like Greenpeace? Use of the law to suppress ecological activism is not confined to Britain. In April 2002 Greenpeace activists boarded a freighter transporting mahogany cut illegally in Brazilian rainforests to Miami. Stumped for a way to bring Greenpeace to heel, the US Attorney's Office eventually hit upon the idea of charging then with "sailor-mongering"—a law last used in 1890 against brothel owners who tried to abduct drunken sailors. In

Australia in 2004, Gunns timber corporation tried to silence critics of its logging of old growth forests through lawsuits against Green Party politicians, leaders of The Wilderness Society, and other activists, claiming $6.9 million as compensation for damage to its business. Five years later the Gunns case failed but not before a heavy psychological toll exacted on the defendants.

• In the United States and Canada the last three decades have seen intense conflict over the logging of remnant old growth forests, especially in the Pacific Northwest. In the United States, logging was impeded by the presence of the spotted owl, an endangered species whose only habitat is old growth forest. Why is there legislation to protect a species such as the spotted owl (the Endangered Species Act), but no legislation to protect ecosystems such as the forest itself? The conflict between companies and logging communities on the one hand and environmentalists on the other is intense and intractable. Attempts to solve the conflict through the courts, through legislation, and through consensus-seeking exercises (such as the timber summit sponsored by and attended by President Clinton in 1993) have all failed. The George W. Bush administration tried to tip the balance in favor of the timber industry, partly through low-visibility administrative changes, more publicly via the "Healthy Forests Initiative" passed into law in 2003, that expanded possibilities for logging on public lands, though the standoff continued. Why was the conflict so intractable? Why does its symbolic importance remain, even as the rate of old growth logging declines substantially? Why do timber workers support logging of old growth to exhaustion instead of sustainable forestry, which would guarantee jobs and incomes in the longer term? Can the simultaneous pursuit of environmental and economic values which sustainable forestry connotes actually be achieved? Would this pursuit be secured, as some economists suggest, by dividing the National Forests into chunks of land and selling each chunk to the highest bidder? Why are such proposals, even when their economic logic seems compelling, resisted so strenuously by both environmentalists and loggers?

In all these conflicts, the different sides interpret the issues at hand in very different ways. At any time, the way the issue is dealt with depends largely (though not completely) on the balance of competing discourses. In this book I intend making sense of the last fifty years or so of environmental concern by mapping these discourses.

A discourse approach

Environmental issues do not present themselves in well-defined boxes labeled radiation, national parks, climate change, biodiversity, rainforest, heavy metal pollution, and the like. Instead, they are interconnected in all kinds of ways. For example, climate change due to buildup of greenhouse gases in the atmosphere connects to air pollution in more local contexts, and so to transportation policy. Climate change also relates to the health of ecosystems (such as tropical forests) which act as carbon sinks, absorbing carbon dioxide from the atmosphere; and to fossil fuel reliance and exhaustion; and so to problems related to alternative sources of energy such as nuclear power. Environmental problems tend to be interconnected and multidimensional; in a word, complex. Complexity refers to the number and variety of elements and interactions in the environment of a decision system. When human decision systems (be they individuals or collective bodies such as governments) confront environmental problems, they encounter two orders of complexity. Ecosystems are complex, and our knowledge of them is limited, as the scientists who study them are the first to admit. Human social systems are complex too, which is why there is so much work for the ever-growing number of social scientists who study them. Environmental problems by definition are found at the intersection of ecosystems and human social systems, thus doubly complex.

The more complex a situation, the larger the number of plausible perspectives upon it—because the harder it is to prove any one of them wrong. Thus the proliferation of perspectives on environmental problems that has accompanied the development and diversification of environmental concern since the 1960s should come as no surprise. It is my intention here to make sense of this proliferation through looking at environmental discourses, which like any discourses contain "representations and systems of meaning" (Howarth, 2009: 311). This system gives context and sense to any particular use of words (Fairclough, 2003).

A discourse is a shared way of apprehending the world. Embedded in language, it enables those who subscribe to it to interpret bits of information and put them together into coherent stories or accounts. Discourses construct meanings and relationships, helping define common sense and legitimate knowledge. Each discourse rests on assumptions, judgments, and contentions that provide the basic terms for analysis, debates, agreements, and disagreements. If such shared terms did not exist, it would be hard to imagine problem-solving in this area at all, as we would have continually to return to first principles. So discourses both enable and constrain communication. Discourses coordinate the actions of large numbers of people and organizations who do not otherwise need to interact. This role is especially important where more formal sources of coordination are weak or absent—such as in global politics, where (as we will see in Chapter 7) environmental affairs have been coordinated by the discourse of sustainable development. The way a discourse views the world is not always easily comprehended by those who subscribe to other discourses. However, as I will show, complete discontinuity across discourses is rare, such that interchange across discourse boundaries can occur, however difficult.

Discourses are bound up with political practices and power (Hajer and Versteeg, 2005: 175). Discourses can themselves embody power in the way they condition the perceptions and values of those subject to them, such that some interests are advanced, others suppressed, some people made more compliant and governable (Foucault, 1980). Discourses are also intertwined with some material political realities. Governments in capitalist economies have to perform a number of basic functions whether they want to or not (see Dryzek, 1992a): first and foremost, ensuring continued economic growth. Corporations can stop investing in response to government policies they do not like. The increasing mobility of capital and finance intensifies this pressure, because businesses can threaten to transfer operations to countries with less stringent environmental policies and practices. As China, long a haven for polluting manufactures, begins to take pollution seriously, it too feels this kind of pressure. If governments make investors unhappy—through (say) tough antipollution policy—then they are punished by disinvestment, which in turn means recession, unpopularity in the eyes of voters, and falling tax revenues. Often the reason investors take such actions is that they subscribe to a market-oriented globalization discourse that defines some government policies as right, others as wrong.

Now, trying to make sense of the Earth's politics through reference to discourses is not the only way of going about the task. Other analysts look at the institutions (markets, government bureaucracies, legal systems, etc.) that have been developed for handling environmental issues.[1] Some look at the policies that governments have pursued. Some care little about the details of real-world practices, focusing instead on the political philosophies that can be applied in environmental affairs. Some look only at particular case studies of environmental issues. I shall have plenty to say about institutions, policies, political philosophies, and case studies, for all owe much to the discourses in their vicinity.

This inquiry rests on the contention that language matters, that the way we construct, interpret, discuss, and analyze environmental problems has all kinds of consequences. My intent is to lay out the basic structure of the discourses that have dominated recent environmental politics, and present their history, conflicts, and transformations. Environmental discourse is broader than environmentalism, extending to those who do not consider themselves environmentalists, but either choose or find themselves in positions where they are handling environmental issues, be it as politicians, bureaucrats, corporate executives, lawyers, journalists, or citizens. Environmental discourse even extends to those hostile to environmentalism. My geographic coverage is uneven, for this is a short book. I emphasize Europe, North America, Australasia, and the global arena; but occasionally look to China, Japan, and developing countries.

Some studies examine discourse carefully in the context of a particular issue. That such an approach is productive is demonstrated by three giants of environmental discourse analysis. Maarten Hajer studied transformations in discourse on acid rain in Britain and the Netherlands in the late 1980s and early 1990s (Hajer, 1995), and the rise of a discourse of "nature development" in Dutch environmental policy (Hajer, 2003). Karen Litfin elucidated changing international discourse about global ozone layer depletion in the 1980s (Litfin, 1994). Charlotte Epstein (2008) shows how an antiwhaling discourse rose to global dominance. My own accounts lack the rich detail of Hajer, Litfin, and Epstein. However, there is room for breadth as well as depth in analyzing environmental discourse, looking at the big picture rather than the details.

In offering a view of a much bigger territory, I will be guided by some analytical devices and distinctions (to be introduced shortly) that give me some confidence in painting such large and complex discursive terrain in broad strokes. I seek vindication only in the plausibility and coherence of the stories I tell (and in being open to counter-examples and challenges to my interpretations). These stories are backed by my own thirty years of working in the environmental field, but others might still carve up the territory somewhat differently. For example, Clapp and Dauvergne (2005) distinguish between market liberals, institutionalists, bioenvironmentalists, and social greens. In histories of US environmentalism, it is standard practice to distinguish between two traditions, heirs respectively to the anthropocentric rational resource management advocated by the US Forest Service's first chief forester Gifford Pinchot and the deeper respect for nature propounded by Sierra Club founder John Muir (see, for example, Taylor, 1992). To Martin Lewis (1992), the only distinction that makes sense is between moderates and extremists, or "Promethean" and "Arcadian" environmentalists as he styles them (I will use the term Promethean somewhat differently). Less worthy of serious attention, former US Secretary of the Interior James Watt distinguished between environmentalists and Americans.

Discourse is important, and conditions the way we define, interpret, and address environmental affairs. This should not be taken to mean that there is only discourse when it comes to environmental problems. Postmodernists believe that there is no escape from specific viewpoints (for an environmental application, see Bennett and Chaloupka, 1993), such that "nature" and "wilderness" are mainly social constructions, understood culturally as the product of societies that have, among other things, removed indigenous peoples from their landscapes. But even those such as Cronon (1995) and Soper (1995) who make this argument also stress that their position does not diminish environmental concern. Thus nature should not be treated as merely a subcategory of culture, as an extreme postmodern position would require. Such an extreme position would be just another anthropocentric turn in the colonization of nature for human purposes (Crist, 2004), an arrogance that fails to recognize nature's existence prior to human appropriation. The extreme postmodern lesson has actually been adopted most effectively by organized climate change deniers in the United States, for whom climate science is just a social construction that serves a political purpose, requiring in their response a social construction of nature that does not allow human-caused climate change.

Just because something is socially interpreted does not mean it is unreal. Climate is changing as a result of greenhouse gas emissions, pollution does cause illness, species do become extinct, ecosystems cannot absorb stress indefinitely, tropical forests are disappearing. But people can make very different things of these phenomena and—especially—their interconnections, providing grist for political dispute. The existence of these competing understandings is why we have environmental politics (or any kind of politics) to begin with. Sometimes particular constructions can be exposed as misguided—as, for example, when automobile company executives in the 1950s dismissed the possibility of smog in cities such as Los Angeles by claiming that car exhaust emissions were simply absorbed by the atmosphere. More often, it is hard to prove constructions right or wrong in any straightforward way. But one might say the same about scientific worldviews, political ideologies, or governmental constitutions. It is still possible to engage in critical comparative judgment, to apply evidence and argument, and to hope that in so doing we can correct some errors, and so move toward better overall understanding of environmental issues and problems. As Litfin puts it, it is possible to subscribe to both a hermeneutic epistemology (i.e., an interpretive philosophy of inquiry) and a realist ontology (i.e., a commitment to the actual existence of problems) (1994: 26–7, 50).[2]

Unfortunately, there are plenty of forces that can impair critical comparative judgment. The public relations departments of large corporations are adept here when it comes to "greenwashing" their activities. According to *O'Dwyers PR Services,* the environment was "the life and death PR battle of the 1990s" (*Guardian,* London, September 18, 1996), and this is no less true in the new millennium. Environmental public relations firms flourish. In the 1990s, the Weyerhauser Corporation advertised itself as "the tree growing company"™, before changing its "tagline" in 1999 to "the future is growing"™. In 2012 its website proclaimed "We are inspired by trees." Weyerhauser does plant and grow a lot of trees. But the trees it plants are single-species plantations, managed with herbicides and pesticides. Many of the trees it cuts down are in multi-species old growth forests, which take hundreds of years to mature. The coal industry points to the virtues of "clean coal" as an energy option—though there is no feasible technology to make clean coal a reality. In the 1990s, corporate front groups had names that connote environmental concern. But the real intent of the Global Climate Coalition, mostly financed by oil companies, was to downplay climate change concern. Similar stories applied to the National Wetlands Coalition, National Wilderness Institute, and (in Australia) the Forest Protection Society. All are now defunct; anti-environmental industry now prefers to fund research foundations.

Classifying the main environmental discourses

Environmental discourse begins in industrial society, and so has to be positioned in the context of the discourse of industrialism. Industrialism may be characterized in terms of its overarching commitment to growth in the quantity of goods and services produced and to the material wellbeing that growth brings. Industrial societies have of course featured many competing ideologies, such as liberalism, conservatism, socialism, Marxism, and fascism. But whatever their differences, all these ideologies are committed to industrialism. From an environmental perspective they can all look like variations on this theme. This commonality might surprise their adherents, more conscious of their ideological differences. But all these ideologies long ignored or suppressed environmental concern. If what we now call environmental issues were thought about at all, it was generally in terms of inputs to industrial processes. For example, rational use of such inputs was the main concern of the Conservation Movement founded at the beginning of the twentieth century in the United States, whose key figure was Gifford Pinchot. This Movement did not want to preserve the environment for aesthetic reasons, or for the sake of human health. Instead, the Conservation Movement sought only to ensure that resources such as minerals, timber, and fish were used wisely and not squandered, so that there would always be plenty to support a growing economy.

Environmental discourse cannot therefore simply take the terms of industrialism as given, but must depart from these terms. This departure can be reformist or it can be radical; and this distinction forms one dimension for categorizing environmental discourses.

A second dimension would take note of the fact that departures from industrialism can be either prosaic or imaginative. Prosaic departures take the political-economic chessboard set by industrial society as pretty much given. On that chessboard, environmental problems are seen mainly in terms of troubles encountered by the established industrial political economy. They require action, but they do not point to a new kind of society. The action in question can be quite dramatic and radical. As we will see, there are those who believe that economic growth must be reined in, if not brought to a halt entirely, in order to respond effectively to environmental problems. But the measures endorsed or proposed by these people are essentially those which have been defined by and in industrialism. For example, those who would curb economic growth normally propose that this be done by strong central government informed by scientific expertise—a quintessentially industrialist instrument.

In contrast, imaginative departures seek to redefine the chessboard. Notably, environmental problems are seen as opportunities rather than troubles. Imaginative redefinition may dissolve old dilemmas, treating environmental concerns not in opposition to economic ones, but potentially in harmony. The environment is brought into the heart of society and its cultural, moral, and economic systems, rather than being seen as a source of difficulties standing outside these systems. The thinking is imaginative, but the degree of change sought can be small and reformist, or large and radical. As we shall see, imaginative reformist ways of rendering the basic political-economic structure bequeathed by industrial society capable of coping with environmental issues may be found. On the other hand, imaginative radical changes can also be envisaged, requiring wholesale transformation of this political-economic structure. Combining these two dimensions—reformist versus radical and prosaic versus imaginative—produces four cells, as indicated in Box 1.1.

Environmental problem solving is defined by taking the political-economic status quo as given but in need of adjustment to cope with environmental problems, especially via public policy. Such adjustment might take the form of extension of the pragmatic problem-solving capacities of liberal democratic governments by facilitating a variety of environmentalist inputs to them; or of markets, by putting price tags on environmental harms and benefits; or of administration, by institutionalizing environmental concern and expertise in its operating procedures. Within the overall discourse of environmental problem solving there may be substantial disagreement as to which of these forms is appropriate. So, for example, a debate between proponents of administrative regulation and market-type incentive mechanisms for pollution control has been under way since the 1970s, with market proponents gradually gaining ground.

Limits and Survival took hold in early 1970s, retaining many believers, though today they are more likely to speak of planetary boundaries rather than limits. The basic idea is that unchecked economic expansion and population growth will eventually exceed the Earth's stock of natural resources and the capacity of its ecosystems to support human agricultural and

BOX 1.1	Classifying environmental discourses	
	Reformist	Radical
Prosaic	Problem solving	Limits and survival
Imaginative	Sustainability	Green radicalism

industrial activity, or the ability of the Earth system to accommodate stress. The limits discourse is radical because it seeks a wholesale redistribution of power within the industrial political economy, and a wholesale reorientation away from perpetual economic growth. It is prosaic because it sees solutions in terms of the options set by industrialism, notably, greater control of existing systems by administrators, scientists, and other responsible elites.

Sustainability rises in the 1980s, and is defined by imaginative attempts to dissolve the conflicts between environmental and economic values that energize the discourses of problem solving and limits. The concepts of growth and development are redefined in ways that render obsolete the simple projections of the limits discourse. In global affairs, sustainability became what Fairclough (2006: 39) calls a "nodal discourse," around which other discourses cluster. Without the imagery of apocalypse that defines the limits discourse, there is no inbuilt radicalism. The arrival of the era of sustainability was confirmed by the Brundtland Report in 1987 (World Commission on Environment and Development, 1987). At the same time, ideas about ecological modernization, seeing economic growth and environmental protection as essentially complementary, arose in Europe.

Green radicalism is both radical and imaginative. Its adherents reject the basic structure of industrial society and the way the environment is conceptualized therein in favor of a variety of quite different alternative interpretations of humans, their society, and their place in the world. Given its radicalism and imagination, it is not surprising that green radicalism features deep intramural divisions—to which I shall attend. In the United States, social ecologists with a pastoral vision and a concern for social justice debate deep ecologists, who prefer landscapes without humans. Everywhere, green romantics disagree with green rationalists, and advocates of green lifestyles disagree with those who prefer green politics. These debates are lively and persistent; but the disputants have far more in common with each other in terms of basic dispositions, assumptions, and capabilities than they do with either industrialism or with the three competing discourses of environmental concern just introduced.

These, then, are the four basic environmental discourses, and I will organize the chapters that follow according to how they fit with these four categories.

Questions to ask about discourses

So far I have identified the four basic categories of discourses in fairly general terms. But in order to see why and how these discourses have developed, and to what effect, it is necessary to pin down their content more precisely. This I shall do in the chapters that follow. To this end, let me now develop a set of questions for the analysis of discourses.

Discourses enable stories to be told; in fact, the title of a discourse can be an abbreviated story line (the concept of environmental story lines is deployed by Hajer, 1995). To refer back to the four categories just enumerated, limits connotes a story about the need to curb ever-growing human demands on the life-support capacities of natural systems. Problem solving connotes a different story—indeed, can subsume a number of different stories—about the unpleasant side-effects of particular economic activities requiring piecemeal remedies. Each discourse constructs stories from the following elements.

Basic entities whose existence is recognized or constructed

This is what is meant by the "ontology" of a discourse. Different discourses see different things in the world. Some discourses recognize the existence of ecosystems, others have no concept of natural systems at all, seeing nature only in terms of brute matter. At least one other entertains the idea that the global ecosystem is a self-correcting entity with something like intelligence. This is the idea of Gaia, which I will address in my analysis of green radicalism. Some discourses organize their analyses around rational, egoistic human beings; others deal with a variety of human motivations; others still recognize human beings only in aggregates such as states and populations. Most believe it is fruitful to deal with "humans" as a category, a few that it is necessary to break down on the basis of gender. Some assume governments and their actions matter; others believe it is the human spirit that is crucial.

Assumptions about natural relationships

All discourses embody notions of what is natural in the relationships between different entities. Some see competition, be it between human beings in markets or between creatures locked in Darwinian struggle, as natural. Others see cooperation as the essence of both human social systems and natural systems. Hierarchies based on gender, expertise, political power, species, ecological sensibility, intellect, legal status, race, and wealth are variously assumed in different discourses; as are their corresponding equalities.

Agents and their motives

Story lines require actors, or agents. These actors can be individuals or collectivities. They are mostly human, but can be nonhuman. In one discourse we may find benign and public-spirited expert administrators. Another discourse might portray the same people as selfish bureaucrats. Still others might ignore the presence of government officials altogether. Many other kinds of agents and motives put in appearances. They include enlightened elites, rational consumers, ignorant and shortsighted populations, virtuous ordinary citizens, a Gaia that may be tough and forgiving or fragile and punishing, among others.

Key metaphors and other rhetorical devices

Most story lines, in the environmental arena no less than elsewhere, depend crucially on metaphor. Key metaphors that have figured in environmental discourse include:

- spaceships (the idea of "spaceship Earth")
- the grazing commons of a medieval village ("the tragedy of the commons")
- machines (nature is like a machine that can be reassembled to better meet human needs)
- organisms (nature is a complex organism that grows and develops)
- human intelligence (ascribed to nonhuman entities such as ecosystems)
- war (against nature)

- goddesses (treating nature in benign female form, and not just as Mother Nature)

Metaphors are rhetorical devices, deployed to convince listeners or readers by putting a situation in a particular light. Many other devices can perform the same tasks. These include appeal to widely accepted practices or institutions, such as established rights, freedoms, constitutions, and cultural traditions. For example, the rights of species, animals, or natural objects can be justified through reference to the long-established array of individual human rights in liberal societies. Appeals can be made to deeper pasts, such as pastoral or even primeval idylls, as a way to criticize the industrial present. The negative and discredited can be accentuated as well as the positive and treasured. For example, it is possible to collect horror stories about government mistakes on environmental issues, and sprinkle these horror stories into arguments. On the other hand, some discourses collect and accentuate success stories.

This completes my checklist of items for the scrutiny and analysis of discourses. The items are summarized in Box 1.2. If my discussion of each element has been brief, matters should become clearer when I deploy this checklist in subsequent chapters in order to capture the various discourses more precisely. Beyond capturing the essence of the various discourses and their subdivisions, it is important to determine what difference each of them makes. I have already asserted that the language we use in addressing environmental affairs does make a difference, but this needs to be demonstrated for particular discourses, rather than just asserted as a general point.

The differences that discourses make

With this need to demonstrate the implications of different discourses in mind, I will take a look at the history as well as the content of each discourse. This history can generally be traced back to some aspect of industrialism—if only as a rejection of that aspect. With time, environmental discourses develop, crystallize, bifurcate, and dissolve. So a discourse of limits evolves into planetary boundaries. The Promethean antithesis to limits analyzed in Chapter 3 eventually accommodates recognition of environmental problems, and a high-technology response to them. Administrative rationalism

> **BOX 1.2**   Checklist of elements for the analysis of discourses
>
> 1. Basic entities recognized or constructed
> 2. Assumptions about natural relationships
> 3. Agents and their motives
> 4. Key metaphors and other rhetorical devices

eventually accommodates networked governance. Sustainable development moves in the direction of business-friendly "green growth." Ecological modernization changes to stress "transition" to a different kind of energy system. Green radicalism moves gradually to greater stress on justice.

The impact of a discourse can often be felt in the policies of governments or international organizations. For example, the flurry of environmental legislation enacted in many industrialized countries around 1970 mostly reflected a discourse of administrative rationalism (a subcategory of problem solving). Since 1970, problem-solving discourse has also been embodied in a number of institutional innovations that extend the openness and reach of liberal democratic control of environmental affairs (in the form of devices such as public inquiries and various procedures for consensual dispute resolution). Beyond affecting institutions, discourses can become embodied in institutions. When this happens, discourses constitute the informal understandings that provide the context for social interaction, on a par with formal institutional rules. Or to put it slightly differently, discourses can constitute institutional software while formal rules constitute institutional hardware. Sometimes, though, discourses do not have direct effects on the policies or institutions of governments, but take effect elsewhere. For example, green radicalism has helped some individuals and communities to distance themselves from both government and corporate capitalism in putative attempts to create an alternative political economy relying on self-sufficiency. Impacts can also be felt directly on society and culture without having to pass through formal institutions or public policies. Contemporary social movements often target the way ordinary people think and behave, and much of their success can be judged in these terms. For example, feminism has changed the division of labor in households. Environmentalism has led many people to change their lifestyles so as to reduce their ecological impact, be it through recycling, not eating meat, avoiding genetically modified organisms, planting native vegetation around their houses, using public transport rather than private cars, or boycotting companies with a poor environmental record.

To assess more fully the worth and impact of a discourse requires attention to its critics as well as its adherents. Sometimes, adherents of different discourses will ignore and dismiss rather than engage one another. Nevertheless, dispute does occur across the boundaries of different discourses. Frequently, this occurs between the environmental discourse in question and the older discourse of industrialism. Occasionally, debate is engaged between the problem-solving, limits, sustainability, and green radical discourses. One goal of this book is to promote such interchange.

Attention to the arguments of critics will facilitate identification of flaws in the discourse. Such identification will also be helped by attention to experience of the practical implications of the discourse, in politics, policies, institutions, and beyond. The tools of discourse analysis which I have enumerated enable further critical analysis of the promise and peril attached to each discourse in its contribution to environmental debate, analysis, and action.

The set of questions I will ask in order to assess the impact, plausibility, and attractiveness of each discourse is summarized in Box 1.3.

The uses of discourse analysis

As should be clear, my intent is to advance analysis in environmental affairs by promoting critical comparative scrutiny of competing discourses of environmental concern. This intent distances me from some other discourse analysts.

BOX 1.3   **Checklist of items for assessing the effects of discourses**

1. Politics associated with the discourse
2. Effect on policies of governments
3. Effect on institutions
4. Social and cultural impact
5. Arguments of critics
6. Flaws revealed by evidence and argument

The concept of discourse owes something (but not everything) to the efforts of Michel Foucault (for example, 1980), who revealed the content and history of discourses about illness, sex, madness, criminality, government, and so forth. Foucauldians are generally committed to the idea that individuals are for the most part subject to the discourses in which they move, and so are seldom able to step back and make comparative assessments and choices across different discourses. It should be evident that I disagree. Discourses are powerful, but they are not impenetrable (as Foucault and his readers have themselves demonstrated in their own exposé of the history of various discourses). Foucault and his followers also often portray discourses in hegemonic terms, meaning that one single discourse is typically dominant in any time and place, conditioning not just agreement but also the terms of dispute. Along these lines, Luke (1999) crudely treats environmentalism mostly in terms of an "environmentality" that actually serves rather than disrupts the established order of industrial society. In contrast, I believe that the variety found in environmental discourses is important. The environmental arena reveals that the discourse of industrialism was indeed hegemonic, to the extent that "the environment" was hardly conceptualized prior to the 1960s. However, this hegemony eventually began to disintegrate, yielding the range of environmental discourses now observable. While in its totality environmentalism can be positioned as a challenge to industrialism, it does not constitute a unified counter discourse. Rather, environmentalism is composed of a variety of discourses, sometimes complementing one another, but often competing. A discourse is not like a tribe. Particular individuals may partially inhabit competing discourses that make claims upon them (see Edwards and Potter, 1992 on discursive psychology). An individual working in a government environmental agency may be an administrative rationalist at work, a green radical in conversations with friends, an economic rationalist in buying and selling. This individual may sometimes have to think long and hard when these discourses pull in different directions, opening space for reflection which I will argue in the concluding chapter is actually vital when it comes to thinking about effective societal response to environmental issues.

With the necessary preliminaries over, it is to a mapping of environmental discourses and their consequences that I now turn.

NOTES

1. For my own contribution to this genre, see Dryzek, 1987.

2. The position I take here is consistent with a critical realist philosophy of science (Bhaskar, 1975), for which real structures exist, while our understanding of them is limited by selective inquiry, exposure, and experience.

PART II
GLOBAL LIMITS AND THEIR DENIAL

....

Environmental issues can be as local as the dog droppings on the grass in front of my house, or as global as climate change. When environmental issues made their first dramatic leap to the top of the political agenda in the late 1960s, it was the global issue that really captured public attention. Not coincidentally, this was also the first time the Earth was photographed from space, and a beautiful, fragile place it looked. For the first time in human history the Earth could be conceptualized readily as a finite planet, and for the first time a true politics of planet Earth became conceivable. Environmental problems were soon cast in terms of threats to the capacity of this planet to support life—especially human life.

The threats in question involved degradation of the global environment through pollution, and exhaustion of the Earth's natural resources (fossil fuels, minerals, fisheries, forests, and croplands). Urgency came from population explosion and economic growth. Exponential growth in both human numbers and the level of economic activity meant that there was no time to lose, for humanity seemed to be heading for the limits at an ever-increasing pace. Hitting these limits would mean global disaster and a crash in human populations.

This discourse of limits and survival was given a major boost by the Club of Rome, an international organization composed of industrialists, politicians, and academics. The Club's most famous product was a set of computer-generated projections of the global future published in 1972 in the international best seller *The Limits to Growth*. These projections showed in graphical terms that if humanity continued on its profligate course then it had at the very most a century before disaster would strike. There were many calls for radical action to stop this headlong rush to destruction, though the political repertoire turned out to consist mainly of some tried-and-tested practices, especially strong governmental control.

The discourse of limits and survival met with immediate counterattack from defenders of the established industrial economy, whose taken-for-granted order of things was challenged. These defenders argued that humans are characterized by unlimited ingenuity, symbolized in Greek mythology by the progress made possible by the theft of fire from the gods by Prometheus. Prometheans asserted that the Earth was in truth unlimited; that as soon as one resource threatened to run out, ingenious people would develop a substitute. This had always happened in the past, and it would continue to happen in the future. The Promethean reaction gathered speed in the 1980s, for it fit quite well with the ideological climate of the Reagan years in the United States. The administration of President George W. Bush beginning in 2001 was still more open to Promethean assumptions. While most Prometheans favor markets, Promethean environmentalists have emerged to argue that high-technology renewable energy will not emerge without substantial government intervention.

The dispute between the two camps continues, and neither shows any sign of conceding. Rather than limits, many environmental scientists now stress planetary boundaries, which refer to the capacity of the Earth system to absorb stress. There is a well-financed organized movement (based in the United States) to deny that one such limit, climate change, could ever be a problem. It matters crucially which side is right. If the market-committed Prometheans are correct, then environmentalism of any kind simply loses its urgency. So: who is right?

2

Looming Tragedy: Limits, Boundaries, Survival

The origins of survivalism

Population biologists and ecologists have long deployed the concept of "carrying capacity"—the maximum population of a species that an ecosystem can support in perpetuity. According to Garrett Hardin, the ecologist's Eleventh Commandment is "Though shalt not transgress the carrying capacity" (1993: 207). When the population of a species grows to the point where carrying capacity is exceeded, the ecosystem is degraded and population crashes, recovering only if and when natural processes restore the ecosystem to its previous capacity. Such crashes are readily observable in relatively simple ecosystems, for example when large herbivores such as deer are introduced to environments with no predators. Their populations soon explode to the point where the food supply is exhausted.

When population biologists turned to human affairs they saw identical possibilities (see especially Catton, 1980; Pengra, 2012). Humans are not like deer: we can adapt more readily in response to environmental stress. But we do not always succeed. Jared Diamond in his 2005 bestseller *Collapse* shows how societies such as the Maya, Anasazi, Greenland Norse, and inhabitants of Easter Island perished rather than adapt to environmental change.

The waters are muddied still further when it comes to contemporary human populations, because trade and aid mean that human societies can escape constraints imposed by geographically bounded ecosystems. For example, biologists may show that the carrying capacity of East African ecosystems for human beings has been exceeded; but continued food aid from overseas means that population does not crash. This sort of analysis is controversial, as it calls into question some basic humanitarian (population biologists would say soft-headed) impulses on the part of donors, not to mention some radical analyses of international political economy; but those critiques can wait.

Given trade and aid, it makes more sense to talk in terms of the human carrying capacity of the global ecosystem. It really matters little that Singapore, New York City, London, and Los Angeles have vastly exceeded the carrying capacity of their local ecosystems, so long as they can exploit distant resources and sinks for their pollutants in order to support large and sometimes growing human populations. This is not to excuse such cities for their vast "ecological footprints."

The other complicating factor when it comes to applying population biology to human societies is the possibility of economic growth. Unique among animals, the ecological burdens imposed by each human are not roughly constant—indeed, they can seem virtually unbounded, as shown by the conspicuous consumption of the super-rich. So if the number of humans is growing and the amount consumed per human is growing, the ecological news is not good. Now, there are those who argue that economic growth is good for the environment because it allows some of the financial fruits of growth to be diverted to conservation; but such arguments belong in a different discourse, and will be dealt with in the next chapter. Let me stick for the moment to the discourse of ecological limits.

Analysis that anticipates misery, starvation, and death resulting from unconstrained human procreation and consumption, and that sees the main political challenge as ensuring human survival at an adequate level of amenity, is not new. It goes back to William Forster Lloyd (1794–1852) and, more famously, Thomas Malthus (1766–1834), widely reviled as the "dismal parson." Free-market liberal economists dismissed him because he doubted cherished Victorian notions of material progress and wealth accumulation leading to general social improvement. Marxists and other socialists were more scornful still, as he cast doubt on their postulate of material plenty in a free and equal post-capitalist society. Ultimately, Malthus's argument was falsified by two hundred years of population growth combined not with misery, but with rising living standards (at least in what is now the developed world). Or so it would seem.

In 1968 Garrett Hardin published his enormously influential essay, "The Tragedy of the Commons." Hardin's analysis quickly became part of the toolkit for analysts of environmental problems. His analytics had in fact been a staple of resource economics for some time (see Gordon, 1954). Hardin himself paid homage to his more distant precursor, William Forster Lloyd.[1] Unlike the economists, Hardin had the good sense to give the analysis a catchy name, publish in the large-circulation journal *Science,* refrain from graphs and algebra, and put it out just as the widespread perception of environmental crisis hit for the first time.

Hardin's logic of the commons is straightforward. Facing a decision about whether or not to put an extra cow on the village commons, each rational self-interested peasant will recognize that the benefits of the extra cow accrue to himself alone, whereas the costs (stress upon the commons) are shared with the other villagers. Thus all villagers will quickly put more cows on the commons, which will in turn be destroyed. Hardin was using the commons of a medieval village as a metaphor for all kinds of environmental resources (the process he described never actually happened in any medieval village, to our knowledge). So each decision maker deciding whether or not to catch an additional netful of fish, or dump an additional ton of sewage, or cut down a tree, or drive an extra mile in Los Angeles, or get that malfunctioning catalytic converter fixed, is facing essentially the same decision: private benefit and the public interest point in opposite directions. Hardin made a connection to childbearing decisions: if the world is a commons, each additional child adds stress to the commons, even though calculations of private interest may determine that the child should be conceived, born, and raised.

Of course, all this is only tragic if the commons is finite—that is, if there are limits. If there are no limits, we can populate, grow, and consume at will. For several centuries it seemed that unconstrained economic growth was the natural order of things, and social survival in finite systems was simply not conceptualized. But come 1970, everything changed in a hurry. The world looked as though it was being hit by what Paul Ehrlich (1968) sensationalized as a population bomb, more powerful than nuclear bombs. Combined with economic growth, population explosion was going to exhaust stocks of energy, cropland, clean water, minerals, and the assimilative capacity of the atmosphere and oceans. Matters were dramatized further by the energy crisis which arrived suddenly in 1973 with the oil embargo organized by the Organization for Petroleum Exporting Countries, to pressure the industrial world to take an anti-Israel line in the Middle East conflict.

To the limits—and beyond

This discourse of limits and survival was not all there was to environmentalism circa 1970. Many concerns were more local, more aesthetic, about quality of life not its mere perpetuation. But this discourse did set the apocalyptic horizon of environmentalism, the basic reason why concern about the environment was not just desirable, but also necessary. One of the most heated debates in the history of environmental concern began in 1972 with the publication of *The Limits to Growth* (Meadows et al., 1972), which within four years had sold four million copies.

This famous study was sponsored by the Club of Rome, founded in 1968 by well-heeled industrialists and sympathetic academics concerned with the "predicament of mankind." Curiously, these industrialists were keen to show that industrialism itself might be unsustainable. The Massachusetts Institute of Technology (MIT) team commissioned by the Club of Rome to undertake the study were not population biologists who knew about carrying capacity, or economists who might know a bit about economic growth, but systems modelers (with business school backgrounds). Systems dynamics was a new technology rendered useful by the development and availability of computers. The MIT team was in a sense "Malthus with a computer" (Freeman, 1973), though unlike Malthus they believed the predicament of mankind had more causes than just population growth. The exercise was legitimated by computers—for both analysis and salvation. As Torgerson (1995: 9) notes, the film version of *The Limits to Growth* portrays a dramatic contrast between the chaos and misery of a world seemingly hell-bent on using resources to exhaustion, polluting till it choked, with population exploding into misery, on the one hand, and the calm authority symbolized by a computer and the experts who could run it on the other. Computers in those days were large, slow, and complicated.

The computer runs themselves were simulations over a hundred years or more into the future of predicted pathways of key aggregates, which interacted with one another through a host of interrelated variables. The key aggregates were resources, population, industrial output, food supply, and pollution. (Critics quickly pointed out the absence of technology and prices.) All variables were measured at the global level. The predictions varied somewhat depending on the assumptions built into different computer runs, but given postulated limits to resource availability, agricultural productivity, and the capacity of the ecosphere to assimilate pollution, some limit was generally hit within a hundred years, leading to the collapse of industrial society and its population. The policy prescription was obvious: humanity needed to change its profligate ways to avoid the apocalypse of overshoot and collapse. Meadows and colleagues envisaged an alternative "stationary state" global economy, at a fixed level of throughput of resources, with a stable population. As they note, this state had been envisaged more than a hundred years earlier by the political economist John Stuart Mill (Meadows et al., 1972: 175). Quite how humanity could move to this steady state was less clear, though as we shall see others quickly supplied the political prescriptions.

The elaborate computer simulations really stated the obvious: exponential growth cannot go on forever in a finite system. Exponential growth is growth at a constant percentage rate. This produces a growth curve over time of the sort depicted in Figure 2.1. With this curve, it matters little whether a limit such as the global supply of natural resources is doubled, tripled, or quadrupled; a little more time may be bought, but the limit is hit soon enough (see Figure 2.2). Nor should we expect much advance warning, for under exponential growth the limit will (by definition) be approached at an absolute speed unprecedented in human history.

Lester Brown (1978) deploys the metaphor of *The Twenty-Ninth Day* to ask on what day a pond will be half-covered with lilies if the coverage doubles every day, and will cover the whole pond on the thirtieth day. The answer is, of course, the twenty-ninth day. It would be very easy to look

FIGURE 2.1   **Exponential growth**

Resource use

Time

FIGURE 2.2 **Exponential growth with limits**

Note: Doubling the available supply of resources from L1 to L2 buys very little time.

at the pond on the twenty-ninth day and conclude there is plenty of clear water. The challenge is to figure out how to build a capacity for foresight into collective decision making, before any evidence of global collapse is apparent. Currently, decision making in government and business is almost entirely geared to the short term.

Global modeling continued under the auspices of the Club of Rome, the United Nations, and the United States government, among others. Under President Jimmy Carter, the US government's various global modeling enterprises were integrated in the *Global 2000 Report to the President,* a gloomy report for a gloomy presidency. With exquisitely bad timing, *Global 2000* was released in 1980, just in time for the arrival in Washington DC of Ronald Reagan, with a worldview that could not fathom such pessimism. Still, the Reagan presidency and the exuberant era it symbolized did not completely silence the discourse of limits and survival, even in the United States, even in its capital.

In Washington, focus on the parlous state of key global aggregates was kept alive by the Worldwatch Institute, under the leadership of Lester Brown. With its annual *State of the World* reports, begun in 1984, the Institute reminds us that indicators of environmental quality and resource availability point in the wrong direction, and that disaster is just around every corner. Though its view of the world is more nuanced than that of the *Limits to Growth,* the emphasis remains on monitoring systems and aggregates at the global level. The main systems are forests, grasslands, fisheries, and croplands. The overall limit identified by the Worldwatchers is the photosynthetic energy these systems can make available for human use. Humans currently appropriate a large and growing proportion of this energy, wasting much of it. The challenge is to use photosynthetic energy more efficiently.

In 2002 the US National Academy of Sciences published a report concluding that total human demands on the biosphere exceeded carrying capacity (Wackernagel et al., 2002). Authors such as Paul Ehrlich, Lester Brown, Norman Myers, and Garrett Hardin continued to contribute to the survivalist discourse in the 1990s and 2000s (Brown, 2003; Ehrlich and Ehrlich, 2004). They were joined by others: so Elizabeth Hannah (2011: 217) could say "Widespread anthropogenic degradation of ecological systems and new interruptions to global climate are creating an environment that does not suit our physiology, and hence is challenging survival of our species." The Club of Rome organized a forty-year commemoration of *The Limits to Growth* in Washington DC in 2012 to remind people of the core message. Nørgård et al. (2010) likewise conclude that the basic message of *Limits* still holds. Looking back on his involvement in the 1980 *Global 2000* report, Gus Speth (2008: 18) concluded "now, sad to say, *Global 2000*'s forecasts are coming true."

In 1995 a few leading economists broke ranks with their colleagues (once near-unanimous in their dismissal of limits) to announce that economic growth sooner or later must encounter the environment's carrying capacity (see Arrow et al., 1995). These ecological economists endorsed the basic tenet that the Earth's resource base is finite, and called for institutional redesign to reduce stress on natural systems.

The field of ecological economics should not be confused with an older environmental economics. Environmental economics is the handmaiden of economic rationalism, discussed at length in Chapter 6. Ecological economics conceptualizes ecosystems as the fundamental entities within which human economic systems are embedded. Thus, environmental problems are to be thought of as shortfalls in the capacity of interdependent ecological systems and economic systems acting in conjunction to sustain human— and possibly nonhuman—life. Ecological economics treats natural systems as finite. The main challenge is to figure out how economic systems could be sustainable within these constraints.

While meeting resistance (or indifference) within the mainstream discipline of economics, ecological economics has acquired academic respectability, through the International Society for Ecological Economics and its journal *Ecological Economics,* both founded in 1989.

The pioneers of ecological economics included Nicholas Georgescu-Roegen (1971) and Herman Daly (1977). Georgescu-Roegen explored the implications of the second law of thermodynamics, which specifies that any closed system will over time deteriorate in the direction of sameness or disorder without external input of energy. The fact that there is only a limited supply of low entropy or order on this planet has major economic implications. Low entropy is really the ultimate form of scarcity. It exists in mineral structures, concentrated fossil fuels, in ecosystems; but human economic activity is running down the supply of low entropy.

Herman Daly worked out principles of steady state economics. Conventional economics is committed to perpetual economic growth, and indeed sees economic health and normality in terms of the presence of growth. Daly rose to the challenge presented by limits, describing how an economy could be run on steady-state lines, without requiring ever-increasing environmental and natural resource inputs (Daly and Farley 2010; Czech, 2000).

From limits to planetary boundaries

The discourse of limits and survival undertook a subtle shift after the Secretary-General of the United Nations in 2000 commissioned the Millennium Ecosystems Assessment (MA), which reported in 2005. "The bottom line of the MA findings is that human actions are depleting Earth's natural capital, putting such strain on the environment that the ability of the planet's ecosystems to sustain future generations can no longer be taken for granted."[2] The emphasis shifted to stressed ecosystems. Building on this kind of thinking, around 2010 the concept of planetary boundaries shot to prominence in the environmental science community and beyond. As formulated in the classic statement of Rockström et al. (2009) there are nine boundaries, each representing a vital life support system, that together define "a safe operating space for humanity." The nine boundaries refer to:

- Carbon dioxide in the atmosphere
- Ocean acidity
- Stratospheric ozone

- Biogeochemical nitrogen and phosphorus cycles

- Freshwater use

- Land system change

- Biodiversity loss

- Chemical pollution

- Atmospheric aerosol loadings

The first seven of these were quantified; for example, the boundary for land system change was placed at converting 15 percent of the world's land area to cropland. Three of the limits were judged as already exceeded by 2009. They were carbon dioxide in the atmosphere (at 394 parts per million (ppm) and rising fast, compared to a boundary of 350 ppm), biodiversity loss (massively exceeding the boundary of 10 extinctions per million species-years), and human interference in the nitrogen cycle. Figure 2.3 reproduces the famous planetary boundaries diagram. The inner two circles represent the safe operating space, the shading on the climate change segment shows this space has already been exceeded, while the shading for biodiversity loss and the nitrogen cycle extends much further out, suggesting these two are in still greater trouble than the global climate.

There is even an environmental advocacy group named after the carbon dioxide limit: 350.org, founded by well-known US environmentalist Bill McKibben. Stabilizing carbon dioxide at 350 ppm would have the truly radical implication that the world's use of fossil fuels must soon cease (because currently around half the carbon dioxide emitted from burning these fuels stays in the atmosphere for good). Even stretching to 450 ppm would require carbon dioxide emissions to fall to near zero by the late twenty-first century; currently these emissions are increasing rapidly.

Boundaries are not the same as limits. None of the boundaries refers to extractive resources such as oil or fish. And there is no simulation of overshoot and collapse, just a warning that crossing a boundary puts humanity in danger. The precise quantity at which the boundary is placed draws on collective scientific judgment, about which there is some room for disagreement. Boundaries can interact, so changes in land use can affect biodiversity and carbon dioxide in the atmosphere. Efforts to stay within one boundary may mean threatening another. So geoengineering efforts to reduce atmospheric carbon dioxide (which I will discuss in Chapter 3) may increase ocean acidity.

FIGURE 2.3   **Planetary boundaries**

Source: Röckstrom et al., 2009.

Reprinted by permission from Macmillan Publishers Ltd: *Nature,* 461: 472–5, copyright 2009

Overall, though, the picture given by boundaries is similar to that of limits, involving transgression and peril (though the acknowledged success of the 1987 Montreal Protocol for the protection of the ozone layer alleviates the gloom on the stratospheric ozone boundary). As the final declaration of the big Planet Under Pressure conference in London in 2012 put it, "In one lifetime our interconnected and interdependent economic, social, cultural and political systems have come to place pressures on the environment that may cause fundamental changes in the Earth system and move us beyond safe natural boundaries." Such changes might take the form of a sudden state shift as a result of a global "tipping point" (Barnosky et al., 2012). Planetary boundaries were also recognized in the draft declaration of the 2012 United Nations Conference on Sustainable Development in Rio—but were removed before the final draft, much to the chagrin of environmental scientists and activists alike.

While the language of boundaries became more prominent, limits did not go away. In a book sponsored by the UK government's Sustainable Development Commission, Tim Jackson (2009: 2) asserted that "There are some immutable constraints on our prospects for a lasting prosperity. The existence of ecological limits to human activity may be one of these." Jackson points to the limited capacity of sinks (such as the ability of the atmosphere, oceans, and forests to absorb carbon dioxide). But unlike the planetary boundaries authors, he also points to limited resources—such as "peak oil," the idea that global oil production peaks around 2010–2020, despite increasing demand. There may be more oil out there, but it lies in increasingly marginal places that are expensive to access, such as the Arctic Ocean, the deep ocean off Brazil, tar sands in Canada. Jackson wants us to redefine prosperity so we can seek it without economic growth, "within the ecological limits of a finite planet" (p. 16).

Ideas about limits and boundaries sit uneasily with another scientific concept that became popular after 2000, the idea that the Earth system has entered an "Anthropocene" era where human activity is decisive (the concept was first named by ecologist Paul Crutzen). In other words, the Earth system is not just a set of constraints on human activity as implied by limits and boundaries; the content of the system itself is affected in fundamental ways by what humans do. The Anthropocene, which got going with industrialization, can be contrasted with the Holocene, the previous 10,000 years of unusual climate stability, during which human civilization arose.

The political philosophy of survival

Many of the more prominent figures who initially advanced the discourse of limits and survival have a background in biology. Their severe policy prescriptions can obliquely commit their authors to particular political structures. For example, Ehrlich (1968) countenanced compulsory sterilization in countries such as India, which could hardly be effective without a more authoritarian politics than India featured then or now.[3] However, in 2011 Worldwatch Institute President Robert Engelman recognized that the key to population control is improvement in the status and wellbeing of women, together with access to contraception (Engelman, 2011)—not coercive control. By 2011, population was actually close to stabilization everywhere except sub-Saharan Africa and a few countries elsewhere (such as Iraq and Afghanistan).

Especially in the 1970s, political prescriptions were often centralized and authoritarian. If, as Garrett Hardin avers in his classic essay, "freedom in the commons brings ruin to all" (1968), then obviously freedom, including the freedom to breed, needs to be curtailed. The solution to the tragedy of the commons in situations characterized by limits is "mutual coercion mutually agreed upon," whether the commons is a local fishery or the global atmosphere. Hardin (1977) expresses skepticism about effective central authority above the level of the nation-state. He recommends that the more developed countries abandon the underdeveloped world if governments in the latter wish to continue policies that promote population explosion and ecological devastation. Developed nations would then constitute "lifeboats" afloat in a world otherwise drowning in misery. Hardin's argument here downplays the fact that it is the rich, not the poor, that impose the greater stresses on the world's ecosystems. Recognition of limits could equally support a program of wealth reduction in rich countries to support redistribution to poor countries within global ecological limits (Reuveny, 2002: 84).

Others are less obviously callous than Hardin, though in basic agreement with him that abuse of the commons, resource exhaustion, and environmental despoliation are largely a matter of individuals and other actors pursuing material interests in decentralized systems. Decentralized systems have no cohesive leadership directing them: examples include markets, governance networks, and the international system. In such systems there is no incentive to care about collective goods like environmental quality or long-term human wellbeing. Thus Robert Heilbroner in 1974 concluded that the only hope for humanity lies in monastic government combining "religious orientation with a military discipline" (Heilbroner, 1991: 176–7; first edn. 1974) in order to cure humanity's profligate ways. Such totalitarian government would control economic transactions as well as politics. Obviously, authoritarian governments committed to industrialism rather than environmental conservation are no help, as the disastrous environmental records of dictatorships around the world testify.

The need to control access to the commons is just one prop for authoritarian government in the limits discourse. A second prop comes with the fact that the discourse places great emphasis on scientific expertise. In some cases, the relevant knowledge is quite hard to master: ecology does, of course, deal in very complex systems. This sort of recognition leads William Ophuls, in the most comprehensive and sophisticated analysis of the political ramifications of ecological crisis to appear in the 1970s, to recommend establishment of a governing class of "ecological mandarins" (1977: 163). The expertise is "on top" rather than "on tap," because ecology's claim to primacy means that there is no room for tradeoff against competing values of the sort that ordinary politicians routinely seek.[4]

Much later, David Shearman and Joseph Wayne-Smith (2007) argued that climate change among other global environmental challenges exposes the limitations of democracy and the liberal capitalism that controls it, meaning authoritarian green government controlled by the relevant experts is necessary. James Lovelock, best known for his Gaia hypothesis that treats the Earth as a self-regulating system (see Chapter 9), concurred: "Even the best democracies agree that when a major war approaches, democracy must be put on hold for the time being. I have a feeling that climate change may be an issue as severe as a war. It may be necessary to put democracy on hold for a while."[5] Such thoughts can draw support from the apparent ability of China to move decisively on environmental issues once its government has decided they are important (Beeson, 2010). Within a few years China came from nowhere to become the clear world leader in renewable energy production and technology (though that achievement remained outweighed by huge growth in coal-burning power plants).

Shearman and Smith, Lovelock, and admirers of China notwithstanding, with time any authoritarianism accompanying the discourse of limits and survival has softened substantially. Richard Barnet (1980) proposed democratic mobilization, not authoritarianism, to confront limits. Norman Myers called for citizen action to confront limits (in his contribution to Myers and Simon, 1994). Lester Brown has consistently placed greater faith in localized citizen action than in national leadership (Brown, 1981; Brown et al., 1992: 180). Czech (2000: 114) hopes in the face of all evidence to the contrary that: "In the world's model democracy [the United States], the steady state revolution must be a revolution in public opinion, a process by which the virtually ubiquitous cherishing of economic growth is transformed into an equally ubiquitous castigation of economic growth." Such calls to citizen action are far indeed from the oligarchy proposed by survivalist political theorists in the 1970s. These theorists did, though, remain unrepentant in the 1990s (see Hardin, 1993; Heilbroner, 1991; Ophuls and Boyan, 1992). Thirty-four years after his original book, in 2011 Ophuls reiterated his condemnation of contemporary liberal democratic capitalist societies and their futile pursuit of sustainability, arguing for small-scale republics that cultivate the virtues of their citizens, governed by anything "from tribal monarchy to direct democracy" (Ophuls, 2011: xii).

To see why citizen action can only fit uneasily into the discourse of limits and survival, a closer examination is in order, using the tools of discourse analysis introduced in Chapter 1.

Discourse analysis of limits and survival

The basic story line of limits and survival is that human demands on the life support capacity of ecosystems threaten to explode out of control, and drastic action needs to be taken in order to curb these demands. This story line is in turn constructed from the following components.

Basic entities whose existence is recognized or constructed

The resources upon which human beings depend for their existence include stocks of nonrenewable resources, such as oil, gas, coal, metallic ores, and cropland. Ecosystems are recognized in the original ontology, but only in limited fashion: as sources of renewable resources such as firewood, timber, soil, and fish, or as sinks for the absorption of pollution. The broader functions ecosystems perform, and the interrelationship between them, do however receive recognition in the more recent planetary boundaries concept. Crucially, stocks of nonrenewable resources and the capacity of ecosystems to produce renewable resources and assimilate and recycle wastes are treated as finite. The discourse also emphasizes human population as an aggregate entity (i.e., it is something other than just "people"), whose size and growth has all kinds of implications for human destiny. Finally, elites—especially those associated with governments, and especially those with pertinent expertise, be it in systems modeling, ecology, atmospheric science, or population biology—play a central role.

Finite stocks of resources, ecosystems as founts of renewable resources and sinks for pollutants, population, and elites—all these might sound unremarkable, just what one would expect to find in environmental talk. In fact, these items together constitute a highly selective and, as I will show later in this chapter, problematical set. For the moment, though, it should be noted that this basic ontology is not exhaustive (ontologies never are). Missing, for example, are individual problem solvers, human beings as social creatures capable of devising cooperative arrangements, markets (except to be criticized), social movements, genders, resilient ecosystems (at least until recognized in planetary boundaries thinking), states, and interest groups.

Assumptions about natural relationships

The relationships assumed by early survivalists to be the most natural in human affairs are conflict and hierarchy. Conflict ranges from rivalry in access to the commons to struggle over scarce resources. Often conflict and hierarchy are taken for granted. In contrast, the early survivalists I have discussed who analyze alternative forms of political-economic organization, such as Hardin, Heilbroner, and Ophuls, reason their way toward hierarchy rather than take it for granted. The basis for hierarchy can be expertise, or virtue, or both. Certainly, human beings conceptualized en masse as "population" do not have the required virtue to control their appetites or their procreation—unless these virtues are inculcated by government, as suggested by Ophuls (2011). Garrett Hardin argues at length that conscience is self-eliminating, for those without a conscience will have more children (1968). (This argument relies on the controversial premise that desired number of children is a hereditary trait.) Lester Brown, Norman Myers and others later softened this hierarchical commitment to include pleas for widespread citizen action. These pleas notwithstanding, the discourse of limits and survival deals ultimately in aggregates such as population, resource stocks, global pollution levels, and, crucially, monitoring and control of these aggregates. Such control is hard to envisage on anything other than a hierarchical basis. The hierarchy does not need to be the tight, authoritarian style of government proposed by some survivalists; but it does require management by elites.

Agents and their motives

It is, then, elites who have agency, the capacity to act. Their motivations are up for grabs. Elites can choose to operate national political economies according to established principles of maximizing economic growth, leavened by a touch of social justice and the need to placate special interests; or they can choose to listen to scientists, be it to oversee the transition to a stationary state through coordinated global action, or to bring humanity back to a "safe operating space." "Populations," be they national, global, or class-specific, have no agency; they are only acted upon, as aggregates to be monitored through statistics and controlled by government policy. At most, their component individuals can only follow their shortsighted desires, however rationally.

Key metaphors and other rhetorical devices

Survivalism is rich in metaphors. These include, first and foremost, the notion of overshoot and collapse, drawn from models of simple ecosystems where one species breeds to excess and then experiences a crash. The tragedy of the commons is rooted in metaphor: Garrett Hardin made his original argument in the context not of any resource currently threatened with exhaustion, but rather the common land of a medieval village. Another favorite metaphor is the spaceship, introduced by Kenneth Boulding (1966). If the life-support systems of the spaceship are not maintained, the crew dies. "Spaceship Earth" became a credible notion as real spaceships left the Earth with humans aboard for the first time and—crucially—these humans photographed the Earth from space. This image gave powerful impetus to thinking about the Earth as a whole system—and a finite, fragile one at that. A photograph of the Earth from space graces the cover of many books on my "environmental" shelf (but not this one).

Other metaphors capture the nature of exponential growth: the pond whose surface covered by lilies doubles every day, the population bomb, population explosion. Czech (2000) compares resource exploitation to "shoveling fuel for a runaway train" destined for a crash. In 2012, Worldwatch Institute Director Øysten Dahle said "Growth is the economy of the cancer cell."[6] The idea that humans are essentially cancerous is perhaps not a metaphor calculated to have broad appeal beyond (tiny) VHEMT, the Voluntary Human Extinction Movement (whose slogan is "May we live long and die out."). But Paul Ehrlich did once draw the further inference that "the

---

BOX 2.1   Discourse analysis of limits and survival

1. **Basic entities recognized or constructed**
   - Finite stocks of resources
   - Carrying capacity of ecosystems
   - Planetary boundaries/safe operating space
   - Population
   - Elites
2. **Assumptions about natural relationships**
   - Conflict
   - Hierarchy and control
3. **Agents and their motives**
   - Originally elites; motivation is up for grabs
   - More recently, greater variety
4. **Key metaphors and other rhetorical devices**
   - Overshoot and collapse
   - Commons
   - Spaceship Earth
   - Lily pond
   - Cancer
   - Virus
   - Images of doom and redemption

---

cancer itself must be cut out" (Ehrlich, 1968: xi). In a 2003 speech, UK Environment Minister Michael Meacher likened the human race to a virus that could destroy the Earth.[7] A vivid medical metaphor is invoked by Shearman and Smith (2007: 6–7), who speak of "the environment in intensive care" and the "multiorgan failure" of the living Earth demanding leadership by (environmental) doctors who certainly do not consult public opinion.

Box 2.1 provides a summary of the discourse analysis of limits and survival.

Limits and survival in practice

What difference has the discourse of limits and survival made in environmental affairs? And has any such influence been for the better or for the worse? Survivalism once provided the apocalyptic horizon of environmental concern, raising the stakes in environmental affairs. In these terms, its effects may be profound, while hard to trace directly into particular politics, policies, or outcomes. Certainly the bleak authoritarian prescriptions proposed by the survivalist vanguard (especially in the 1970s) find little reflection in political practice or institutional design, and show few signs of being adopted anywhere. The draconian population control attempted briefly and disastrously in India in the mid-1970s, and in China with greater effect since then, may constitute exceptions. The more pervasive political practice associated with survivalism turns out to take a form somewhat different from the original authoritarian political theory.

This form does, though, remain an elitist affair, certainly not that of a social movement, or even interest groups involving large numbers of people. The discourse of limits and survival treats most people as "population," effectively denying them agency, the capacity to act. The politics of limits is exclusive. Now, pressure groups devoted to furthering the survivalist agenda have existed and do exist, in the form of organizations such as Negative Population Growth (NPG), the Club of Rome (which later embraced ecological modernization; see Chapter 7), the Worldwatch Institute, and 350.org. Such groups have generally relied upon the largesse of foundations and a few wealthy benefactors, rather than mass membership (though 350.org styles itself as a grassroots group). The Club of Rome limited its membership to one hundred individuals. More broadly based was the Global Tomorrow Coalition of environmental and future-oriented interest groups in the United States, formed to follow up the *Global 2000 Report to the President* after 1980. Some of these groups had a large membership. But the coalition itself never played an especially visible role in mobilizing public opinion; groups could declare an affiliation to it without really integrating its efforts into their own activities.

Pressure groups advancing limits and survival have for the most part sought the ear of the powerful rather than the mobilization of any broader public (though Worldwatch publications are widely distributed). Sometimes this was successful—as for example, when President Jimmy Carter directed the Council on Environmental Quality and the Department of State to produce *Global 2000*. In a 2012 speech United Nations Secretary-General Ban Ki-Moon endorsed the planetary boundaries concept. UK Environment Minister Michael Meacher in 2003 declared that "this is the first time in the history of the Earth that species by themselves by their own activities are at risk of generating their own demise."[8]

The impact of discourses cannot be reduced to the direct consequences of the efforts of organizations that subscribe to them. Discourses can also take effect in largely impersonal fashion, if they can indeed manage to change the language that significant numbers of people use. So can we trace any initiatives, policies, agreements, social changes, or other phenomena to the limits discourse? Obviously coordinated population control efforts—especially in China—fall into this category. At the all-important global level, perhaps the best example may be found in coordinated international action to halt and reverse ozone depletion in the stratosphere. Meadows et al. (1992: 141–60) believe that the ozone issue shows that we can indeed move at the global level "back from beyond the limits"; similarly, Rockström et al. (2009) say it shows a planetary boundary can be confronted. Peter Haas (1992) argues that a like-minded "epistemic community" of atmospheric scientists was the driving force behind global action, just as it should be in this discourse.

Ozone depletion was first recognized as an issue in the 1970s; the culprit was identified as chlorofluorocarbons (CFCs), chemicals found in aerosol sprays and refrigerators. Stratospheric ozone is vital in shielding life on Earth from solar ultraviolet radiation, which can cause skin cancer in humans and other animals, damage photosynthesis in green plants (so threatening agriculture and forestry), and kill aquatic plankton. The issue was dramatized in the form of an "ozone hole" appearing over Antarctica in the austral winter, identified and named in 1985. The ozone problem did, then, constitute a classic limit, which by the mid-1980s appeared to have been overshot. While global negotiations relating to this issue had been going on for some time, in 1987 there was a dramatic acceleration in global action. The 1987 Montreal Protocol was signed by twenty-four nations, covering the main CFC producers and consumers. The Protocol committed developed nations to freeze consumption of CFCs almost immediately and impose a series of percentage cuts subsequently. Later revisions strengthened the Protocol, eventually specifying that CFCs be eliminated at the end of 1995, at least for developed countries. The rest of the world was given longer, and promised aid from developed countries to introduce substitutes and compensate for economic losses caused by lack of access to CFCs.

Meadows, Meadows and Randers (1992: 159) conclude that the ozone issue shows that "a world government is not necessary to deal with global problems, but it is necessary to have global scientific cooperation, a global information system, and an international forum within which specific agreements can be worked out." Litfin (1994) explains the Montreal Protocol in terms of a global discursive shift on this issue, toward a discourse of limits, or, as she refers to it, precaution. The key event to Litfin was the rhetorical force of the "ozone hole" idea. The hole referred to seasonal and variable (though substantial) reductions in ozone concentrations over Antarctica. A "hole" could capture the imagination in the way reams of data from monitoring stations could not. By 1987 there was no empirical evidence that CFCs actually damaged the ozone layer, though the required chemical reactions had been demonstrated in laboratory settings.

There is no denying that the ozone issue does represent an environmental success, and by 2010 there were signs of recovery in the ozone layer. However, some caution is in order before making too much of it, or seeing it as a prototype for global action on other issues, for three reasons. First, the stakes were comparatively small: CFCs are useful chemicals, but substitutes for them exist. Second, it is possible to reconstruct the history of negotiations on the ozone issue in terms not of rational solving of a collective problem (Meadows), nor of science-driven policy making (Haas), nor a discourse shift (Litfin), but rather in terms of the material interests of key actors, as Berejikian (2004) shows. The negotiations were dominated by two key actors: the United States and the European Community (EC). The United States already had legislation restricting CFCs at the national level. Corporations such as Du Pont feared that lack of any global controls on CFCs would put them at a competitive disadvantage, as they were devoting resources to the development of substitutes. (Meadows et al. (1992: 159) praise the role played by "flexible and responsible corporations" such as Du Pont.) So an international agreement was desirable from the point of view of Du Pont and, by extension, the United States. The EC initially dragged its feet on the issue. However, once it became clear that the United States might ban imports from the EC of products containing CFCs, the EC was much more willing to negotiate. On the ozone issue, it was fortuitous that the material interests of key players could eventually be brought into line with global environmental concerns. This coincidence should not be expected as a general rule.

If ozone layer protection is the most prominent (qualified) success in addressing a global limit, climate change is to date the most prominent failure. The economic stakes on this question are much higher, as the foundation of industrial economies in fossil fuels is at issue. Climate change resulting from increased concentrations of greenhouse gases (notably carbon dioxide and methane) in the atmosphere promises greater frequency of extreme weather events such as hurricanes. However, the kind of catastrophe over-dramatized in the 2004 film *The Day After Tomorrow* is less important than chronic and insidious changes: gradually rising sea levels, slow melting of the permafrost underlying tundra in Arctic regions, changes in rainfall patterns leading to either flood or drought. Some uncertainty remains concerning the timing of these effects, though there is scientific consensus on the existence and severity of climate change. The Intergovernmental Panel on Climate Change set up by the United Nations General Assembly in 1988 summarizes the scientific consensus in periodic reports.

The Kyoto Protocol of 1997 committed developing countries to reducing their carbon dioxide emissions to 5.2 percent below 1990 levels by 2012. Developing countries (including emerging industrial giants China and India) were exempt. Most of the countries that ratified the protocol did not reach its targets. In 2001 President George W. Bush took the United States out of Kyoto on the grounds that US economic interests were more important than global environmental protection. Since then the US federal government has been prevented from taking any action on climate change by Congressional Republicans, for whom climate change denial eventually became an article of faith. Political forces in the United States that still care about climate change include state governments (notably California), insurance companies worried about extreme weather wiping out profits (Gaffney and Höppe, 2012), and national security specialists in the Pentagon and elsewhere who warn of civil conflicts, population movement, and instability conducive to terrorism and war that could result from climate-related catastrophes (Gilman et al., 2011).

Every year since 1995 there has been a Conference of the Parties (COP) to the United Nations Framework Convention on Climate Change (UNFCCC) with a view to negotiating a comprehensive global agreement to reduce emissions of greenhouse gases. Almost all of the world's countries send a delegation. But agreement has proven elusive; and many countries seem to be fighting for their economic self-interest, paying only lip service to global climate concerns. The UNFCCC is nothing like the global steering system seen as necessary in a discourse of limits and boundaries, and global emissions of greenhouse gases continue to rise.

Limits and survival: an assessment

The lack of international action on climate change illustrates what is perhaps the biggest challenge confronting the limits discourse. In this discourse, agency is for elites, and most importantly for elites operating on a coordinated global basis. The slogan "Think globally, act locally" is a frequent exhortation in environmental circles; but for the discourse of limits and survival, the appropriate slogan is "think globally, act globally." Though the ozone issue illustrates potential for coordinated global action, as things stand the requisite global authority is missing. Some recent work on "Earth system governance" promotes strengthened global institutions (Biermann et al., 2012). But existing institutions for global environmental governance are weak, especially in comparison with those for economic governance. The World Trade Organization is perhaps the strongest body for global governance yet established. Though sustainable development appears in the preamble to its constitution, and it has a Committee on Trade and the Environment, in practice it subordinates environmental values to economic ones. Within free-trade regimes, nation-states are compelled to pursue policies to encourage footloose investors to locate capital in their countries rather than their rivals, and this means removing environmental restraints on trade. Within states, liberal democracy is the most popular model (though it is challenged by China's vision of an authoritarian "harmonious society"). This model is a far cry indeed from the centralized authoritarian forms favored by the more austere old survivalists, though real-world liberal democracies are not necessarily so far from the more pervasive elitism of the discourse.

The discourse of limits and survival does not, then, sit easily in the real world. It also has to struggle with some powerful competing discourses. Rome is home to a Church as well as a Club. The Roman Catholic Church has consistently opposed any efforts to control human population, inasmuch as such efforts countenance contraception and abortion. The Church played an obstructive role at the 1994 United Nations International Conference on Population and Development in Cairo, in unholy alliance with Islamic fundamentalists and mostly Protestant fundamentalists from the United States.

From the left, opposition comes from those who see talk of population as inherently racist (for the United States, see Chock, 1995; for Australia, see White, 1994). An ontology that stresses "population" and the denial of agency to members of that population looks, from this left/multicultural direction, as if it were designed to control and discriminate against those ethnic groups whose numbers are increasing most rapidly. In the United States, these are generally nonwhites and especially Hispanics, whose numbers are bolstered by immigration both legal and illegal. In 2004 a group opposed to immigration attempted to gain control of the Sierra Club's governing board, but was defeated in a membership election.

An assault on the discourse of limits has also come from ecofeminism. Ecofeminists affirming pre-patriarchal symbols of fertility contend that population control means control of women by a male power structure (Diamond, 1994), in the interests of producing the kinds of consumers required by global capitalism (Sandilands, 1999: 88). For women to regain their places in harmony with a living, fertile earth it means breaking free from all patriarchal shackles—including population control experts and their political masters. The survivalists once gave them plenty of ammunition, as for example when Garrett Hardin (1993: 258) states that "we need to devise acceptable ways of influencing the desires of women in the light of community needs." But today it is abundantly clear that population growth can be curbed through empowerment and education of poor women, and so the limits discourse can happily shed such associations.

The religious, left multiculturalist, and ecofeminist arguments against the limits discourse miss their target. Religious arguments reduce to dogma concerning fundamental tenets of faith for individual (micro) behavior combined with insensitivity to how these tenets play out at the macro level. Left multiculturalists, in exposing racist and sexist aspects of limits discourse, do not thereby solve the problem of population pressure; they sweep it under the carpet, or implicitly assume that the interests of particular ethnic groups must always trump any global interest. In other words, they advocate maintenance and expansion of a commons in the interests of social justice. They actually have nothing to say about the reality or otherwise of limits, beyond dismissing them as social constructions that serve established political power—which is obviously false, given that global capitalism is so much better served by Promethean discourse that denies limits. A better deployment of social justice concerns here would begin by noting that it is the prosperous peoples of the world who impose the greatest burden on the ecosphere.

There does exist a discourse that has engaged limits and survival more directly, and on ground where arguments can be made, as opposed to dogma asserted. This opponent is Promethean, and its defining feature is the denial of limits. Given that it is rooted in industrialism, but only makes sense as a reaction against the limits discourse, it is appropriate to discuss this Promethean discourse and the challenge it presents to survivalism at length in the next chapter.

The limits discourse has, then, had limited impact in its own terms. Recall that this discourse seeks coordinated, central action, with foresight built in. Very little such action is apparent. The time horizons of governments and corporations remain short. The global political economy is thoroughly inhospitable to any ideas about limits and boundaries that could threaten the very idea of perpetual economic growth. The limits discourse is in evidence at the periodic United Nations conferences (notably the Conference on the Human Environment in Stockholm in 1972, the Conference on Environment and Development in Rio in 1992, the International Conference on Population and Development in Cairo in 1994, the World Summit on Sustainable Development in 2002, and the Conference on Sustainable Development in Rio in 2012), though these gatherings became increasingly dominated by the competing discourse of sustainable development. Eventually we find laments about time wasted as a result of prior warnings unheeded—which is why Meadows et al. (1992) believe the world has now gone "beyond the limits" (see also Nørgård et al., 2010).

Nothing in this patchy record means that the discourse is erroneous in its stress on limits, and it may yet find vindication if, for example, the planetary boundaries identified by Rockström et al. (2009) are seriously violated. Politically, there has never been enough imagination as to how the agenda might be pursued, and the discourse took a long time to shake off the simplistic draconian authoritarianism of the 1970s survivalists. Its partisans do not quite know what to say or do about global capitalism, especially given that some of their financial sponsors are global capitalists. These problems notwithstanding, the impact of the discourse of limits and survival should not be dismissed. If nothing else, it raised the stakes in the establishment of the environment as a key issue, perhaps *the* key issue for the twenty-first century.

NOTES

1. His analysis was also formally identical to the account of the seventeenth-century political philosopher Thomas Hobbes of the "war of each against all."

2. <http://www.maweb.org/en/About.aspx> (accessed July 11, 2012)

3. Countries such as the United States, in contrast, require relatively restrained policies, such as heavy taxes on diapers and toys to discourage people from having children. Later, Paul and Anne Ehrlich (1974) give up on the possibility of any government doing much right, and propose only that individuals prepare themselves for the coming crunch by laying in stores of food and practicing self-sufficiency. With this suggestion, the Ehrlichs find common ground with the right-wing, gun-toting survivalists in the United States. But such aggressive individualism is generally absent from the environmental discourse of limits and survival.

4. Later, Ophuls protests that he raises the specter of authoritarianism simply as a warning of what might have to happen unless humanity gets its political-ecological house in order through less draconian means (Ophuls and Boyan, 1992: 312). In addition to this authoritarian model, his book contains, in uneasy juxtaposition, a decentralized, Jeffersonian political economy of self-reliant small-scale communities.

5. Interview with James Lovelock. Online at <http://www.guardian.co.uk/environment/2010/mar/29/james-lovelock> (accessed March 29, 2010).

6. <http://www.worldwatch.org/node/10496> (accessed May 6, 2012)

7. "Michael Meacher: End of the world nigh – it's official," *Guardian*, London, February 14, 2003.

8. "Michael Meacher: End of the world nigh – it's official," *Guardian*, London, February 14, 2003.

3

....

Growth Unlimited: The Promethean Response

The Promethean background

Discourses do not need conscious articulation. They can be so ingrained and taken-for-granted that it would never occur to anyone to mention them. (Analogously, most speakers of the English language could not articulate the basic principles of grammar and syntax they use every day.) Such was long the case for the environmental discourse which can, now that it has been articulated, be styled Promethean. In Greek mythology Prometheus stole fire from Zeus, and so vastly increased the human capacity to manipulate the world. Prometheans have unlimited confidence in the ability of humans and their technologies to overcome any problems—including environmental problems.

The term "cornucopian" is sometimes associated with this denial of environmental limits. Cornucopia means abundant natural supply: unlimited natural resources, unlimited ability of natural systems to absorb pollutants, and unlimited corrective capacity in natural systems. However, Julian Simon protests that this is a misnomer: "The school of thought that I represent here is not cornucopian. I do not believe that *nature* is limitlessly bountiful. . . . our cornucopia is the human mind and heart not a Santa Claus natural environment" (1981: 41). Simon's protests notwithstanding, I will show that members of this school, including Simon himself, do portray a Santa Claus natural environment at key junctures. So strictly speaking this discourse should be styled Promethean/cornucopian. But that is too much of a mouthful, so let me just call it Promethean, which really does capture the essence better than "cornucopian."

For several centuries, at least in the West, the dominant Promethean order had been taken for granted. The Industrial Revolution produced technological changes that made materials close to home (such as coal and later oil) into useful resources. At the same time, European colonial expansion opened up new continents and oceans for exploitation. Capitalist economic growth could be taken as the normal condition of a healthy society. Even those who looked forward to a future beyond capitalism, notably Karl Marx, applauded technological progress, economic growth, and the conquest of nature.

Today, just about every government sees its first task as promoting economic growth. The entire way in which economic news is reported assumes that growth is good. This refers to growth in wealth, growth in income, growth in profits, growth in the stock market, growth in employment, growth in housing starts, growth in passenger miles traveled. That economic growth usually means increased stress on environmental systems—more pollution, more congestion, faster depletion of resources—is never reported along with these economic aggregates (though this stress is reported elsewhere). The political-economic discourse of liberal capitalist systems still generally floats free from any sense of environmental constraints.

Promethean argument to the foreground

The recognition of ecological limits described in the previous chapter meant that Promethean discourse had to be articulated and defended, rather than just taken for granted. Economists have been at the forefront of the Promethean counterattack. The economists' basic argument was established as early as 1963 with the publication of *Scarcity and Growth* by Harold Barnett and Chandler Morse, produced under the sponsorship of the Washington think tank Resources for the Future. Economists have always said that price is a measure of scarcity: if the real price of a good goes up, that means demand in relation to supply is increasing. Conversely, if the price of a good falls, then demand relative to supply is falling. This logic can be applied to the goods we call natural resources. Barnett and Morse gathered long-term trend data for the prices of a number of "extractive goods": agricultural products, minerals, fisheries products, and timber. In every case except forest products the story was the same. Barnett and Morse showed that since at least the beginning of the twentieth century, the real price (i.e., after adjusting for inflation) of natural resources had been falling. If price measures scarcity, this means natural resources are becoming more abundant with time. Updates of the Barnett and Morse analysis continued to tell a similar story (Smith, 1979; Taylor, 1993).

When the limits to growth argument arrived with such a bang in the early 1970s, Promethean economists did, then, have a ready-made argument and plenty of data to throw back at the survivalists. Wilfred Beckerman (1974) deployed long-run evidence from price trends against the *Limits to Growth* global modelers to argue that there was nothing wrong with projecting economic growth into an indefinite future. It became the standard criticism of the *Limits* modelers that their computer models did not include any role for either prices or technology. Twenty years later, Beckerman saw no difficulty in deploying the same kind of evidence against another generation to argue that *Small is Stupid* (Beckerman, 1995; the title's allusion is to E. F. Schumacher's *Small is Beautiful*). Later still, his *A Poverty of Reason* (Beckerman, 2002) took aim at sustainable development as well as limits. Julian Simon put his money where his mouth was in a famous bet with population biologist Paul Ehrlich in 1980. Simon bet that the real price of any set of natural resources that Ehrlich cared to name would be lower at any time in the future than in 1980. Ehrlich specified copper, chrome, nickel, tin, and tungsten, with 1990 as the date. Come 1990, the price of copper was 24 percent lower than in 1980, chrome 40 percent lower, nickel 8 percent lower, tin 68 percent lower, and tungsten 78 percent lower. Ehrlich sent Simon a check for $1,000 (see Michaels, 1993: 368–9). Later, Simon would renew his challenge in the context of a debate with Norman Myers; he was so confident that he increased the offer to a month's pay, and extended it to any measure of human welfare in any country or region of the world (Myers and Simon, 1994: 20–1, 115; see also Simon 1996: 33–6). This time, Simon found no takers.

Why do the prices of natural resources keep falling, suggesting increasing abundance? If a shortage threatens, there is money to be made in either finding new sources of the resource in question, or in developing substitutes. In this light, there is nothing new about resource scarcity, or about response to it. In sixteenth- and seventeenth-century Europe, wood was the key energy resource, and so when wood supplies seemed to be running out an energy crisis looked imminent. The response was the development of coal as a fuel, which in turn made the technologies of the Industrial Revolution possible—and coal itself came to be mined more cheaply using these technologies (Nef, 1977). Come the mid-nineteenth century, the economist William Jevons (1865) predicted that coal would soon run out, and that the wheels of British industry would stop turning. He need not have worried; not only were more deposits of coal continually discovered, but oil was soon developed as an energy resource.

Economists such as Barnett, Morse, Beckerman, and Simon see no problem in projecting such happy trends in resource and energy availability and price into the future. Just how far into the future? "We expect this benign trend to continue at least until our sun ceases to shine in perhaps 7 billion years, and until exhaustion of the elemental inputs for fission (and perhaps for fusion)" (Simon and Kahn, 1984: 25). No modesty here! Those not convinced that economists can forecast inflation and unemployment over the next year or so might be a bit hesitant about accepting the seven-billion-year forecast.

In the 1980s Julian Simon established himself as the leading American Promethean, and broadened the argument beyond resource prices to encompass trends over time of indicators of human wellbeing such as life expectancy, food supply per capita, amount of arable land, air and water quality, amount of parkland, forest cover, and fish catch. The indicators he sought were mostly global, though national and regional data were adduced too. Life expectancy plays a key role for Simon as a surrogate for pollution. He allows that with time some forms of pollution increase as others decrease; so the introduction of the internal combustion engine saw an increase in pollutants such as carbon monoxide and ozone, but a massive decrease in the horse droppings in which city streets were often quite literally awash. What matters, Simon says, is the net overall effect of offsetting pollution increases and decreases on human health—and the best summary measure of that is life expectancy (1981: 130–1). The long-term trend evidence is that in all parts of the world people are living longer; therefore in all parts of the world pollution is falling. (However, AIDS would cause falling life expectancy in much of sub-Saharan Africa.) Easterbrook (1995) declared that "In the Western world, the Age of Pollution is nearly over." Bradley (2003) argues that all the pollution issues associated with energy production have now been solved (though climate change resulting from fossil fuel use may still require a bit of attention). For Ridley (2010), such trends are not just positive—they are accelerating.

Simon is not always as scrupulous as he might be in the kinds of evidence he adduces. For example, in 1984 he tried to show that the United States was becoming less crowded through reference to a graph showing a massive increase in the amount of land in national parks over the 1950–80 period (Simon and Kahn, 1984: 8). In fact, almost the entire increase occurs in 1979. What happens in 1979, which Simon fails to mention, is passage of the Alaska National Interest Lands Conservation Act, which for the first time classified federal government lands in Alaska. Some of these lands were classified as national parks. Many are accessible only by bush plane. One can imagine the sighs of relief in 1979 echoing around the Bronx, South Central Los Angeles, and Chicago, as suddenly their residents all felt less crowded.

Julian Simon died in 1998. His place as the public face of Prometheanism was soon taken by Bjørn Lomborg. Lomborg is a political scientist and statistician rather than economist, and so says little about the underlying economic mechanisms that alleviate scarcity. He focuses narrowly on the trends themselves, and reaches exactly the same conclusions as Simon on global aggregates (though like Simon he uses regional data when it suits his purposes). Lomborg made a splash in 2001 with the publication of *The Skeptical Environmentalist* ("Environmentalist" because he claims to be a former Greenpeace member). Extracts and summaries of the book quickly appeared in the *New York Times, Guardian* (London), and *The Economist*. The claims echoed Simon: natural resources, energy, and food are becoming more abundant, fewer people are starving, life expectancy is increasing, pollution is eventually reduced by economic growth, species extinction presents a limited and manageable problem, forests are not shrinking.

Lomborg met a storm of criticism from environmentalists and scientists (in some cases those whose work he drew on in the book).[1] Environmentalists (e.g., Burke, 2001) objected that Lomborg begins with a caricature. In Part I of his 2001 book, Lomborg sets out an alleged "Litany" of environmentalism:

The environment is in poor shape here on Earth. Our resources are running out. The population is ever growing, leaving less and less to eat. The air and water are becoming ever more polluted. The planet's species are becoming extinct in vast numbers . . . the forests are disappearing, fish stocks are collapsing. . . . We are defiling our Earth, the fertile topsoil is disappearing, we are paving over nature, destroying the wilderness, decimating the biosphere and will end up killing ourselves in the process. The world's ecosystem is breaking down. We are fast approaching the absolute limits of viability, and the limits to growth are becoming apparent. (Lomborg, 2001a: 4).

Lomborg goes on to say about the Litany: "There is just one problem: it does not seem to be backed up by the available evidence." But there is in fact another problem: hardly any environmentalists actually subscribe to it. The Litany captures only an extreme position in the survivalist discourse, more popular in the early 1970s than in the early 2000s. Lomborg's main targets are the Worldwatch Institute and the early works of Paul Ehrlich (which predate *Global 2000*, Simon's main target). Lomborg fails to recognize the variety of environmentalist positions—not least one that would credit environmental improvements of the kind he charts to the political efforts of environmentalists influencing public policy.

Natural scientists objected that Lomborg presented selective and distorted interpretations of their data. A special issue of *Scientific American* (January 2002) was devoted to debunking Lomborg. Aside from ad hominem remarks about a political scientist trespassing on scientific territory, the authors criticized Lomborg's misinterpretation of scientific sources, selective presentation of evidence, stress on the quantity as opposed to quality of resources such as forests (equating old growth ecosystems with timber plantations), and insensitivity to uncertainty about complex systems. Charges against Lomborg were taken to the Danish Committee on Scientific Dishonesty, which found against him in that "the objective criteria for scientific dishonesty have been met," but excused him on the grounds he didn't know what he was doing.[2] In December 2003 the Danish Ministry of Technology overturned the Committee's negative verdict. This episode reveals much more about the peculiar politics of science in Denmark than it does about the veracity or falsity of Lomborg's analysis.

Subsequently Lomborg turned his attention to climate change, arguing in *Cool It!* (2007) that the world would be better off devoting money to (say) the eradication of malaria than to reducing greenhouse gas emissions. While many Prometheans would deny the existence of climate change caused by humans, Lomborg accepted that climate change was real—and could be combatted on a vast Promethean scale through geoengineering, which requires abandoning the idea of self-correcting markets in favor of big, planned projects. According to Lomborg (2010), cost-benefit analysis shows that the most effective way to curb climate change is through marine cloud whitening, which requires creating mists from sea water. The consequently whiter clouds would reflect more sunlight into space, and so help cool the Earth. Lomborg also endorsed the injection of sulfate aerosols into the atmosphere to simulate the cooling effects of volcanic eruptions in blocking sunlight. The third geoengineering option often proposed (but not endorsed by Lomborg) would involve seeding the oceans with iron so they can absorb more carbon dioxide. These sorts of giant projects reflect the Promethean faith in technology—but not in prices and markets, for it would surely need government of some kind to organize them.

Promethean environmentalism

While most Protheans believe environmental affairs can be left to the market, Lomborg's support for high-technology, large-scale geoengineering points to a new kind of Promethean environmentalism, which recognizes the severity of problems but would confront them with technology, developed and deployed by governments as well as markets. So for example leading British environmentalist George Monbiot has embraced nuclear power as essential, given that it produces hardly any greenhouse gas emissions. The nuclear revival received a setback with the earthquake and tsunami that hit power plants at Fukushima in Japan in 2011, leading to meltdown and substantial radiation release. Japan subsequently took all its reactors offline (thus increasing greenhouse gas emissions). After Fukushima, the conservative government in Germany under Chancellor Angela Merkel changed course to confirm Germany's planned abandonment of nuclear power. Monbiot (2011) insisted that the real lesson of Fukushima was quite different: that if old plants using obsolete technology with poor safety standards in a vulnerable location did such little harm when hit, think how safe nuclear power plants could be if built to higher specifications in secure places.

Promethean environmentalism is advanced most forcefully by the Breakthrough Institute in the United States, founded in 2003. Opposing an environmentalism of limits and complaints, Breakthrough sees a future of high-technology, clean energy abundance (Shellenberger and Nordhaus, 2007). In the introduction to their manifesto *Love Your Monsters* (the allusion is to the unloved Frankenstein, who turned to evil only after being abandoned by his creator), Shellenberger and Nordhaus (2011) proclaim:

By 2100, nearly all of us will be prosperous enough to live healthy, free, and creative lives. Despite the claims of Malthusian pessimists, that world is both economically and ecologically possible. But to realize it, and to save what remains of the earth's ecological heritage, we must once and for all embrace human power, technology, and the larger process of modernization.

The Breakthrough Institute has as little faith in self-regulating markets as in self-regulating ecosystems. Rather, it seeks governmental direction of the search for new technologies. Sarewitz (2011) in his contribution advocates massive investment in cheap low-carbon energy—as an alternative to increasing the price of fossil fuels through carbon taxes or emissions trading schemes (which I will discuss in Chapter 6). Sarewitz departs from conventional market economics, which would see the development of low-carbon sources being spurred by high fossil fuel prices.

Analysis of Promethean discourse

Basic entities whose existence is recognized or constructed

For Prometheans, natural resources, ecosystems, and indeed nature itself, do not exist. This denial can explain just about everything there is worth knowing about Promethean discourse. This claim about nature's nonexistence, at least as anything more than a store of matter and energy, might seem startling. Consider, though, Simon's basic argument about natural resources. He affirms, time and again, that the supply of natural resources is infinite. Why? Because there is no fixed supply of resources: "Resources are only sought and found as they are needed" (1981: 40). Thus there is no point in measuring the quantity of reserves remaining: if more is needed, more will be sought and found. But just what are these things we call natural resources anyway, if, as one Promethean argues, "Not a single natural resource has ever been created by 'nature'" (Taylor, 1993: 378)? The answer is that "natural" resources are created by humans transforming matter. Nature is, indeed, just brute matter; and in their wilder moments (as in the Simon and Kahn seven-billion-year projection mentioned earlier)

Prometheans believe matter is infinitely transformable, given enough energy. The medieval alchemists believed base metals could be turned into gold. Prometheans believe that with enough energy iron can be turned into copper (Myers and Simon, 1994: 100n)—which indeed it can be, though the amount of energy required is massive. Similarly, deserts can be turned into cropland, outer space can be colonized.

With enough energy, with the fruits of economic growth, we can also take care of pollution (see Lewis, 1992: 184). Pollution is, in Promethean light, just matter in the wrong place in the wrong form, and with enough skilled application of energy, that can be corrected. As Lomborg puts it: "only when we are sufficiently rich can we afford the luxury of caring about the environment" (2001a: 33). Ridley (2010) argues that if climate change is a problem, poor countries should become richer in order to finance adaptation to it.

Though Prometheans might occasionally use the word "ecosystem," the concept plays no real part in their discourse, in which ecosystems do not constrain human activity. Accordingly, "the term 'carrying capacity' has by now no useful meaning" (Simon and Kahn, 1984: 45). Lomborg's position on limits is a bit different from Simon's: he accepts that when it comes to fossil fuels and minerals, "there must be some limits to the amount . . . that can be extracted," but "That limit is far greater than many environmentalists would have people believe" (2001b).

Having dealt with absences from the Promethean ontology, what basic entities does it recognize or construct? In short: people, markets, prices, energy, technology. (Promethean environmentalists of the Breakthrough Institute variety would replace markets with states.) Prometheans talk a lot about population—Julian Simon became famous mostly as a result of his intervention in debates over global population, in which he celebrated population growth. But population is not constructed in the way it is for survivalists, as an aggregate entity to be controlled. I will return to the implications of this difference shortly.

Assumptions about natural relationships

I have already noted that the Promethean discourse comes close to denying the very existence of nature, which is at most seen in inert, passive terms. The most important natural relationship taken for granted is therefore a hierarchy in which humans (and, in particular, human minds) dominate everything else. This domination does not need to be organized, or consciously maintained; it just exists. In their more extreme moments, Prometheans believe that a total control of nature is within our grasp (for an early explicit statement, see Murphy, 1967).

Beyond human domination, the other relationship seen as natural is competition between humans (again, with the exception of Breakthrough Institute statists), through which innovative means for overcoming emerging scarcities can best be generated. So when the Organization for Petroleum Exporting Countries organized oil embargoes in the 1970s it was competition which spurred the search for non-OPEC sources of oil, and for cars that would use less gasoline. This emphasis reveals an affinity between the Promethean discourse and proponents of the market. Prometheans see little need for government to do much in the way of environmental and natural resources policy: if long-term trends are improving, the best thing government can do is leave well alone (Ridley, 2010). Inasmuch as they attend to government, Prometheans see mostly sources of ill. As the Promethean physicist Bernard Cohen (1984: 566) puts it in reference to the United States, "Given a rational and supportive public policy, science and technology can provide not only for the twenty-first century but for ever." But, he avers, the necessary support for nuclear energy and other constructive endeavors is missing. For:

our government's science and technology policy is now guided by uninformed and emotion-driven public opinion rather than by sound scientific advice. Unfortunately, this public opinion is controlled by the media, a group of scientific illiterates drunk with power, heavily influenced by irrelevant political ideologies, and so misguided as to believe that they are more capable than the scientific community of making scientific decisions. (p. 566)

Agents and their motives

In the Promethean discourse, agency—the capacity to act—is for everyone, mainly as economic actors. People going about their business, pursuing their selfish interests, will together ensure a bright environmental future. This is an application to resource and environmental issues of the "invisible hand" working in the market system, first celebrated by Adam Smith in the late eighteenth century.

As seen in the preceding chapter, the discourse of limits and survival denies agency to populations, which are treated as problems to be controlled. Promethean discourse, in contrast, celebrates the people who compose populations. If individuals are problem solvers, all potentially contributing to the betterment of humanity's lot, then the more people the better. In denying the existence of limits, Prometheans generally also deny the need to worry about rising populations, be it on a national, regional, or global scale. Rising populations have been accompanied by rising, not falling, life expectancy, and increased, not reduced, income per head. Certainly this is true at the global level: the same decades which have seen population explosion have also seen life expectancy rising to historically unprecedented levels on a global scale, and the prices of natural resources continuing to fall. Individuals, Julian Simon believes, make good decisions about the number of children they have, such that "population size adjusts to productive conditions rather than being an uncontrolled monster" (1981: 162–3). For Simon, "the ultimate resource is people—skilled, spirited, and hopeful people who will exert their wills and imagination for their own benefit, and inevitably they will benefit not only themselves, but the rest of us as well" (1996: 589). If people are good, then more people will always be better. Implicit here is the idea that the supply of ingenuity is proportional to the number of people (an assumption questioned by Homer-Dixon, 2000, who suggests limits to this supply).

Not all Prometheans share Simon's cavalier position on population. Easterbrook (1995) calls for world population stabilization in the short term, while allowing that in the long term the Earth could support several times its current population. Beckerman (1995: 63, 173–4) allows that developing countries have a population problem. He believes (as does Lomborg, 2001b) that the world's most pressing environmental problems are associated with the poor in these countries lacking access to clean water and good sanitation. The obvious solution is for them to become rich, and that may be easier the fewer of them there are.

Key metaphors and other rhetorical devices

The key Promethean metaphor is mechanistic. Machines are constructed from simple components—ultimately, simple resources—through the application of human skill and energy. Thereafter they do useful things. A solution to any kind of problem can be pieced together in like manner for Prometheans, be it the restoration of malfunctions in the human environment (such as pollution or wilderness destruction), or the creation of natural resources for human use.

The main weapon in the Promethean rhetorical arsenal is the trend. Prometheans are at their happiest when presenting graphs depicting declining resource prices, increasing parklands, croplands, and forests, increasing life expectancy, increasing crop yields and fisheries catches, and so forth. The explicit accompanying message is: the trend can be extrapolated indefinitely into the future—more than seven billion years into the future, as we have seen for Simon. Lomborg is slightly more cautious, saying that "trends provide the best information about how things have progressed and are likely to progress" (2001a: 6). Note how different this is from the modeling of the interaction of different variables (such as population growth, resource use, and environmental damage) reported in the previous chapter. The trends presented in graphs or figures by Prometheans are single-variable, and no attempt is made to model interactions. Prometheans would say that the interactive models found in the discourse of limits and survival are inaccurate, simplified, and speculative. The difference underscores the Promethean neglect of the existence of eco*systems,* in which by definition many factors interact.

Box 3.1 provides a summary of the Promethean discourse analysis.

BOX 3.1 Promethean discourse analysis

1. **Basic entities recognized or constructed**
   - Nature as only brute matter
   - Markets
   - Prices
   - Energy
   - Technology
   - People
2. **Assumptions about natural relationships**
   - Hierarchy of humans over everything else
   - Competition
3. **Agents and their motives**
   - Everyone; motivated by material self-interest
4. **Key metaphors and other rhetorical devices**
   - Mechanistic
   - Trends

The impact of Promethean discourse

Promethean discourse flourished alongside capitalism and the Industrial Revolution, with its unbounded faith in the ability of humans to manipulate the world in ever more effective fashion. Such was human progress. Thus the first place to look for the impact of the discourse would be in our dominant institutions: a capitalist economy geared to perpetual economic growth, and a political system whose main task is to facilitate the conditions for that growth. Discourse and institutions co-evolved. When it comes to political institutions, the Promethean discourse constitutes much of their software, if the hardware is composed of formal laws and constitutions. That is, institutions of government such as parliaments, executives, and bureaucracies require sets of understandings shared by the people who work within them in order to coordinate their operations. The main shared understanding in the capitalist democracies has long been that growth is good. And we find that political elites in these countries generally exhibit a much more Promethean attitude to the technological risks that must be taken to facilitate growth than do publics, who are more risk averse. This difference is especially striking for publics that get a chance to deliberate and reflect upon risks (for a demonstration of this difference in the case of genetically modified foods, see Dryzek et al., 2009).

Once the environmental challenge arrived in the late 1960s, and especially with the limits terms of debate set in the early 1970s, the Promethean discourse was very much on the defensive, and so pressured to articulate its key tenets for the first time. These newly articulated tenets eventually found a ready and sympathetic ear in the form of President Reagan and his associates, and later in the presidency of George W. Bush. These presidencies are the high points of influence of Promethean discourse on policies and institutions, though we can also see Promethean influence at work in conservative governments in Australia (1996 to 2007) and Canada (after 2006).

Two key appointments symbolized the Reaganite Promethean approach. James Watt was appointed Secretary of the Interior, responsible for overseeing the vast bulk of federal lands. Anne Gorsuch (later Burford) was appointed Administrator of the Environmental Protection Agency (EPA), charged with administering the nation's antipollution policy. Both Watt and Gorsuch Burford were hostile to most of the legislation they were supposed to administer. Watt was by background a "Sagebrush Rebel," identified with a movement in the rural west of the United States keen to transfer ownership of federal lands (including national parks and wilderness areas) to the states, hoping that the states would open these areas (ironically, with public subsidy) to loggers, miners, and ranchers. Watt's view was clearly Promethean: resources were there to be used for human benefit, not locked away. He characterized environmentalists as Nazis or Bolsheviks, and anyone who did not share his views as un-American. In 1990 he suggested that "if the troubles with environmentalists can't be solved in the jury box or the ballot box, perhaps the cartridge box should be used" (quoted in Dowie, 1995: 97).

Burford for her part attempted to purge the EPA of individuals who actually believed in the agency's mission, and turned policy making over to the polluters the EPA was supposed to regulate. She left behind an agency with its budget and personnel slashed, its morale shattered, and its mission compromised.

The later Reagan years saw a retreat from some of the excesses (and flamboyance) of the Watt–Burford era. No longer was the Promethean agenda in the hands of clowns and criminals at the highest level of government (criminality being evident at the EPA). Yet Promethean discourse set the tone for US actions in the international arena, where wholesale reversal of US commitment to international environmental governance took place (see Caldwell, 1984). The United States withdrew support and finance for international treaties or programs concerning the law of the sea, transboundary air pollution (especially acid rain), trade of nuclear materials, and the United Nations Environment Program. This attitude continued for the next three decades, with the US Senate the guarantor of opposition to international environmental agreements, even as Presidents Clinton and Obama were personally in favor of international cooperation. In the 1980s, the only real exception to US foot-dragging on international environmental affairs came with the issue of ozone layer depletion, discussed in the previous chapter.

Promethean discourse returned to the White House with a vengeance with the installation of George W. Bush in 2000. Though radical, the attack on environmental policy was often low-key and subtle, with no flamboyant figures to act as lightning-rods and recruiting agents for environmentalists. The EPA was initially headed by moderate Christine Whitman, Interior by the low-profile Gale Norton. The best hate figure for environmentalists was Vice-President Dick Cheney, who brought the values of the unreconstructed wing of the oil industry into government. Cheney headed a task force on energy policy composed of executives from the oil, coal, and vehicle manufacturing industries. In introducing its report in 2002, Cheney declared that "conservation may be a sign of personal virtue, but it is not a sufficient basis for a sound, comprehensive energy policy." "Sound and comprehensive" meant increasing the supply of traditional energy sources, especially fossil fuels. This in turn meant promoting oil and gas development on federal lands—most controversially, the Arctic National Wildlife Refuge in Alaska—and removing restrictions on the use of fuels. The emphasis on supply over conservation could be linked to the 2003 invasion of Iraq, though in the short term at least the effect on oil supply was the opposite of that intended.

Promethean discourse backed US withdrawal from the Kyoto Protocol on climate change in 2001, on the grounds that US economic interests took precedence over environmental considerations. As Wapner (2003: 7) put it, "the hegemon has essentially checked out of the business of global environmental protection." The administration had little to fear from a Republican-dominated Congress. The courts eventually proved more of a check. Notably, in 2007 the Supreme Court, in a case brought by Massachusetts and other states, ruled that carbon dioxide was a pollutant, and so the federal EPA should regulate its emission (despite the opposition of EPA Administrator Stephen Johnson). In addition, the administration still feared the environmental leanings of public opinion. So domestically, policy actions were cloaked in the language of environmentalism. Opening federal forests to (uneconomic) logging was justified by fire protection, and described as the "Healthy Forests Initiative" (signed into law in 2003). Similarly, a weakening of air pollution controls was styled the "Clear Skies Initiative." In 2004 Interior Secretary Gale Norton spoke of her department's "new environmentalism."

Most policy changes took effect "below the radar," in administrative interpretation of legislation and regulation, reduced enforcement of regulation, funding cuts at the EPA, and the politicization of scientific advice. Government scientists were expected to toe the line and suppress unwelcome evidence and advice. Few species were listed as endangered, and few designations of critical habitat made. Some administrative decisions were profound in their effects. Examples include a 2003 decision to allow coal-burning electrical utilities to upgrade old and dirty plants without meeting current antipollution standards, the attempted removal of Clean Water Act protection for vast areas of "isolated" waters, and the attempted exemption of the US military from all environmental laws (for a catalog, see Environment 2004,2003). Mountaintop removal to access coal seams was made easier, with devastating consequences in Appalachia.

In February 2004 an e-mail sent to all Republican members of Congress recommended they reply to Democratic criticisms of Bush's environmental policy with rosy quotes from Lomborg.[3] But Lomborg proved reluctant to embrace Bush. Right-wing think tanks continued to push the Promethean agenda in the United States (for example, *Bailey's Earth Report 2000* is linked to the Reason Foundation).

It is, then, mainly in the United States that explicit Promethean discourse has gained significant influence (though there are Promethean publicists in other countries, such as Wilfred Beckerman in the UK and Bjørn Lomborg in Denmark). This American exceptionalism was highlighted in the 1980s and after 2001. In the 1980s, the United States sometimes found itself casting the sole vote in the United Nations General Assembly against particular environmental measures—such as the World Charter for Nature in 1982, and a motion against trade in hazardous substances in 1983. (Of course, not all of the countries voting for these measures could be said to be paragons of environmental virtue.) In 2001, the United States stood almost alone in renouncing the Kyoto Protocol (accompanied only by Australia, whose foreign policy at the time was to follow US instructions; in 2011 Canada withdrew). In the United States, Promethean discourse resonates with the interests of both capitalist market zealots and Christian conservatives, not to mention miners, loggers, and ranchers accustomed to subsidized access to resources. Such constituencies are smaller or absent in other countries, except for Canada and Australia.

After 2010, massive Promethean energy and finance were devoted to attacking and undermining the science of climate change, in favor of a cornucopian idea that the environment is infinitely forgiving of what humans might do to it. Corporations such as Koch Industries and Exxon Mobil pour money into compliant think tanks such as the Heritage Foundation and Heartland Institute, and seek out and fund scientists who depart from the scientific consensus (Dunlap and McCright, 2011). In the United States, organized climate change denial proved successful, and by 2012 no Republican presidential candidate could possibly allow that human-induced climate change was real. Republican members of Congress also fell into line. The attacks on mainstream climate scientists were bitter and personal; in 2010 Senator James Inhofe (R-Oklahoma) argued for criminal investigation of climate scientists. In 2009 the organized denial movement received a major boost with the publication of stolen e-mails from the University of East Anglia in the UK that suggested breakdown of scientific objectivity. A subsequent parliamentary inquiry cleared the scientists in question of any wrongdoing, but the public damage was done.

The climate denial movement works not by generating any body of counter-evidence, but by sowing doubt in the minds of the public. As Oreskes and Conway (2010) point out, many of the tactics—and indeed some key individuals—were taken from the tobacco industry's long-standing campaign to discredit scientific findings linking smoking to cancer and other diseases. Organized denial receives enthusiastic backing in the right-wing media (such as Fox News), and can even take advantage of the "balance doctrine" in the more serious media—the idea that two sides on an issue must be presented (Boykoff and Boykoff, 2004). While the organized denial movement has successfully halted US federal government action on climate change, its impact elsewhere is mostly limited to two other Anglo-American frontier societies that depend heavily on fossil fuel exports—Canada and Australia.

On the face of it, it seems odd that these Prometheans should attack the science and argue climate change is not a problem—rather than show that it is a problem that could be solved by human ingenuity and markets. But the issue may be that the organized denial movement is right in thinking that climate change, if it exists, can only be confronted by strong governmental action (Klein, 2011). Thus climate change cannot be allowed to exist, and no amount of science can possibly induce organized climate change deniers to change their mind. The term "skeptic" is sometimes used to describe those who think anthropogenic (human-caused) climate change does not exist, but that is a misnomer. A true skeptic is someone who takes nothing on trust, requiring evidence and argument to be convinced. In this sense, Bjørn Lomborg is a true skeptic; but organized deniers are not. In subordinating science to politics, truth for the organized deniers becomes a subcategory of power. The organized denial movement therefore embodies extreme postmodernism, destabilizing the idea that there can be any such thing as scientific truth that is not driven by a political agenda. The whole Enlightenment ideal of a society guided by reason is lost. There is no reason, no truth—only a fight between political positions, which the organized denial movement is determined to win.

Promethean discourse: an assessment

Assessment of the Promethean discourse may begin by noting that without a cornucopian adjunct, the discourse is radically incomplete, the protestations of its adherents, such as Julian Simon, notwithstanding. Why is this?

Prometheans believe that humans left to their own devices will automatically generate solutions to problems—and that an invisible hand guarantees good collective consequences. To substantiate this claim, they return time and again to examples such as the introduction of motor vehicles leading to cleaner and healthier city streets with the removal of horses and their droppings. But there is no guarantee that such benign side-effects of individual actions will always occur. It is not only survivalists who stress the centrality in environmental affairs of the tragedy of the commons, the essence of which is that materially rational individual decisions can produce disastrous macro-level consequences. What can Prometheans say about, for example, climate change, where millions of rational individuals contribute to the buildup of carbon dioxide in the atmosphere by burning fossil fuels? The most common Promethean answer is simply to deny that climate change is a problem, and to attack the science that suggests otherwise. Bradley (2003: 20–1) even argues that climate change is mostly benign, bringing "warmth, moisture and carbon fertilization."

The Promethean Aaron Wildavsky goes through a series of environmental risks to show that really the scientific evidence shows there is no cause for alarm—and happily generalizes this conclusion to all risks, including ones he has not studied (1995: 447). Similarly, Simon suggests that we extend his conclusions from cases where good evidence is available to cases where at the time he was writing it was unavailable, such as "the ozone layer, the greenhouse effect, acid rain, and their kin" (Myers and Simon, 1994: xvi). When it comes to loss of biodiversity through species extinction, Prometheans again deny the problem, arguing that there are no reliable statistics to show wholesale extinctions caused by human activities such as deforestation (see Simon's contribution in Myers and Simon, 1994: 40; Lomborg, 2001a: 255).

What is coming to the rescue of the Prometheans here? Julian Simon claims that the difference between himself and those who see limits is that he bases his arguments on evidence, whereas his opponents rely on theory (Myers and Simon, 1994: 148). But the Promethean argument can only stand with not just a theory of human ingenuity, but also a theory of nature's abundance. The required theory is that nature is replete with negative feedback devices that correct for human abuses. (Negative feedback is by definition automatic corrective action in a system which restores it to equilibrium when it is disturbed, so usually a good thing.) So when Simon discusses biodiversity, he refers to the fact that nature is always creating species, as well as extinguishing them (Simon and Kahn, 1984: 23). Unfortunately for Simon the rate of species extinctions caused by environmental destruction far exceeds the speed with which nature can create species; it is the difference between years and millennia. Wildavsky (1995), in his discussion of global warming, alludes to such feedback devices in ecosystems. If the Promethean position is to stand, such devices must have unbounded capacity to correct for human abuses. In short, what is needed here is an infinitely forgiving nature. Earlier, I noted that Simon referred disparagingly to Santa Claus cornucopians. Yet Promethean discourse requires nature to be more generous still than Santa Claus, who brings only coal and no presents to children who misbehave. For the Prometheans—more properly styled Promethean–Cornucopians—nature will bring good things to us even, and especially, when we misbehave.

Who is right? Are there limits, or are there not? The world of limits and survival described in Chapter 2 consists of finite ecosystems with fixed stocks of resources, where human population explosion and economic growth threaten to overshoot the limits of these systems or transgress the boundaries of a "safe operating space." In the Promethean world, nature does not exist, save as a source of matter to be rearranged in the human interest through application of energy and technology (though an infinitely forgiving nature eventually comes to rescue the otherwise incomplete Promethean worldview). Where Prometheans see benign trends heading off into a happy future, their opponents see looming boundaries into which these trends will eventually crash.

On the trend evidence so far, the Prometheans are clear winners. Now, as we have seen, Prometheans are not always overly scrupulous about a little sleight of hand when it comes to presenting statistics. And given complexity and interdependence in environmental affairs, improvement on one indicator in one place may mask deterioration in another. This is the phenomenon of displacement (see Dryzek, 1987: 16–20). Displacement occurs when, for example, a country exports its toxic wastes, or its polluting industry. A cleaner environment in developed countries, for which we have more and better figures to compose trends, has been purchased in part by transferring manufacturing to developing countries with comparatively lax standards, so if we look at the emissions embedded in the goods *consumed* in developed countries, the overall trend may be in the wrong direction. Displacement across space can also occur when tall smokestacks are constructed on coal-burning power stations to reduce local pollution—only to cause acid rain elsewhere, as a result of sulfur dioxide spending longer in the atmosphere. Displacement can take place across the media, as when a water pollution problem is solved by capturing effluent, drying, and burning it; or disposing of it as toxic sludge. Promethean statistics should be believed only when they refer to global trends. Caution may be warranted there too—if, for example, growing global agricultural production has been purchased at the expense of the long-term productivity of land (through excessive use of fertilizers and pesticides, or farming techniques that hasten soil erosion). This example shows that displacement can occur across time too. Prometheans ignore this issue (or, in Lomborg's case, attempt to refute it by ridiculing one poor example of displacement; 2001a: 11). Their confidence in the veracity and power of statistical indicators of environmental trends represents refusal to recognize complexity and uncertainty in ecological affairs.

These issues notwithstanding, when it comes to long-term global trends in natural resource prices, agricultural production, and life expectancy, most of the lines on the graphs have indeed been pointing in benign directions. Thus those who stress limits are tactically mistaken in taking on Prometheans in arguing about which direction the global trends are pointing—sometimes ending up with egg on their faces as a result (or, in the case of Paul Ehrlich, a wallet $1,000 lighter). However, the fact that a trend has persisted in the past is no guarantee that it will persist indefinitely into the future. The driver of an accelerating car about to hit a brick wall might well say "so far, so good"— but that does not mean the wall is not there. In Chapter 2 we saw there are all kinds of good arguments for the existence of walls—even if it is hard to see how far in front of the car they are located.

One way to resolve this issue might be to compare the answers to two questions. First, if we believe the Prometheans and they are wrong, what are the consequences? Second, if we believe there are limits or boundaries and that proves wrong, what are the consequences?

As a footnote to this analysis of Promethean discourse, on dimensions unrelated to limits and survival Prometheans can be found on the environmentalist side. Julian Simon says that he enjoys the outdoors, especially likes bird-watching, and looks back fondly on the nature study merit badge he earned as a boy scout (1996: xxxiv). Aaron Wildavsky concludes his Promethean exposé of environmental risks with the question, "What, in my vision, is left of environmentalism? There is respect for nature, for all life. There are moral questions of human relationships to all creation" (1995: 447). Given that there is little in Promethean discourse about aesthetics, there is nothing to stop Prometheans being aesthetic environmentalists. Aesthetics aside, if the Prometheans are right then all other discourses of environmental concern are rendered irrelevant and unnecessary.

NOTES

1. Lomborg's replies to his critics can be found at <**http://www.Lomborg.com**>

2. "Debunker of global warming found guilty of scientific dishonesty," *Guardian*, London, January 9, 2003.

3. "Bush attacks environment 'scare stories,'"*Observer*, London, April 4, 2004.

PART III
SOLVING ENVIRONMENTAL PROBLEMS

....

The clash of survivalists and Prometheans detailed in Part II is full of drama, and the stakes appear massive—nothing less than the fate of the Earth. Yet if we look for specific changes in institutions, policies, and practices directly traceable to these discourses, we are often likely to be disappointed. Prometheans committed to the market would say that the whole point is that nothing much needs changing, though there are a large number of public policy practices they would like to see eliminated, involving fairly radical changes. In practice, we find more limited policy responses in an environmental context. Governments have not engaged in draconian population control or sought to limit (let alone end) economic growth. Instead, they have opened their doors to environmental lobbyists, passed laws to conserve resources or ameliorate pollution, and created bureaucracies to implement these laws.

I turn then to a less apocalyptic category of discourse that has had obvious consequences in the way societies, and especially governments, have gone about characterizing and attacking environmental problems. The discourses of environmental problem solving recognize ecological problems, but treat them as tractable within the basic framework of the political economy of industrial society. The basic story line is that of problem solving rather than heroic struggle. Human interactions with the environment generate a range of problems (rather than one big problem like overshoot of limits threatening social collapse, or planetary boundaries being transgressed), to which human problem-solving devices can be turned. Different varieties of this discourse reveal different conceptions about how best to organize problem solving, especially when social problems require coordination of large numbers of individuals. The three main ways to coordinate such efforts are by bureaucracy, democracy, and markets. Corresponding to these three coordination mechanisms are the three discourses I address in Chapters 4, 5, and 6: administrative rationalism, democratic pragmatism, and economic rationalism. However much partisans of these three variations may disagree with each other, they share the basic story line of problem solving; and their differences with the limits discourse, Prometheans, sustainable developers, and green radicals are striking. Of the three, I will deal with administrative rationalism first because it captures the dominant governmental response to the onset of environmental crisis, remaining prominent in the ambitions of some scientists in global politics, and looming large in China. Democratic pragmatism emerged as a corrective to administration, and in the form of networks eventually extends across national boundaries. And economic rationalism builds on its advances in all areas of political life to generate alternatives to and remedies for the pathologies it identifies in both administration and liberal democratic governance. All three eventually take on global environmental problems, if in very different ways.

4

Leave it to the Experts: Administrative Rationalism

Environmental issues are typically complex. They also involve systems that have long been the objects of study of natural scientists (and public health engineers). Thus when these issues came to prominence in the 1960s they could be associated with a public policy tradition that accorded substantial status to scientific expertise harnessed by administrative structures. Administrative rationalism may be defined as the problem-solving discourse which emphasizes the role of the expert rather than the citizen or producer/consumer in social problem solving, and which stresses social relationships of hierarchy rather than equality or competition. As an institutional style, administrative rationalism figures more strongly in some political systems than in others. So it is very strong in France, Germany, and China, slightly less strong in Britain (where it has been leavened by a culture of generalism among high-ranking civil servants), and it has had a somewhat patchy but none the less significant presence in the United States.

In 2012 there was a concerted push by environmental scientists to render global environmental governance more closely guided by scientific expertise, culminating in the 2012 Planet Under Pressure conference in London. As Lovejoy (2012) put it in a *New York Times* op-ed, "The moment has come to realize that this planet which brought us into existence must be managed as the biophysical system that it is. It is time to get our hands on the steering wheel, not to save the planet, but to keep it habitable." This of course assumes there is a global steering wheel somewhere; the subsequent 2012 United Nations Conference on Sustainable Development held in Rio seemed to confirm that there is not, as the governments in attendance could agree on very little of substance.

When environmental issues first rose to prominence on the political agenda, their assimilation to administrative rationalism was not planned or debated against the alternatives (such as those that might be generated by the alternative discourses that appear in other chapters). It was simply taken for granted that this was how issues should be handled. Thus the onset of environmental problems was met by institutional and policy responses remarkably similar in both content and timing across the nations of the developed world.[1] If one seeks the essence of most other environmental discourses, it is to be found in the writings and speeches of theorists and activists. But for administrative rationalism, that essence can be captured by looking at actual practice in the development of policies, institutions, and methodologies. Administrative rationalism does have its theorists, but they tended to come later. In this chapter we will encounter some of them, but it is more appropriate to begin with a survey of practices, policies, and institutions.

The repertoire of administrative rationalism

Administrative rationalism manifests itself in the following institutions and practices.

Professional resource-management bureaucracies

"Natural resource management" has been around much longer than "environmental policy," especially for developed governments with resource-rich territory and significant economic activity in the resource sector, notably the United States, Canada, and Australia. The oldest professional resource management bureaucracies are to be found in the United States, the legacy of its Conservation Movement at the beginning of the twentieth century (Hays, 1959). This movement was infused with some German ideas about conservation ecology via its key figure, Gifford Pinchot, who studied in Germany. The movement's main argument was that the American endowment of natural resources was in danger of being squandered in a free-for-all, such that more rational scientific management coupled with government ownership was required to put those resources to more efficient human use. The movement had no interest in wilderness preservation, environmental aesthetics, or pollution reduction, and sought only to achieve maximum sustainable yield from renewable resources such as forests and watersheds. The Conservation Movement achieved ascendancy in Washington DC, and Gifford Pinchot lent his guidance to the administration of President Theodore Roosevelt. The main organizational legacy was the US Forest Service, located within the Department of Agriculture, which was reorganized by Pinchot. However, the Forest Service's ethos of professional resource management based on scientific principles could not withstand sustained political pressure from the timber industry. Today, the US Forest Service functions mainly to service the industry—for example, by constructing logging roads into national forests at public cost, so providing enormous public subsidy to the industry. Welfare logging of this sort presumably has Gifford Pinchot turning in his grave.

Later, President Franklin Roosevelt's New Deal in the 1930s saw the establishment of several federal resource management agencies, notably the Civilian Conservation Corps, the Tennessee Valley Authority, and the Soil Conservation Service. Creations of a confident presidency, these agencies were deliberately insulated from congressional influence, thus giving professional managers space without having to worry about political oversight. Ackerman and Hassler (1981: 4–6) define a New Deal agency in terms of the "affirmation of expertise," insulated from both political control and judicial oversight. Today, the US federal government is home to resource management bureaucracies such as the Bureau of Land Management, the Fish and Wildlife Service, the National Park Service, the National Oceanic and Atmospheric Administration, and the US Geological Survey. None of these is a paragon of scientific management to the exclusion of political influence—especially the influence of extractive industry, be it miners, loggers, oil companies, ranchers, or fishers. But all operate according to at least a public justification of administrative rationalism, however much that may be violated in practice. All employ individuals with relevant scientific and professional expertise.

Pollution control agencies

Not every country has a vast national estate of natural resources. But every country suffers from pollution; and so every country that can afford it has a pollution control agency. Many subnational governmental units such as states, provinces, and cities also possess such agencies; they have even emerged at the international level (for example, the United Nations Environment Program).

The oldest such agency is Britain's Alkali Inspectorate, created in 1864. The Alkali Inspectorate is one of the ancestors of the unified Inspectorate of Pollution established in Britain in 1987 as part of the Department of the Environment. This Inspectorate was itself later merged into a still more inclusive Environment Agency. This unification was a bit belated; most developed countries gained such an agency in the early 1970s. So the Netherlands gained a Department for Public Health and Environmental Hygiene in 1971, the US Environmental Protection Agency was established in 1970, and in Germany antipollution policy was centralized in the Interior Ministry in 1969, later passing to a free-standing agency. Such agencies are typically charged with implementing laws. Landmark pieces of legislation here include the 1956 Clean Air Act in the United Kingdom (passed in response to London's "killer fog" in December 1952). More recently, a number of governments have set up specialized agencies to deal with climate change (for example, the UK's Department of Energy and Climate Change, Australia's Department of Climate Change and Energy Efficiency).

The US Environmental Protection Agency (EPA) is sometimes regarded as the paradigmatic antipollution agency, but in fact it is a bit of an anomaly, for its professional discretion is highly constrained. The members of Congress who set up the EPA in 1970 had in mind the experience of regulatory agencies that had been captured by the industries they were supposed to be regulating (so the trucking industry controlled the Interstate Commerce Commission, the food industry controlled the Food and Drug Administration). To prevent such capture, Congress specified in a number of statutes (such as the Clean Air Act, Water Pollution Control Act, Toxic Substances Control Act) in great detail exactly what the EPA must do, setting precise targets and dates for pollution reduction and the means for achieving them. This micro-management on the part of Congress intensified in the 1980s when congressional leaders perceived that the Reagan administration wished to dismantle the EPA (Rosenbaum, 1995: 208–9). The EPA's counterparts in other countries typically have much more discretion in setting standards and deadlines, and in formulating measures to apply in particular cases.

Resource management bureaucracies and regulatory pollution control agencies rest claims to authority on the scientific and professional expertise they mobilize. Such claims to impartial expertise have come under attack from right wing conservatives and postmodernists, united in a belief that scientific neutrality is impossible, that all science (and especially climate science) is ideologically colored. The politicization of science in the administration of George W. Bush was criticized in a 2004 report by the Union of Concerned Scientists: *Scientific Integrity in Policymaking: An Investigation into the Bush Administration's Misuse of Science.* This politicization involved replacing scientists on advisory committees with pro-industry partisans, selective release of the findings of scientific studies of proposed antipollution legislation in order to discredit proposals unfavorable to industry, and the suppression of discussions of climate change in EPA publications.

Regulatory policy instruments

Whether as a matter of legislation (as for the US EPA) or of choice on the part of the agency, the most popular policy instrument for pollution control has, in developed countries, been regulation (see Burleson, Lye, and Robinson, 2012 for a survey). Regulation traditionally involved the staff of the agency formulating knife-edge standards for particular polluters, who are punished (usually by fines) if and when these standards are not met. Regulators could also specify the kinds of pollution-control equipment that must be installed to cut emissions (for example, catalytic converters on car exhausts, or scrubbers for coal-burning power plants), the kinds of materials that can be used (for example, unleaded gasoline, or low-sulfur coal), and the kinds of practices that must be followed (such as inspections and safety checks). Normally regulation has been "end of pipe" in character—that is, regulators have not intervened to specify changes in production processes to make them produce less noxious waste. Instead, the focus is on reducing discharge of that waste into the environment once the waste has been produced.

Regulation of this sort entails substantial discretion on the part of the regulators, even in the United States. That said, national approaches to regulation vary. In the United States, regulation proceeds in adversarial fashion, and both sides rely a great deal on lawyers to advance cases for more or less stringent pollution standards. Many decisions end up in the courts: polluters sue the EPA for excessive stringency in enforcing the relevant law and for arbitrary action violating the principles of the US constitution; environmentalists sue the EPA for not enforcing laws with enough vigor; the EPA sues polluters for not complying; corporations sue individuals for defamatory criticisms (so-called SLAPP suits—strategic lawsuits against public participation). In 2007 the State of Massachusetts and others successfully sued the federal EPA to force it to recognize and so regulate carbon dioxide as a greenhouse gas pollutant. Thus in the United States it is the courts' interpretation of legislation that is decisive, and administrative rationalism in practice is highly constrained by this legalistic, adversarial context. Fiorino (2006) argues that though this approach has had its successes, more flexibility in how polluters can respond to regulatory goals would be desirable.

Matters are very different in countries where administrative rationalism is allowed a freer hand. In Britain, where administrative rationalism traditionally dominated environmental policy (Gray, 2000), regulations are developed in consultation between government officials and polluters. Pollution abatement and environmental quality appear no worse in Britain than in the United States. Regulation in Britain is not simply a matter of political negotiation, for all sides at least in principle accept the authority of scientific expertise in adjudicating disputes. In some cases, a scientific body is called on formally to render a verdict—the Royal Society played this role on acid rain policy in Britain in the 1980s (Hajer, 1995: 144–5). Pollution-control discourse in Britain specifies that no regulatory action be taken until science can demonstrate the harm being caused. As William Waldegrave, Minister of State in the Department of the Environment, put it in 1987: "It is necessary in an area which should be science-based to put up pretty formidable hurdles and tests of a scientific nature if we are to make rational priorities" (quoted in Weale, 1992: 80). This is the exact opposite of the "precautionary principle" applied in countries such as Germany and the Netherlands, which specifies that scientific uncertainty is not a good reason for delaying action (see Chapter 8).

A particular kind of regulation involving a lighter touch is "nudge," sometimes classified as "libertarian paternalism." Cass Sunstein, one of its originators (Thaler and Sunstein, 2008) went on to become Director of President Obama's Office of Information and Regulatory Affairs. The idea of nudge is not to tell people what to do, but to change the context in which they act so as to induce them to make different decisions. To date the environmental applications have been fairly minimal: for example, making recycling bins much larger than garbage bins, labeling the latter "goes to landfill," providing feedback to householders along with their energy bills on how much they have used in comparison with previous years and what the associated greenhouse gas emissions are. The impact has been fairly minimal too. Sunstein himself points to the possibility of big nudges—for example, a well-publicized list of the biggest corporate greenhouse gas emitters in a country.

Environmental impact assessment

Environmental impact assessment specifies that government departments (and, in some cases, private developers) must prepare a systematic assessment of the environmental damage likely to be caused by any major project, be it an airport, a mine, a shopping mall, a sale of oil or mining or timber leases, a freeway, or a pipeline. The US National Environmental Policy Act of 1970 (NEPA) is a landmark in establishing this kind of process, but again the US turns out to be slightly anomalous. Large numbers of impact statements have been prepared in the US, perhaps the most famous being the two prepared for the Trans-Alaska Pipeline immediately following the passage of NEPA. The first was a few pages long; after being ruled inadequate by the courts, a second was prepared in multiple volumes which would occupy many feet of shelf space (ironically, the pressure of the energy crisis in the wake of the 1973 Organization of Petroleum Exporting Countries oil embargo eventually led Congress to exempt the pipeline from NEPA requirements). Again, the courts have played a large role in determining what US legislation actually means. In the case of NEPA, the courts' interpretation has been that an impact statement must be prepared, not that it must actually be used in decision making. Thus US environmental impact statements became long and unreadable documents, designed to defend agencies against accusations that environmental concerns were not being taken seriously. Environmentalist and community objectors to proposals could file suit only on the basis of the adequacy of the impact statement, not on the basis of the substantive merits of the agency's decision. Observers of the environmental impact process in the US are divided on whether it has indeed improved policy making as intended. Even Lynton Caldwell, largely responsible for crafting the NEPA legislation, could not make up his mind on whether the Act had the desired impact (for a pessimistic assessment, see Caldwell, 1978; for a more positive verdict, see Caldwell, 1982).

Environmental impact assessment soon spread to Canada, Australia, Germany, France, and elsewhere. The UK eventually accepted environmental impact assessment at the behest of the European Community in 1985. In these other countries the path of administrative rationalism in environmental impact assessment has been less strewn with legal and political obstacles than in the United States. Not that matters are always smooth. For example, in Melbourne (Australia) the state government (Victoria) routinely exempted the biggest and most controversial projects from assessment. In the mid-1990s these included construction of a Grand Prix motor-racing circuit in an inner-city park, a freeway network around the city center, and the world's biggest casino. High-profile exemptions can happen in the United States too. In 2009 the Obama administration exempted BP's Deepwater Horizon project in the Gulf of Mexico. In 2010, disaster struck the project with a massive oil spill into the Gulf.

Environmental impact assessment is not unalloyed administrative rationalism. Typically the process also mandates opportunities for public comment on impact statements and so public participation in the policy process. This latter aspect is more easily joined to democratic pragmatism, and will be discussed in the next chapter.

Expert advisory commissions

The United States also pioneered the idea of an expert commission to offer advice on environmental affairs. The President's Council on Environmental Quality (CEQ) was set up in 1970 in a section of the National Environmental Policy Act. Quite what the commission would do (aside from offer comment on the environmental impact processes established under NEPA) was never entirely clear, and the role of the CEQ has varied substantially across different presidencies. It fell into virtual disuse in the 1980s. The CEQ might act as a counterweight to the longer-established and more influential Council of Economic Advisors (CEA). Both report directly to the President. But the CEQ has never attained the standing of the CEA. In 1993 President Clinton merged the CEQ into an Office of Environmental Policy (OEP) in the White House. This arrangement continued under President George W. Bush, though the CEQ/OEP profile continued to fade, and its membership was skewed to people with a background in polluting industry. Bodies such as Germany's Council of Environmental Experts, established in 1972 and modeled on the US CEQ, have achieved greater centrality in policy making. Special-purpose commissions can also be set up; in 2011 the Australian government established a Climate Commission to advise on greenhouse gas emissions control policy.

In Britain, there is a long tradition of deference to scientific expertise, and so to expert advisory bodies, though that tradition is now waning. Notable among such bodies was the Royal Commission on Environmental Pollution, established in 1971 but abolished in 2011. In addition, the Royal Society (of scientists) is occasionally called upon to play a key role in policy determination (indeed, its advisory role began with a 1664 report on forests to King Charles II). None of this means that environmental policy in Britain is made by administrative rationalism untarnished by politics, for science is expected to fall into line with the policy priorities of the government of the day.

Planning

Planning is not confined to administrative rationalism, and different varieties are covered in other chapters of this book. However, administrative rationalism is home to a particular kind of top-down planning that sets targets centrally then specifies the means to achieve them. This sort of environmental planning is prominent in China, whose government now speaks of "building ecological civilization" as part of its "harmonious society" (Morton, 2009: 32–4). In the 1990s China began to reconsider its policy of industrial development at all costs to at least recognize the need for pollution control and natural resource management, establishing a series of plans and targets.

Engineers are heavily represented in the Chinese Communist Party leadership, and they tend to think in terms of big projects. In the past this meant projects to conquer nature that ignored social and environmental impacts, such as the Three Gorges Dam. More recently, it means projects to protect or repair the environment, such as tree planting programs to restore watersheds, even bigger plans to restore the ecological health of river basins, five year plans to promote the energy efficiency of industry, and massive development of renewable energy (in which China is now the world leader). Such projects by no means exhaust the repertoire of Chinese environmental policy. But they are attractive to the leadership because when it comes to environmental laws and regulations, China suffers a chronic problem of weak enforcement, especially when they collide with local economic development imperatives. Big projects and plans seem to fare better.

Should geoengineering to combat climate change ever come to pass (see Chapter 2), it would almost certainly be accompanied by planning on a huge scale. Projects such as cloud whitening, seeding the oceans with iron, and inserting aerosols into the atmosphere will be global in their scope and in their investment requirements, and so would have to be organized globally.

Rationalistic policy analysis techniques

The expertise that legitimates administrative rationalism comes largely in the form of environmental science and engineering. Relevant disciplines include forestry, oceanography, meteorology, ecology, hydrology, geology, fisheries biology, biochemistry, and toxicology. But administrative rationalism also involves application of general-purpose policy analysis techniques, most of them geared to identification of the optimal policy in a given situation. The most widely used are cost–benefit analysis and risk analysis. Other available techniques include technology assessment, decision analysis, and a range of forecasting methods. Cost–benefit analysis can be either forward-looking, in informing the choice of policy or project, or backward-looking, to evaluate policies already in place. Forward-looking cost–benefit analysis involves the following steps:

1. Identify policy options (including "do nothing").

2. For each option, list both desirable effects (benefits) and undesirable effects (costs).

3. Attach monetary values to all costs and benefits, using "shadow pricing" when the item in question has no market price.

4. Convert all costs and benefits occurring in future time periods to the present time period using a discount rate.[2]

5. Add up the monetary costs and benefits to give the net benefit associated with each alternative.

6. Choose the option with the greatest net benefit (provided that this net benefit is positive).

The real substance of a piece of cost–benefit analysis is shadow pricing. Obviously some items can easily have a monetary cost pinned onto them. For example, if the analysis is of a proposal to build a dam, construction costs can easily be expressed in terms of dollars. So can the benefits of the electricity generated by the dam. Other items are more difficult. How does one value in monetary terms the loss of a free-flowing river? Or the benefits to recreational users yielded by the artificial lake that will be constructed? Many shadow-pricing techniques can be brought to bear. A lost environment (such as a drowned river valley) can be valued by conducting a survey and asking individuals how much compensation they would require to consider themselves no worse off than before. Alternatively, they can be asked how much they would be willing to pay to prevent the drowning. Or the amount of time and money individuals expend to reach the valley for recreational activities can be observed and summed and used to calculate how much individuals actually pay to get to the valley. Valuing lives saved is still more controversial. In a cost–benefit analysis conducted by the US EPA in connection with the George W. Bush administration's Clear Skies initiative in 2003, a "senior discount" was applied that reduced the value of the lives of old people, leading to a political storm (Schmidt, 2003).

Cost–benefit analysis was pioneered in the siting and construction of dams in the United States, starting in the 1950s. The main sponsors were the US Army Corps of Engineers and the Bureau of Reclamation. One of the more famous pieces of cost–benefit analysis was conducted in the late 1960s in Britain by the Roskill Commission, set up to recommend a site for a third major airport for London. Roskill's recommendation in favor of a site at Wing in Buckinghamshire was reached via a cost–benefit analysis of the alternative sites. In its efforts to monetize all costs and benefits associated with each site, the Commission provided plenty of ammunition for its opponents. For example, the price put on a centuries-old church which would have to be demolished was determined by the increased travel time churchgoers would have to spend to go to more distant churches. (The recommendation in favor of Wing was not accepted by the government.)

Cost–benefit analysis received a major boost with the promulgation in 1981 of Executive Order 12291 by President Reagan, which specified that all significant federal regulations, including environmental ones, had to pass a cost–benefit test administered by the Office of Management and Budget. The idea was to use cost–benefit analysis as a tool to free corporations from regulations that harmed profitability. The Clinton administration reaffirmed the application of cost–benefit analysis to regulation. Under the George W. Bush administration, cost–benefit analysis was forced on the EPA and other agencies by the Office of Information and Regulatory Affairs within the Office of Management and Budget (Schmidt, 2003). Again, the next Democratic president (Obama) affirmed that existing and proposed regulations should be subjected to cost–benefit analysis (in a 2011 executive order).

Cost–benefit analysis on a grand scale appeared in the landmark 2006 Stern Review on climate change commissioned by the UK government. Stern carried out a global analysis, concluding that coordinated global action to reduce greenhouse gas emissions would yield benefits far in excess of the costs (Stern, 2006). Mainstream economists criticized Stern on the grounds that his conclusions rested on a low discount rate (0.1 percent per annum), and that a more conventional market-determined rate of around 3 percent per annum would change the conclusions (Nordhaus, 2007a). Economist Ross Garnaut (2008) produced a report for the Australian government reaching similar conclusions to Stern. The popularity of cost–benefit analysis then extended to biodiversity with the idea that the benefits that nature yields to humans can be monetized in the form of "ecosystem services" (see Norgaard, 2010 for a critique). In 2012, ninety countries jointly established an Intergovernmental Platform on Biodiversity and Ecosystem services that used this kind of language.

Planetary-scale cost–benefit analysis is also advocated by leading Promethean Bjørn Lomborg (2010: 2), who believes that "an informal ranking of solutions to the world's big problems is possible, and that cost-benefit analyses (CBAs)—much maligned by some—can lead to a clear and compassionate focus on the most effective ways to respond to the real problems of the world's most afflicted peoples." Lomborg's conclusions point to geoengineering solutions to climate change—not emissions reductions as favored by Stern.

Cost–benefit analysis is the subject of a huge literature, both technical in terms of how to do it (see, for example, Boardman et al., 2010), and critical in terms of why it should not be done (Sagoff, 1988; Vatn, 2000). From the discourse analyst's perspective, one large impact of cost–benefit analysis may be in legitimating the idea that public policy is a matter for technical, expert choice and not a question on which non-specialists such as elected officials, still less any broader public, have any rightful say. And this is why cost–benefit analysis rests more easily in a discourse of administrative rationalism than it does in economic rationalism. For this technique uses markets only to provide prices for the balance sheet of costs and benefits. Once such prices have been input, expert-guided governmental actions are central. Thus cost–benefit analysis has an implicit faith in the welfare-maximizing virtues of government officials, which true economic rationalism lacks, preferring instead that market mechanisms be utilized wherever possible.

Risk analysis covers a family of procedures and techniques, to quantify the potential harm from environmental hazards, such as ingesting pollutants, living downwind of a nuclear power plant, or being exposed to additional ultraviolet radiation as a result of ozone depletion in the stratosphere. The main sources of information in risk assessment are animal studies and epidemiology. Animal studies are based on the assumption that exposing animals to high doses of a pollutant can yield useful information about what happens when human beings are exposed to much lower doses (in terms of cancer rates, etc.). Epidemiological studies are statistical analyses of human populations that relate degree of exposure to a risk (for example, quantity of suspended particulates in the air) to the incidence of particular kinds of death and disease (for example, lung cancer). Both instruments can be very blunt. As Wildavsky (1995: 254, quoting David Ozonoff) puts it, "a good working definition of a catastrophe is an effect so large that even an epidemiological study can detect it." Thus it is no surprise when the claims of activists about health damage from a toxic dump in the neighborhood, electromagnetic radiation from power lines, or herbicide spraying are not confirmed. The number of cases is usually too small to enable demonstration of population-level effects required for statistical significance in an epidemiological study; but this does not mean the activists are wrong (Tesh, 2000). Also, risk assessment is not very good at dealing with the interaction effects of multiple environmental hazards.

Risk analysis also involves study of perceptions by ordinary people. Almost invariably, the scientific evidence shows that people wildly overestimate the potential damage to them from environmental risks such as having a toxic waste dump in the vicinity (Wildavsky, 1995), and behave quite inconsistently in relation to risks. Given that both animal studies and epidemiology are extremely blunt instruments, public skepticism and alarmism become a bit more understandable. Still, thinking of the place of risk analysis in environmental discourse, its political function is quite clear: the assessment of true risks is a matter for the experts, and the ordinary public usually gets it wrong.

Many of the psychologists who study risk give greater credence to public skepticism (Fischoff and Kadvany, 2011). Public skepticism can be explained by, for example, distinguishing between risks that are borne voluntarily, like driving a car, and those that are incurred involuntarily, like being exposed to fumes from a nearby factory. People have a much higher tolerance for risks they bear voluntarily. They also tend to have low tolerance for low-probability catastrophic events (such as the meltdown of a nuclear reactor), and so overestimate the risks from them.

Discourse analysis of administrative rationalism

Administrative rationalism seeks to organize scientific and technical expertise into bureaucratic hierarchy in the service of the state. As such, it rests on the following components.

Basic entities whose existence is recognized or constructed

Administrative rationalism is a problem-solving discourse, and so takes the structural status quo of liberal capitalism as given. Government is the administrative state, treated in unitary terms. Governing is therefore not participatory, but about rational management in the service of a clearly defined public interest, informed by the best available expertise.

The best real-world approximation to this monolithic imagery could long be found in Germany, home to a "legal corporatist" conception of government under which law is seen as an expression of state authority. In environmental administration, law was to be based on the best science. The Prussian administrative tradition views state and society as an organic whole, and the public interest in abstract legal terms, so not something that interest groups should bend. Opponents of the implementation of law could be styled as obstructionists and cranks, even if they were denied input to the formulation of law. While this system of government began to break down in the 1980s, residues lingered in the new century (Dryzek et al., 2003: 35–42).

Administrative rationalism is quite agnostic about many of the entities that so energize the discourse of limits and its Promethean critics—entities such as ecosystems, finite stocks of resources, population, energy (at least in the key role Six Prometheans construct for it).

Assumptions about natural relationships

While not explicitly concerned with the fundamental character of relationships between human and nonhuman worlds, administrative rationalism does assume that nature is rightfully subordinated to human problem solving, though not in the forthright and confident celebration of human domination of nature found among Prometheans.

Within human society, administrative rationalism assumes two complementary kinds of hierarchy. The first subordinates the people to the state (or, potentially, a transnational authority). The second puts experts and managers in their properly dominant places in the state's own hierarchy, which is justified on the basis of expertise. The discourse pretty much denies the existence of politics of any sort.

Agents and their motives

Agency is granted to both collective and individual actors. Government as a collective actor is the primary agent, but this does not imply that all individuals working for the state have an equal capacity to act. Technical experts and managers have a greater capacity than anyone else. Motivations are treated as entirely public-spirited, and the public interest is conceptualized in unitary terms. Thus discovery and application of the public interest is itself a technical procedure (see Williams and Matheny, 1995: 11–17), which is why (for example) cost–benefit analysts or risk assessors know better than the public itself what is in the public interest.

Key metaphors and other rhetorical devices

Administrative rationalism is much less vivid in its metaphors than survivalist and Promethean discourses. Doom and redemption are not at issue, which makes for muted rhetoric. Environmental problems are serious enough to warrant attention, but not serious enough to demand fundamental changes in the way society is organized.

If there is a metaphor that characterizes the discourse, it is that of a unitary administrative mind. This is like the human mind, only collective and embodied in the administrative state. Just as the human mind controls the body, so the administrative mind controls the state. As Torgerson (2005: 98) puts it: "The image of the administrative mind is one of an impartial reason exercising unquestionable authority for universal wellbeing; it is an image that projects an aura of certain knowledge and benign power." Accompanying this imagery is the idea that society can be steered in the right direction, that effective navigation through the complexities of the social-ecological environment is possible.

Box 4.1 provides a summary of the discourse analysis of administrative rationalism.

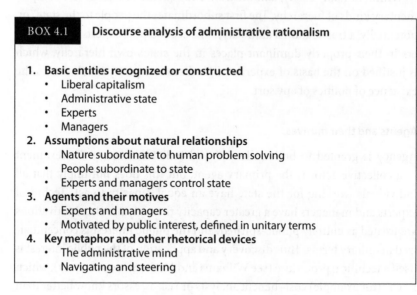

BOX 4.1   **Discourse analysis of administrative rationalism**

1. **Basic entities recognized or constructed**
   - Liberal capitalism
   - Administrative state
   - Experts
   - Managers
2. **Assumptions about natural relationships**
   - Nature subordinate to human problem solving
   - People subordinate to state
   - Experts and managers control state
3. **Agents and their motives**
   - Experts and managers
   - Motivated by public interest, defined in unitary terms
4. **Key metaphor and other rhetorical devices**
   - The administrative mind
   - Navigating and steering

The justification of administrative rationalism

I argued earlier that the search for administrative rationalism should begin not with the writings of theorists and the proclamations of activists, but with an examination of actual policy practice. I have defined that practice in terms of the sevenfold repertoire of administrative rationalism. These items are for the most part institutional and policy hardware, with very tangible existence. As bits of hardware, some of them can be appropriated by competing discourses, at least by the other problem-solving discourses set out in the next two chapters. The essence of administrative rationalism is to be found in the discursive "software" that unites these seven items around a common purpose. As a problem-solving discourse, administrative rationalism takes the political-economic status quo of liberal capitalism as given. It then puts scientific and technical expertise, organized into bureaucratic hierarchy, motivated by the public interest, to use in solving environmental problems without changing the structural status quo. With this characterization in hand, it is possible to identify more clearly the justification on which administrative rationalism rests.

The twentieth century was greeted by the German sociologist Max Weber with an announcement that bureaucracy was the supremely rational form of social organization (see Gerth and Mills, 1948). Weber was not happy about this, but saw increasing rationalization of society through bureaucratic organization as inevitable. Increasing complexity in social and economic problems could not be confronted by individuals acting in isolation, only by coordinated problem-solving efforts of large numbers of individuals. The best way to cope with a large, complex problem is to break it down into smaller sets and then into still smaller subsets. Each subset should then be assigned to an individual or small group to craft a solution. These partial solutions are then aggregated into a solution for the complex problem as a whole (see H. Simon, 1981). Clearly, somebody needs to formulate the initial breakdown into sets and subsets; somebody needs to keep an eye on the people dealing with each subset; and somebody needs to piece together the elements. That "somebody" is the apex of organizational hierarchy. Hierarchy is justified on the basis of access to both principles of administrative management and substantive expertise in the issue area in question. The structure of problem disaggregation and solution aggregation describes too the standard organization chart of a bureaucracy.

When Weber was writing, environmental problems were not conceptualized as such. But when these problems did reach the agenda, Weberian bureaucracies were constructed to deal with them. How is an antipollution agency organized? It is normally divided into offices dealing with air pollution, water pollution, hazardous wastes, and solid wastes. Each of these offices is then disaggregated further, perhaps on a regional basis, perhaps to deal with different kinds of pollutants, perhaps to deal with different industries. For example, the air pollution office could be divided into "stationary sources" (smokestacks) and "mobile sources" (vehicles). The stationary source unit could then be divided further into units dealing with power generation and manufacturing. Power generation could be divided into suspended particulates (smoke), greenhouse emissions (carbon dioxide), and sulfur dioxide (acid rain). Particular kinds of scientific and engineering expertise can then be assigned to the appropriate unit or subunit.

In practice, political factors often intervene to confuse the organizational chart. These factors include interventions by elected officials, political parties, lobbyists, and, occasionally, even the public. The politicization of science reached a high point in the presidency of George W. Bush. When politicization happens, policy making can become more complicated and messy. The response by structural reformers is often to try to depoliticize and centralize decision making. For that especially politicized agency, the US EPA, Walter Rosenbaum (1985: 299–300) recommends four measures along these lines: a fixed five- or seven-year term for the Administrator (head of the EPA) so that he or she cannot be dismissed at will by the President; the replacement of political appointees by professional civil servants; the establishment of an inspector-general to oversee the professional conduct of the EPA and its employees; and an external scientific review of the EPA's use of technical information in decision making.

If political conflict cannot be banished from environmental administration, the next best thing for the administrative rationalist may be to channel it more productively. Kai Lee (1993) argues that the proper function of political conflict is to raise issues which managers might otherwise miss. Lee's ideal is "ecosystem management," in which professional resource managers trained in ecology take charge of whole ecosystems. He regards the Northwest Power Planning Council, responsible for the Columbia River Basin (and on which he served) as exemplary, though it was not in fact governed by ecologists. For Lee, ecosystem management cannot be entrusted to politicians, who do not have the patience to learn, the willingness to tolerate failure for the sake of learning, the ability to operate on a biological rather than an electoral timescale, or to look beyond the short-term interests of their constituencies. But recognizing that political conflict cannot be eliminated, he suggests taming it by establishing alternative dispute-resolution forums where people can reason through their differences, rather than waste energy in adversarial processes that produce only stalemate or uncreative either/or decisions. Unfortunately, ecosystem management in the Columbia basin ended in the face of legal challenges from environmentalists under the Endangered Species Act.

Administrative rationalism in crisis

Among those who have reflected upon administrative rationalism, few have done so in order to defend it. Part of this is due to the association with bureaucracy. It is hard to find anyone who actually likes bureaucracy, which is generally defended as necessary rather than attractive. Still, a discourse can soldier on without reflective defenders—indeed, particular discourses may persist precisely because nobody at all is reflecting on them.

Prosaic and uninspirational though it might be, administrative rationalism could always sustain itself so long as it delivered the goods. These goods would include cleaner air and waters, fewer toxins circulating in the human environment, an environmentally secure future, improving aesthetic standards in city, suburb, countryside, and wilderness, more securely protected ecosystems and species. But the administrative state's performance on these standards has been called into question. This questioning can often be put under the heading of "implementation deficit"—a substantial gap between what legislation and high-level executive decisions declare will be achieved and what is actually achieved at street level (Weale, 1992: 17–18). Implementation deficit was originally a German expression. Germany was long the exemplar of administrative rationalism in environmental policy, but it only became an environmental leader once its administrative system began to open up in the 1980s (Dryzek et al., 2003).

The administrative state may be running out of steam in the environmental arena, or experiencing diminishing returns to effort. This would accord with experience in other policy areas such as crime, public health, industrial development, and education. It is relatively easy to achieve substantial initial gains, because the easier and most visible problems will be attacked first. It is very hard to show sustained improvement on any dimension once initial gains have been made. For example, in air pollution control it tends to be suspended particulates in cities that get attacked first: these are (literally) visible and easily remedied by technical fixes (such as mandating smokeless fuels). More insidious pollutants such as lead from car exhausts take longer to come to attention and receive their fix—but eventually they get it in the form of unleaded gasoline. Acid rain eventually gets tackled through regulation of sulfate emissions from power stations. To date the more complex problem of climate change has eluded effective administrative response. It becomes increasingly hard to sustain science-driven policy without acknowledging complexity and attendant political conflict (Ascher, Steelman, and Healy, 2010).

What lies at the root of these problems? To begin, administrative rationalism implies hierarchy based on expertise, with both power and knowledge centralized at the apex. Those at the apex are assumed to know better than subordinate levels, so as to be able to assign tasks and coordinate operations. But problems of any complexity defy such centralization: nobody can possibly know enough about the various dimensions of an issue such as acid rain, global climate change, ozone depletion, or the interacting cocktail of urban air pollutants, not to mention the social and economic aspects of these issues, to sit with any confidence at the apex. As the philosophers Karl Popper (1966) and F. A. von Hayek (1979) argued at length (though never in the context of environmental problems), the relevant knowledge is dispersed and fragmentary. The closed, hierarchical style of administrative rationalism has no way to aggregate these pieces of information in intelligent fashion. Popper's solution is the give and take of liberal democracy; Hayek's is the market. Popper's critique is especially devastating because it is rooted in a model of science as the exemplary problem-solving activity. To Popper, the hallmark of the scientific community is not authority based on expertise, but free, open, and equal criticism and test of the conjectures of scientists by other scientists. Just as hierarchy and deference to expertise can only obstruct scientific problem solving, so they can only obstruct problem solving in policy and politics.

The Weberian approach to problem disaggregation and assignment of chunks of the problem to different units within the organization requires that such disaggregation be done in intelligent fashion. The main principles here are that interactions within problem subsets as defined should be rich, and interactions across different subsets should be weak (Alexander, 1964). But for truly complex problems, those with a large number and variety of elements and interactions facing a decision system, no intelligent disaggregation may be possible. For defensible disaggregation requires minimization of interactions across the problem chunks. High orders of complexity mean that such interactions will always occur, no matter how intelligently the disaggregation is done. When that happens, there is little problem solving, but a great deal in the way of problem displacement (see Dryzek, 1987: 16–20, 99–100; Wapner, 2002b). Such displacement occurs when an air pollution problem is solved by creating a water pollution problem—for example, prohibition of the burning of waste may lead a company to discharge the waste in watercourses instead. It occurs when tall smokestacks are built to alleviate air pollution in the vicinity of a factory, thus leading emissions to fall somewhere else and, in the case of coal-burning power plants, for sulfur dioxide to stay in the atmosphere long enough to constitute acid rain. Most antipollution agencies operate under single-medium statutes such as clean air and clean water acts, which facilitate displacement across the media. Displacement also occurs when a rich country's pollution is reduced as a result of production for its consumers moving to poor countries with weak or non-existent environmental controls. Offsets for carbon dioxide emissions are also a form of problem displacement from rich to poor countries (even if the latter are compensated for taking on the problem). As Wapner (2002a) points out, problem displacement can cause environmental injustice, as it is often the problems of the rich that are displaced to the poor.

This question of displacement has been recognized by administrative rationalists, but rarely answered effectively. The US EPA has experimented with a "cluster" approach to pollutants, to coordinate rules coming from different pieces of legislation for (say) an industry (Fiorino, 1995: 210). The EPA has also tried "integrated environmental management" of particular geographical pollution hot spots (see Mosher, 1983). But these efforts have been unable to transcend the divisions across the single-medium statutes under which the EPA continues to operate.

In Britain, the unified Inspectorate of Pollution was created in part to integrate antipollution efforts, and so help identify courses of action that would best reduce environmental damage for any given cost to society. But this Inspectorate was still composed of single-medium units, dealing with industrial air pollution, "wastes," radioactivity, and water quality. For a number of years its water operations faced competition from the single-medium National Rivers Authority, though eventually the competitors were merged into the Environment Agency. Legal changes that would have allowed the Inspectorate and its successor to try to operate in holistic fashion were very slow in coming.

More effective integration was developed in Sweden, initially at the plant level (Weale, 1992: 98–9). Later, Sweden pioneered integration across areas with large implications for the environment, but traditionally dealt with separately, by creating a Delegation for Ecologically Sustainable Development made up of the ministers responsible for agriculture, environment, education, labor, and taxation. But such integration remains an uphill struggle in traditionally compartmentalized governments (Lafferty and Hovden, 2003), and remains underdeveloped everywhere (Bührs, 2009).

A more straightforward reason that helps to explain implementation deficit under administrative rationalism is the problem of compliance with policy decisions. Compliance is required in two stages: first, "street level" agency officials must comply with legislative direction and the desires of their superiors, and second, polluters, developers, and resource users must comply with directives emanating from the administrative structure. Both kinds of compliance are problematical. As Weale (1992: 18–19) notes, the latter kind of compliance is rarely a matter of actors being told what to do by public officials and then doing it; more often, compliance is negotiated. So, for example, the degree of pollution reduction, the timetable at which it is achieved, and the kinds of equipment to be installed can all be a matter for negotiation. Negotiated compliance makes sense for street-level bureaucrats because they need to cultivate working understandings with polluters, and there is every reason for them to make discretionary judgments about who is to blame and what negotiation strategy is likely to pay off in the long run. Policies made centrally are rarely sensitive to the local circumstances in which street-level bureaucrats operate.

Learning about what works in practice is most easily achieved at this street level. Administrative learning in an environmental context has been pursued in the form of "adaptive management" of ecosystems, requiring some ecosystem-specific authority to begin with (there are connections to bioregionalism; see Chapter 10). Ideally, this authority would proceed under "learning by doing," modeled on scientific experimentation and recognizing high levels of uncertainty. Adaptive management has found its way into the rhetoric of the US Forest Service, among other agencies (Lee, 1999). While attractive to scientists, it sidelines both politicians impatient with the long timescale adaptive management requires, and also administrators uneasy with explicit recognition of uncertainty.

The structure of administration often prevents learning being communicated up the administrative hierarchy. As one ascends the administrative hierarchy, the limited time and information-processing resources of individual administrators means that much information is inevitably lost. So administrative rationalism is faced with a conundrum: the more an organization is disciplined, the less it can be expected to learn (see Torgerson and Paehlke, 2005: 6). The more it learns (by developing an open and decentralized structure), the less easy will it be to maintain discipline by administrative means, and so the more likely becomes implementation deficit.

From government to governance?

Can administration both learn locally and remain coordinated by adherence to central goals and principles? Sabel et al. (2000) suggest this can be done through what they call a "rolling rule regime" kind of regulation, under which a central agency sets standards, while compliance is negotiated locally with activists and corporations. The central agency holds the locals to account, but is willing to adjust standards in light of feedback. Sabel et al. point to US cases where this approach has worked, such as watershed protection in Chesapeake Bay and management of toxic pollutants in Massachusetts. This approach is consistent with the principles of "national standards, neighborhood solutions" and "collaboration, not polarization" endorsed by federal EPA Administrator Mike Leavitt in 2004. Administrative rationalism is diluted. Skeptics would say there is also an abdication of public authority in favor of unrepresentative private interests powerful enough to secure a place in the dialogue, raising the old specter of capture by industry.

The rolling rule regime approach is also consistent with widespread enthusiasm for "governance" as opposed to "government" in public policy in general. Government here is seen as top-down and Weberian, while governance is decentralized, informal, and networked. Governance in this sense is more easily linked to democratic pragmatism than to administrative rationalism, and so will be addressed in the next chapter. The move from government to governance is perhaps symbolized by the establishment of the Netherlands Environmental Assessment Agency in 2008. Its Director was none other than pioneering environmental discourse analyst Maarten Hajer. The mission of the agency involves strategic policy analysis, but in practice it promotes decentralized, polycentric, networked governance, facilitated but not controlled by central government (Hajer, 2011)

Any wholesale transition from government to governance would signal the end of administrative rationalism. But there may be life in the beast yet. Vogel (2003) argues that in the United States there is actually movement toward greater use of cost–benefit analysis, risk assessment, and more technocratic policy making in general, accompanied by greater trust in regulators. He believes this return to administrative rationalism results from reactions against regulatory overkill associated with public alarmism about risks. The Superfund clean-up of toxic sites and programs to remove asbestos from schools were hugely expensive and may even have increased risks (by moving hazardous materials that were safely in place). In 1996 Congress modified the Delaney Clause that had long prohibited any substance associated with any risk of cancer in food, in favor of a risk–benefit approach. Vogel notes that the European Union is moving in the opposite direction, as scandals such as mad cow disease (BSE) led to public distrust of government regulators and demands for greater public participation in policy making. Vogel's argument on the United States does not quite add up, because it implies that when regulatory overkill goes, technocracy returns. But overkill itself was often administered technocratically. Still, some aspects of administrative rationalism are tenacious in the face of "new governance" trends.

Given the locally variable and negotiated ways in which administrators now secure compliance, it is ironic that market-oriented opponents of administrative rationalism still try to stigmatize it by attaching the ugly and undemocratic term "command and control" to regulatory policy, a terminology reproduced even by those who take a more balanced approach to the relative virtues of regulation and price incentives (for example, Harrington and Morgernstern, 2004). This is a rhetorical accomplishment, but very little commanding and controlling actually goes on in the implementation of environmental regulations.

Administrative rationalism has had substantial impact in the environmental arena, and shows renewed life in China in particular. In the West it may be running out of steam and facing crisis, perhaps even yielding to governance, but its past achievements should not be forgotten. The countries of the developed world have an environment which is cleaner, safer, and more aesthetically pleasing than it would have been without the last forty years of administrative rationalism. This evaluation does not mean that administrative rationalism was the most effective conceivable response to environmental crisis, or even an adequate one. Nor are past achievements any guarantee of future success. So let me turn to the two other problem-solving discourses, which are presented by their adherents as containing effective remedies for the contemporary ills of administrative rationalism.

....

NOTES

1. For the United States, Hays (1987: 393–4) argues that the high-visibility conflictual environmental politics of the late 1960s and early 1970s yielded to environmental administration and management in the late 1970s, a development he describes as the rise of the environmental professional. In contrast, I would argue that the administration was there all the time in this era, but that in the late 1970s the politics became fairly subdued, leaving the field relatively free for the professionals. Political conflict has certainly made many comebacks since then.

2. A discount rate is like an interest rate, except that it works back from the future to the present. So at a discount rate of 5 percent, $100 expected one year in the future has a present value of $95.

5

Leave it to the People: Democratic Pragmatism

Ours is a democratic age; it is increasingly unfashionable for anyone, anywhere in the world, to proclaim themselves to be anything but a democrat. It is correspondingly hard to proclaim one's faith in bureaucracy and administrative rationalism. Administration is not very popular as an ideal; rather, it is just what a lot of people, and a lot of institutions, actually end up doing. Democracy is different; everyone wants to be a democrat. Whether they truly are democrats is a different question, made harder to answer by the sheer variety of meanings and models of democracy.

In this chapter I treat democracy not as a set of institutions (elections, parliaments, parties, etc.), but rather as a way of approaching problems. I will be concerned with democracy as a problem-solving discourse reconciled to the basic status quo of liberal capitalism. This is the version of democracy which dominates today's world, especially after the revolutions of 1989 destroyed the credibility of some Marxist alternatives. Other discourses of democracy do exist, some of which challenge this status quo, advocating radical participatory alternatives, for example (see Dryzek, 1996a), and I shall return to some of these alternatives in later chapters.

Democratic pragmatism may be characterized in terms of interactive problem solving within the basic institutional structure of liberal capitalist democracy. The word "pragmatism" can have two connotations here, both of which I intend. The first is the way the word is used in everyday language, as signifying a practical, realistic orientation to the world, the opposite of starry-eyed idealism. The second refers to a school of thought in philosophy, associated with names such as William James, Charles Peirce, and John Dewey. To pragmatist philosophers, life is mostly about solving problems in a world full of uncertainty. The most rational approach to problem solving, in life as in science, involves learning through experimentation. For problems of any degree of complexity, the relevant knowledge cannot be centralized in the hands of any individual or any administrative state structure. Thus problem solving should be a flexible process involving many voices, and cooperation across a plurality of perspectives. The degree of participation with which pragmatists are happy often corresponds roughly to that found in existing liberal democracies (though some pragmatists advocate more and better participation), so there is congruence between the demands of rationality in social problem solving and democratic values. In his advocacy of "civic environmentalism," William Shutkin (2000) believes there is an essential affinity between democracy and environmental conservation, so democracy and the environment rise or fall together. For Shutkin, healthy communities cultivate both their social capital and their natural capital in public-spirited, participatory fashion.

Pragmatist philosophy received an explicit environmental twist with the arrival of "environmental pragmatism," which takes its bearings from philosophical debates in the field of environmental ethics. Environmental pragmatism battles attempts to propose moral absolutes to guide environmental affairs, which are treated instead as ripe for tentative problem-solving efforts in which a plurality of moral perspectives is always relevant (see Light and Katz, 1996). In this chapter I will be concerned less with the finer points of environmental pragmatist philosophy, and more with the way democratic and pragmatic discourse plays out in the real world of environmental affairs. This style of problem solving can be found within administrative structures, in negotiations between parties to a legal dispute, in international negotiations, in informal networks, as well as in legislatures.

Democratic pragmatism in action

In the previous chapter I noted that environmental administration is in crisis, indicated by diminishing returns to administrative effort. Democratic pragmatism can speak directly to this crisis, and later I will assess its performance in these terms. Some of the impetus for democratic pragmatism now comes from a desire to make administration more flexible and responsive to varied circumstances (Fiorino, 2004). But the main reason for the democratization of environmental administration has often been a felt need to secure legitimacy for decisions by involving a broader public. The most vivid case of a national legitimation crisis leading to outreach to participation by environmental interests occurred in the United States around 1970. The Nixon administration felt besieged by the antiwar movement, radical elements of the civil rights movement, and the counter-culture more generally. The administration reached out to environmentalists as the least radical elements of the counter-culture, and drew them into government (Dryzek et al., 2003: 57–60).

Several devices are available to democratic pragmatists, as follows.

Public consultation

One important item in the repertoire of administrative rationalism is environmental impact assessment, under which a statement is prepared detailing the anticipated impact of a project (be it a freeway, pipeline, or land-use plan) on the environment (see Chapter 4). Impact assessment is designed to force administrators to consider environmental values and scientific evidence that they might otherwise have excluded or overlooked. But impact assessment is invariably accompanied by opportunities for public comment on the document produced. Sometimes this is mere symbolism, if there is nothing to force the department in question to take into account the substance of public comment in its subsequent decision on the proposal. Still, policy makers must both anticipate and respond to comment. In the process set up in the United States under the National Environmental Policy Act of 1970, the responsible federal agency must produce a draft statement, release that document for comment, compile responses (from other government agencies, other levels of government, environmental and community groups, interested corporations, resource users, and ordinary citizens), and respond to these comments in the final version of the statement. Thus information from a variety of perspectives is systematically sought out. This information will rarely have direct, traceable impacts on agency decisions; but more subtly it may alter the context in which administrative decisions are made and implemented, by changing the discourse surrounding policy determination in a way that makes both environmental and democratic values more legitimate and more visible. The way Bartlett (1990) puts it, environmental impact assessment can constitute a "worm in the brain" of administration, one that moves it in simultaneously more democratic and more environmentally sensitive directions.

Public consultation can also proceed without being tied to particular documents such as impact statements (Stewart, 2009). For example, several

European countries (Sweden, the Netherlands, and Austria) initiated extensive consultative efforts in the late 1970s concerning the future of nuclear power (see Nelkin and Pollack, 1981). These exercises had real consequences: for example, in 1979 the Swedish government decided not to construct any more reactors, and to begin phasing out nuclear energy.

Public consultation has its critics who think that too often it features either uninformed participants or unrepresentative activists and special interests, is vulnerable to the way policy makers frame the exercise, and ultimately has little impact on policy (Smith, 2009: 14–20). Such worries notwithstanding, consultation is now regarded as a necessary accompaniment to environmental policy development in many countries, and on no issue is this more true than genetically modified organisms in agriculture. In 2003 the UK government initiated "GM Nation," a six-week consultative exercise on genetically modified crops and foods. GM Nation involved more than 600 public meetings across the country, and publicization of scientific reviews and analyses of the costs and benefits of genetically modified organisms.[1] Around 36,000 questionnaires were turned in, and opinions could also be submitted via a website. The idea was to involve ordinary people, though self-selection of participants meant activists were over-represented. The summary reported public unease on both health and environmental grounds, together with widespread distrust of government and biotechnology companies. In 2004 Environment Minister Margaret Beckett announced the government's response. GM crops should be evaluated on a case-by-case basis under precautionary guidelines, and GM food products should be clearly labeled.

Alternative dispute resolution

Opportunities for public comment do not formalize any particular role for nongovernmental participants. One way of recognizing and involving interested parties is through alternative dispute resolution (ADR). ADR arose in legalistic systems—notably the United States—as an alternative to the expensive stalemate that prolonged legal actions entail. The idea is to bring the parties to a dispute together under the auspices of a neutral third party (often a professional mediator) such that they might reason through their differences (Susskind, 2009). The target is agreement under which all parties are better off than they would be in the absence of an agreement (Susskind et al., 2000); processes can be creative in generating proposals that serve the core interests of all sides. ADR reached the environmental realm in the 1970s under the heading of environmental mediation, and since then disputes have been mediated on a wide variety of issues, including complex ones. These issues include construction of dams, irrigation schemes, mines, shopping malls, and roads; watershed management; siting of hazardous waste disposal operations; clean-up of existing hazardous waste sites; ecological restoration; and antipollution measures. Mediation functions not just as an alternative to the courts. Government agencies can also use and sponsor it when encountering resistance to their proposals. The relevant participants might include community representatives, environmental groups, corporate developers or polluters, government departments, and local governments. Thus mediation can play a role in policy making rather than dispute resolution narrowly defined. Kai Lee (1993) believes that this is a productive way of channeling political conflict into administrative decisions. In particular, he believes ADR has an essential role in effective ecosystem management, providing creative ways for conflicts to end in learning rather than in victory for one side and defeat of the other. Other observers are more skeptical, seeing ADR mainly in terms of the co-option and neutralization of troublemakers (for example, Amy, 1987). It is perhaps best to accept that ADR has an ambivalent potential. At a minimum, it demonstrates that decisions must be legitimated through participatory procedures. These procedures can involve neutralization and co-option; but they can also involve democratic principles eating away at the administrative state, forcing it to open its ways. So it is up to democratic pragmatists and perhaps even proponents of more radical democracy to make the most of these cracks in the citadel of the administrative state and its legal accompaniments (Torgerson, 2005: 111–16).

Policy dialogue

Environmental mediation and other forms of ADR are often case-specific or site-specific. However, principles of reasoned discussion oriented to consensus can also be applied to more strategic policy issues, though the success rate (in terms of reaching an agreement and having it put into policy practice) is lower than for more circumscribed cases. If partisans are entrenched then agreement can prove elusive. So a 2001–2002 national policy dialogue organized by the German government on agricultural biotechnology did not move any of the participants (farm associations, food processors and retailers, biotechnology companies, environmentalists and consumer groups) to change their solidified positions either for or against genetically modified organisms.

A comprehensive example of environmental policy dialogue may be found in Australia, with the Ecologically Sustainable Development (ESD) process initiated by Prime Minister Bob Hawke in 1990. ESD began with an invitation to the main national environmental groups and relevant industry representatives to participate in discussions oriented to the generation of strategic policy recommendations in a number of areas: agriculture, energy, fisheries, forests, manufacturing, mining, and tourism. In each area a working group was set up, and a report eventually produced. The four invited environmental groups were the Australian Conservation Foundation, World Wildlife Fund, Greenpeace, and the Wilderness Society. The Wilderness Society withdrew immediately due to its unhappiness with other government policies contrary to sustainability; later, Greenpeace withdrew. However, both groups remained in contact with the two groups that continued to participate. When the time came for the ESD groups to report, Hawke had been replaced by a prime minister committed to confrontation rather than consensus, who placed a much lower priority on environmental issues, which had also faded from public prominence with the arrival of economic recession. Thus few of the recommendations found their way into public policy.

A more effective translation of policy dialogue into policy practice may be found in the Canadian province of Alberta, the first place in North America to solve the NIMBY (Not In My Back Yard) problem for hazardous wastes. Nobody wants a hazardous waste treatment facility in their backyard. Given that everywhere is someone's backyard, and given the relative ease of access to veto power in the Canadian and US political systems (reinforced in the United States by the prominent role of the courts), the normal condition of policy on this issue is impasse. Recognizing this problem, the government of Alberta in the late 1980s initiated a dialogue with local community groups and industry, which eventually produced consensus on a site and principles for its development and operation. The process involved a referendum on the basic idea of siting, funding to communities to employ experts, regular seminars and public meetings. Once the Swan Hills site was selected and the treatment plant built, communities in the vicinity received further funding and access to monitoring reports and expert advice (for details, see Fischer, 1993: 176–7; Rabe, 1991). Unfortunately the operation of Swan Hills proved problematic, re-creating a familiar standoff of environ-mentalists and indigenous peoples against operators of the site.

Alberta is a fruitful place for dialogues. The Alberta Climate Dialogue is a multi-year project that began in 2010 to involve thousands of citizens and stakeholders in deliberative processes. The Dialogue addresses climate change at multiple levels of government, as well as what individuals and communities might do. While there is no guarantee its conclusions will be embodied in public policy, the Dialogue established close relationships with the city governments of Edmonton and Calgary in particular. Alberta is a particularly appropriate place for such an exercise given that it is home to some of the most climate-unfriendly energy extraction in the world. Oil from tar sands yields relatively small net energy while producing huge carbon dioxide emissions in the process of extraction.

Policy dialogues have spread worldwide with impetus from the "Local Agenda 21" initiative coming out of the United Nations Conference on Environment and Development in 1992, which encouraged local govern-ments to develop sustainability plans. More recently, China has adopted community environmental roundtables, involving local governments, com-panies, and community representatives (Wang, 2011).

Lay citizen deliberation

ADR and other policy dialogues normally involve partisans, be they environmentalists or developers (though the Alberta Climate Dialogue just mentioned also includes ordinary citizens). But reflective deliberation may be achieved more readily by non-partisan lay citizens, if they are more open to argument and persuasion than are entrenched partisans. This capacity helps explain the rise of deliberative exercises built around lay citizen partici-pation (Smith, 2009). Examples include consensus conferences (invented in Denmark), citizens' juries (which began in the United States but have been used most extensively in the United Kingdom), deliberative opinion polls (created by James Fishkin), 21st Century Town Meetings (invented by the America*Speaks* Foundation), planning cells (found in Germany). The number of participants varies from around fifteen in a citizens' jury to several hundred in a deliberative poll or planning cell to several thousand in a 21st Century Town Meeting. Participants are recruited through random selection or some stratified sampling procedure, and brought together for two days or more to deliberate the issue in question. There are opportunities to question experts and advocates, and plenty of information is provided. The product is normally a policy recommendation (though in deliberative polls, participants simply fill out a questionnaire at the end). Lay citizen deliberations have occurred on issues encompassing genetically modified organisms in agriculture (in many countries), container deposit legislation in Australia, energy policy in Texas, urban planning in Germany, and wetlands protection in England.

A particularly ambitious lay citizen deliberation was held on September 26, 2009 when 100 citizens in each of thirty-eight countries met under a common process to contemplate policy responses to climate change (Rask et al., 2012). Coordinated by the Danish Board of Technology, this World Wide Views project's results were presented at the Conference of the Parties to the United Nations Framework Convention on Climate Change (UNFCCC) in December 2009 in Copenhagen. In almost every country, the lay citizens favored stronger action to reduce greenhouse gas emissions than their own governments were contemplating. Other lay citizen deliberations on climate change include the Citizens Summit of 150 participants conducted by the UK government in 2007 as part of public consultation on a climate change bill. In 2010 Australian Prime Minister Julia Gillard proposed to hold a citizens' assembly to "build consensus" on climate policy, but this was abandoned amidst criticism that it was simply to provide cover for the government's inability to develop an effective policy.

Public inquiries

Public inquiries resemble impact assessment in that they are often oriented by a specific project proposal (though they can also be retrospective; in 2012 the Japanese government set up an inquiry into the 2011 Fukushima nuclear disaster). But rather than just producing a document and allowing public inspection and comment, a public inquiry involves a visible forum where proponents and objectors alike can make depositions and arguments. Much depends upon the terms of reference, and the way these terms are interpreted by the individual presiding over the inquiry. The terms and their interpretation can be narrow and biased toward the project proponent. This is how inquiries into proposed nuclear installations in Britain once proceeded. So Kemp (1985) chronicles the case of a 1977 inquiry into a Thermal Oxide Reprocessing Plant (THORP) proposed for Windscale in northwest England. The project proponent, British Nuclear Fuels Ltd., was allowed to introduce evidence on the economic benefits of THORP, but objectors were not allowed to bring economic evidence against it. The legalistic rules of the inquiry were congenial to the well-funded proponents, not to the resource-poor objectors; and the proponents could deploy the Official Secrets Act at key points. Not surprisingly, Mr. Justice Parker presiding over the inquiry came down in favor of THORP. Contrast this with the contemporaneous inquiry into proposed oil and gas pipeline construction from the Arctic to Southern markets conducted in Canada by Mr. Justice Thomas Berger. Berger took pains to make sure that resource-poor interests, especially indigenous peoples, were provided with funds, access to expertise, and an ability to testify in a forum under conditions with which they were familiar (the inquiry traveled to remote villages). He interpreted the terms of reference broadly, to encompass development strategies for the Canadian North, not just whether or not pipelines should be built. In this sense, the inquiry became more like a policy dialogue. Berger's report (Berger, 1977) proposes a reinvigorated renewable-resource based economy for the Canadian North, in which oil and gas development have little place. Berger pushed democratic pragmatism to its limits—and perhaps beyond, to the kind of participatory process favored by green radicalism.

Another Canadian case that resembles Berger but was styled a "scientific panel" rather than "public inquiry" can be found in the mid-1990s in Clayoquot Sound in British Columbia, where the issue involved logging. The panel was set up to resolve an impasse between logging companies on one side and environmentalists and indigenous people on the other. Science was interpreted broadly to encompass and integrate the traditional ecological knowledge of the Nuu-Chah-Nulth people, and a Nuu-Chah-Nulth chief chaired the panel. The panel shifted policy concern from economic efficiency to ecological integrity (Torgerson, 2003: 128–31). While the Berger and Clayoquot Sound cases provide encouragement to ecological democrats, their rarity should give pause for thought.

Right-to-know legislation

If individuals from outside government are to be effective participants in democratic processes they need access to relevant information. Sometimes access will be facilitated by general freedom of information laws under which governments operate. These apply to some governments more than others. For example, the British counterpart to freedom of information has long been the Official Secrets Act, which presumes that everything is secret if it has the remotest connection to national security (this comes into play, for example, on anything relating to nuclear power). More specific to environmental politics is right-to-know legislation which specifies that corporations must disclose information relating to (say) the risks to workers of particular chemicals, the routes and timetables of shipments of noxious substances, and the toxicity of wastes being stored, transported, and dumped. Such laws exist in a number of Canadian provinces and US states.

These six developments all involve injections of democratic pragmatism into the administrative state. In every case experience has been mixed, and a lot of skepticism remains, especially from those committed to more radical expression of both environmental and democratic values. But in some cases, notably Berger and Clayoquot, we can glimpse the possibility of a more radically participatory and discursive democracy. At any rate, taken together, these six developments indicate the degree to which environmental policy has over the past forty years been accompanied by greater openness and participation in decision making. As Paehlke (1988) notes, all this is a far cry from the gloomy prognostications of 1970s survivalists who argued that environmental limits could only be confronted by centralized and authoritarian government. Survivalists might still say that all the policy effort of the last four decades has not really confronted the issue of environmental limits head-on, and that we are still on course for overshoot and collapse.

Democratic pragmatism as government and governance

Democratic pragmatism describes an orientation to governing in its entirety, not just the inspiration for a variety of specific reforms and exercises of the kind described in the preceding section. This orientation stresses interactive problem solving involving participants from within government and outside it. Such interaction can occur in the context of committee meetings, legislative debate, hearings, public addresses, legal disputes, rule-making, project development, media investigations, and policy implementation and enforcement; it can involve lobbying, arguing, advising, strategizing, bargaining, informing, publishing, exposing, deceiving, image-building, insulting, and questioning. In this light, the real stuff of government is not to be found in constitutions and formal divisions of responsibility. Rather, it is to be found in interactions that are only loosely constrained by formal rules. Quiet conversations in the bar may matter as much as speeches to parliament.

These interactions occur whether or not constitutions, laws, rules, and organization charts say they should. Thus democratic pragmatism can readily assimilate the kind of decentralized networked governance discussed as a corrective to administrative rationalism in Chapter 4. "Government" has a top-down imagery in which administrative rationalism operates once goals and principles have been set. "Governance," in contrast, downplays any central locus of authority, reveling in informal interactions. The actors involved might be public officials, but they might equally well be nongovernmental organizations (NGOs), lobbyists, activists, journalists, corporations, international organizations, or governments in different jurisdictions. The image of the network replaces that of the hierarchy (Castells, 1996). A network can have multiple nodes and feature complex pathways of interactions across participants. Communication in a hierarchy goes up to and down from the apex. In a network, public outcomes can be produced without the stamp of any apex, or even without the approval of any government. This happens when a consumer boycott forces a corporation to change its ways (for example, to catch tuna in a way that does not endanger marine mammals and turtles); or when activists and businesses agree on a corporate code of conduct. Jänicke (1996) calls such actions "paragovernmental."

In the 1990s, the Reinventing Government task force (charged with looking at the structure of policy delivery) headed by US Vice-President Al Gore proposed reforms to the EPA's regulatory system along "governance" lines, to emphasize public–private partnerships and collaborative relationships across regulators, communities, and businesses. Republicans in Congress eager to devolve power from the federal level were supportive. Environmentalists were less eager. Still, the United States in the 1990s saw substantial impetus toward more flexible, decentralized, and cooperative environmental regulation (Fiorino, 2004).

In both the United States and the European Union, networked governance became associated with "new environmental policy instruments" (Jordan et al., 2003). Some of these instruments are market-based (and so will be discussed in Chapter 6). Others are more truly collaborative governance measures. These include voluntary agreements between regulators and corporations, and environmental management and audit systems under which corporations voluntarily set targets for their own environmental impacts and monitor progress, receiving a stamp of approval if targets are met. This stamp does not have to be given by government. Transnational forest certification for wood products is administered by a network of NGOs (including the Rainforest Alliance and World Wide Fund for Nature) and corporations, coordinated by the Forest Stewardship Council, founded in 1993 (Meidinger, 2003). While the Forest Stewardship Council is believed by its enthusiasts to show how effective environmental governance without government can be, Bell and Hindmoor (2012) point out that it regulates only a small proportion of global wood products, and that its coverage is greatest where it is needed least—in government-owned forests in the Nordic countries. Collaborative governance can also be found in natural resource management. Innes and Booher (2003) describe the case of the Sacramento Water Forum, which seeks consensus encompassing businesses, environmentalists, farmers, and local governments in an ecologically degraded setting.

The transnational governance of climate change has also seen a host of collaborative and networked initiatives. The Clean Technology Fund overseen by the World Bank involves cooperation between donor and recipient countries, corporations, and NGOs with the intention of financing low-carbon development. The ICLEI Cities for Climate Protection network facilitates information exchange about policies and mutual encouragement to reduce greenhouse gas emissions. Voluntary schemes for the trading of emissions and offsets are also organized on a network basis. For Hoffman (2011), these initiatives form the basis for a comprehensive approach to the global governance of climate change, an alternative to the failure of intergovernmental negotiations under the auspices of the UNFCCC to produce agreement, let alone action. Nobody is forced to join these initiatives; their voluntary nature means they do not contain obstructionists. The situation is very different in the UNFCCC negotiations, where countries such as Saudi Arabia and Canada can obstruct action. With time, the new forms of networked governance may generate actors with a vested interest in effective emissions control, such as carbon traders, purveyors of clean technologies, and emissions certifiers.

A slightly different decentralized approach to climate governance is advocated by Elinor Ostrom (2009), deploying the considerable intellectual capital she accrued from her 2009 Nobel Prize in Economics that recognized her work on the cooperative management of local resources (such as forests and fisheries). Ostrom believes that communities can devise their own responses to climate change, without top-down management, still less a comprehensive global agreement. She points to cases where cities and subnational governments such as the State of California have developed greenhouse gas emissions programs when national governments have been unable to act. For Ostrom, climate change requires "polycentric" governance, with multiple initiatives in different places.

Skeptics would see in networked governance in particular an abdication of public authority into private hands. Bell and Hindmoor (2009) point out that many governance networks ultimately remain subordinate to the governments that established them. Those distrusting business power would stress the need for governance to be exercised over corporations, not just with them. Along these lines, Braithwaite and Drahos (2000) show how activists and NGOs as well as states have helped to create a global governance web that regulates business beyond the level of the nation-state and beyond the reach of conventional administrative rationalism.

The rationality of democratic pragmatism

Political interaction can, then, involve complex paths of communication. To the administrative rationalist, this might sound like chaos and subversion. But, arguably, this apparent chaos has its own rationality, what Charles Lindblom called "the science of muddling through" (1959), or "the intelligence of democracy" (1965). This "science" is the opposite of administrative science, for it revels in unclear divisions of responsibility, political conflict, bending the formal rules so as to make things work, and substituting ordinary knowledge for professional expertise. Problems are solved piecemeal, usually through compromises among the different actors concerned with an issue. Interaction substitutes for analysis; different actors bring different perspectives and concerns, which are somehow agglomerated into policy decisions.[2]

Pragmatists believe such processes are the best means for attacking public problems. A justification for the essential rationality of decentralized political interaction (though only within the confines of the liberal democratic state) has also been advanced quite famously by Karl Popper (1966). Popper's model problem-solving community is found in successful sciences, where the rational attitude is to advance theories capable of being put to the test, then seek criticism of them through as many tests as possible, especially experiments. Popper believes that this attitude should apply in politics and policy making too. Public policies are like experiments. Nobody knows in advance if a particular policy will succeed or fail. So it should be tried first on a limited scale, and reactions sought from as many different directions as possible about its positive and negative effects. Popper calls this kind of policy making "piecemeal social engineering." The only way to ensure feedback from as many different directions as possible is to have policy proceed in a liberal democratic setting, where different interests and actors (such as environmental and community groups, professional associations, different kinds of scientists, elected representatives, corporations and their officials, labor unions, and journalists) are all able to give their opinions without fear. Real-world liberal democracies and governance networks are only imperfect approximations to Popper's "open society" ideal, but their defenders would say no closer style of politics has yet been found.

Is this sort of policy making by interaction appropriate to an ecological context? The apparent chaos of piecemeal, interactive politics might belie a deeper organization. Interactive politics in one sense resembles ecosystems, for both are self-organizing systems (diZerega, 2000). That is, complex structures of order evolve without anyone designing them, as a result of the relatively simple and shortsighted choices and actions of individual organisms. In this light, the real order of democratic pragmatism is not to be found in constitutions, but in informal, interactive processes. Of course, the precise structure of order in any self-organizing system matters a great deal. By definition, an environmentalist can have little quarrel with the kind of order that ecosystems have produced by evolution. That liberal democracy and governance networks are self-organizing systems (as is the capitalist market) does not mean they are adequate in light of ecological criteria.

Ecosystems are self-organizing systems full of negative feedback devices that correct for disturbances. For example, a forest fire is normally followed by pioneer species of plants springing up in the burned area, which in turn provide the growing conditions for more mature forest species to return. The idea of negative feedback also defines the metaphor of the thermostat. So what kind of "thermostat" does democratic pragmatism possess? The answer lies in the variety of individuals, organizations, parties, and movements which can bring pressure to bear in and on political interaction in response to environmental disturbances. For example, one would expect wilderness advocates to keep their eyes on old growth forests, so that if clear-cutting threatens to get out of hand they can protest, lobby, hold press conferences, issue legal challenges, and so forth. Or if a proposal for a toxic waste incinerator in an urban neighborhood threatens life and health, the local community can organize against it. Those stressing limits and survival would argue that these kinds of actions are reactive and so incapable of anticipating limits before we hit them.

Whether or not these negative feedback devices are ecologically adequate depends crucially on the values of the people through whom the devices act. If people value tangible material goods above all else, then feedback will be impaired (though even these individuals might protest against any immediate environmental threat to their life and health). So is there anything in democratic pragmatism intrinsically conducive to ecological values? Two arguments claim that there is.

Democratic pragmatism involves talk and written communication, not just strategizing and power-plays, and such communication works best when it is couched in the language of the public interest, rather than private interests. Steven Kelman (1987) believes such talk is not cheap, and that people actually internalize public interest motivations. Adolf Gundersen (1995) applies this sort of analysis to public deliberation about environmental affairs. Deliberation is necessary for democratic pragmatism to work. Gundersen believes the very act of discussion or deliberation about issues activates commitment to environmental values, or, more precisely, "collective, holistic, and long term thinking." Gundersen's evidence is a series of forty-six "deliberative interviews" he conducted with a variety of people who did not in the beginning identify as environmentalists. By the end of these discussions, all espoused environmental values more strongly. On this account, everyone has latent positive dispositions which only need to be activated into specific policy commitments. Discussion in democratic settings forces people to scrutinize their own dispositions in a way that promotes such activation. There is some corroborating evidence from citizen forums. In the thirty-eight-country World Wide Views exercise discussed earlier, ordinary people with no history of environmental activism ended up supporting decisive action to reduce greenhouse gas emissions.

The idea that participation in democratic settings activates environmental values is shared by Mark Sagoff (1988, 2008). Sagoff believes that every individual has two kinds of preferences: as a consumer and as a citizen. These preferences may point in quite different directions for the same individual.

His running example concerns the Mineral King Valley in California's Sierra Nevada, where the Walt Disney Corporation wanted to build a ski resort. Confronting his students with this possibility, it turns out that many of them would enjoy visiting such a resort to ski and enjoy the après-ski nightlife. Few had any interest in backpacking into the existing Mineral King wilderness. But when asked whether they would favor construction of the resort, none did. The answer is that while as consumers they would love to ski there, as citizens they object to wilderness destruction. Citizen preferences are more concerned with collective, community-oriented values, as opposed to the selfish materialism of consumer values. While one might dispute the degree to which such public-spirited motivation pervades real-world liberal democratic politics, Sagoff's critique of economic reasoning and market rationality as applied to environmental policy is devastating. He also deploys his argument to excuse some of his more disgusting personal habits, notably driving a car that leaks oil everywhere which sports an "ecology now" bumper sticker (Sagoff, 1988: 53). The sticker proclaims his citizen preferences, the oil slick under his car his consumer preferences. The citizen in him would like the government to crack down on the consumer in him.

Sagoff's distinction makes little sense to advocates of a truly ecological citizenship that emphasizes one's place in and duties toward ecosystems. Ecological duties transcend Sagoff's separation of economic and political action, conditioning consumption decisions as well as voting and other conventionally political acts (Seyfang, 2006).

Discourse analysis of democratic pragmatism

Basic entities whose existence is recognized or constructed

Like administrative rationalism, democratic pragmatism takes the structural status quo of liberal capitalism as given. However, the treatment of government is very different. Government and governance are not treated as monoliths, but rather in terms of a multiplicity of decision processes populated in large part by citizens. *Homo civicus* figures large, *Homo bureaucratis* hardly at all. Democratic pragmatism has little or nothing to say about ecosystems and the natural world; very different conceptions on this score are welcome in debate.

Assumptions about natural relationships

Both administrative rationalism and democratic pragmatism place nature as subordinate to human problem-solving efforts. Whether nature contains self-regulating ecosystems or is just a storehouse of brute matter and energy makes little difference here. The natural relationships within human society postulated by the two discourses are in contrast quite different. Democratic pragmatism celebrates equality among citizens (of course, the reality of liberal democracy may be very different). Everyone has the right to exert political pressure, be they scientists, elected officials, pressure group leaders, ordinary voters, or ordinary non-voters. Beyond this basic equality, political relationships are seen as interactive and far more complex than those in a bureaucratic hierarchy. Interactions feature a mix of competition and cooperation. Certainly cooperative problem solving can occur; but so can conflict between partisans of competing interests (such as environmentalists and developers).

Agents and their motives

Agency in democratic pragmatism is for everyone, be they individual citizens and activists or collective actors such as corporations, labor unions, environmentalist groups, community organizations, and government agencies. Motives are mixed. Starting from theory rather than practice, Wissenburg (1998) argues that the building blocks of green liberalism may be found in agents who accept "ecoduties" as part of their basic social responsibilities. Individuals must also accept a "restraint principle" whereby any environmental damage they do cause requires restoration or compensation on their part. But this specification of principles begs the question of how they might come to the fore.

Many actors much of the time pursue selfish material interests, such as profit, increased property values, higher wages, more secure employment, or subsidized access to a favorite natural area. But the discourse of democratic pragmatism requires that at key junctures agents can be motivated by the public interest, and recognize that there are community interests (such as ecological integrity) that transcend individual interests (de-Shalit, 2000: 92–129). It is here that citizenship comes to the fore. In the first instance, the public interest will have to be defined in plural terms. So what the Wilderness Society takes as the public interest will not necessarily be the same as the Chamber of Commerce. Some democratic pragmatists would leave it at that, arguing that plurality here is irreducible, and that we can expect only piecemeal compromises across partisans of different views. But others, such as Kelman, Gundersen, and Sagoff, hope reasoned public dialogue will produce convergence on a common conception of the public interest (see also Williams and Matheny, 1995). If a single public interest does emerge through dialogue, it is a very different matter from the unitary public interest that exists for administrative rationalists, for whom the public interest is something for analysts to discover, rather than the public to debate. So "environmental sustainability" can be treated as a scientific concept to be administered; or as something to be explored in democratic debate (Arias-Maldonado, 2000).

Key metaphors and other rhetorical devices

Two scientific metaphors are advanced by reflective defenders of democratic pragmatism. The first draws from physics to treat public policy as the result of forces acting upon it from different directions. These forces differ in the direction in which they want to pull public policy, and in their relative power. Such a metaphor is likely to be employed by those who think there can be no unitary public interest. This metaphor was long a staple of pluralist accounts of the US political system developed by American political scientists.

A second metaphor is that of science in its entirety. As we have seen, Popperians believe that public policies are like scientific experiments, and that the proper attitude for scientists and policy makers alike is an open, critical, and democratic one.

Another metaphor I mentioned earlier is that of the thermostat, designed to trigger interventions (heating and cooling) as soon as temperature departs from a desirable range. Democratic pragmatism allows attention to a wide range of target variables analogous to temperature (economic and political as well as environmental ones), and many ways in which negative feedback can be brought to bear. Foremost among these is the possibility for aggrieved citizens and groups to mobilize when they perceive an environmental abuse.

Finally, the network itself is a kind of metaphor, especially when deployed by those who emphasize the information society in which we live. Parallels are drawn between networked information technology (especially the internet) and networked governance. Both proceed without any central controller.

Box 5.1 provides a summary of the discourse analysis of democratic pragmatism.

The limits of democratic pragmatism

Democratic pragmatism has much to be said on its behalf. It accepts many problems that baffle administrative rationalism. This transfer is often made for reasons relating to the need to legitimate policy decisions in the eyes of a broader public, but it can be justified in terms of more effectively resolving problems too. If we look around today's world, we see that the countries that have progressed most in terms of environmental conservation and pollution control are the ones where democratic pragmatism is most common: the capitalist democracies (though the most capitalist are not the best performers). If we extend the analysis to all the world's countries, we find democracy has a positive impact on pollution control (Farzin and Bond, 2006), though there is some dispute as to the strength of this influence once we take into account the wealth of a country (Scruggs, 2009). Christoff and Eckersley (2011: 445) conclude that the best performing countries on greenhouse gas emissions control feature "an advanced economy, a strong civil society, a strong and respected tradition of scientific research, and a diverse media" (all ingredients of democratic pragmatism), though they also note the importance of a strong executive that can face down opposition.

This last piece of evidence is consistent with the finding that acknowledged leaders in the environmental stakes include countries such as Germany and Japan (Scruggs, 2001), where there are limits on who can have access to policy making and under what terms. So in Japan policy is monopolized by business and government elites; in Germany, labor union leaders also have a say (though German policy making has opened up considerably in the last two decades). In each of these cases, usually described as corporatism, participation is through highly formalized channels, allowing little of the self-organizing give and take celebrated by democratic pragmatists. Moreover, some of the best-performing countries are adopting a discourse a bit different from democratic pragmatism, as we will see in Chapter 8.

Prometheans argue that it is the prosperity of the developed capitalist democracies that allows them to cope better with their environmental problems than anyone else, as opposed to the intrinsic problem-solving qualities of democratic pragmatism. And there is always the possibility that these

---

BOX 5.1 **Discourse analysis of democratic pragmatism**

1. **Basic entities recognized or constructed**
   - Liberal capitalism
   - Citizens
2. **Assumptions about natural relationships**
   - Equality among citizens
   - Interactive political relationships, mixing competition and cooperation
3. **Agents and their motives**
   - Many different agents but citizens central
   - Motivation a mix of material self-interest and multiple conceptions of public interest
4. **Key metaphors and other rhetorical devices**
   - Public policy as a resultant of forces
   - Policy like scientific experimentation
   - Thermostat
   - Network

---

countries have offloaded many of their environmental problems onto poorer countries. So a clean and pleasant environment in Japan is purchased in part by the dirtier elements of manufacturing industry being transferred to other East Asian countries, not to mention deforestation of Southeast Asia to meet Japanese timber needs. Greenhouse gas emissions in many wealthy liberal democracies are reduced inasmuch as the goods they now consume are produced in places such as China and Vietnam, rather than at home.

The main limit to democratic pragmatism is the simple existence of political power (which goes unrecognized by enthusiasts such as Gundersen and Sagoff). Political power and the divisive politics fossil fuel interests can unleash are also ignored in Ostrom's (2009) polycentric approach to climate governance, which interprets difficulties only in terms of barriers to collective action on the part of people with a shared interest in the quality of a resource (such as the atmosphere). But politics in capitalist democratic settings is rarely about disinterested and public-spirited problem solving in which many perspectives are brought to bear with equal weight. Often there are powerful interests with large financial resources at their disposal that try to skew the outcomes of policy debates and decision-making processes in their direction (González, 2001a; Speth, 2008: 217–9). Sometimes that direction will coincide with ecological values. More often it will not, as the interests with the greatest amount of resources and the strongest incentives to deploy them are business interests, such as the real estate developers who drive urban sprawl in the United States (González, 2009). Networked governance will not necessarily change matters here. Surveying environmental and natural resource management cases in Scandinavia and the European Union, Bäckstrand et al. (2010) conclude that the environmental performance of new forms of networked and collaborative governance is not demonstrably better than conventional top-down forms, precisely because the new forms remain dominated by state and corporate actors.

In a democratic society, public opinion ought to have a major influence on policy making. But public opinion can be targeted by anti-environmental business; in Chapter 3 we saw how in the United States corporations such as Koch Industries and Exxon Mobil have been remarkably successful in sowing doubt about the existence of damaging human-caused climate change. Industry front groups such as the Global Climate Coalition and Greening Earth Society (now both disbanded) could, despite their names, bolster climate change denial. Less obviously anti-environmental business can influence the terms of debate by producing glossy advertising material to tout the environmental friendliness of its products. It can sponsor Earth Day festivities. It can produce television advertising to promote the corporate environmental image: so in the United States Weyerhauser once promoted itself as "the tree growing company," with film of a bald eagle flying over a forest. The clear-cutting of old growth forests, which is also one of Weyerhauser's activities, is unmentioned. Corporate actors also have greater access to expert counsel in public inquiries. ADR can be manipulated by these actors and their sympathizers in government in order to co-opt and neutralize troublemakers from community and environmental groups. ADR can be oriented toward a "responsible development" gloss on projects which generally go ahead, and toward treatment of environmental values as on a par with business's material interests (Amy, 1987). Participation by environmentalists in impact assessment might dissipate energies that would be better spent on other activities, if the process merely legitimates decisions already made elsewhere on the basis of economic values or corporate profit (Amy, 1990: 60–4). Corporations can even offer employment to environmental activists. For example, leading British Green Jonathan Porritt signed on as an advisor to Sainsbury's, the food retailing giant. Former Australian Conservation Foundation Director Trisha Caswell was subsequently employed by a forest industry association.

Such pressures do not go all one way; public opinion does exist as something more than the creation of business public relations departments, and public interest groups can mobilize expertise and support, even money. Online activism using social media potentially introduces further autonomy in public opinion. Still, so long as the structural status quo of the capitalist market economy is taken as given, business has a "privileged" position in policy making, for government relies greatly upon business to carry out basic functions such as employing people and organizing the economy (Lindblom, 1977: 171–5). Any measures for environmental protection, conservation, or pollution control which threaten to undermine business confidence will be automatically punished by disinvestment. This possibility casts a long shadow over policy deliberations, however democratic they may be (see Press, 1994). And once business publicists realize this, they can make good strategic use of the disinvestment threat, even when there is no real intention to disinvest. As we will see in Part IV, sustainability discourse dissolves such problems by eliminating the conflict between economic and environmental values.

Democratic pragmatism as a discourse recognizes citizens as a basic entity, and a natural relationship of equality across citizens. But this imagery of reasoned debate among equals is in practice highly distorted by the exercise of power and strategy, and by the overarching need of government to maintain business confidence. Matters appear still more doubtful in an ecological light when one further considers the character of actors and their interests. One advantage of democratic pragmatism stressed by its adherents is that it enables views on policy proposals to come from a variety of directions. Some directions represent conceptions of what is in the public interest. These conceptions may vary: to some, the public interest may involve mostly economic efficiency, to others distributional equity in society, to others still ecological integrity, to others social harmony. When enthusiasts such as Gundersen and Sagoff in an ecological context, and Dewey and Popper more generally, think of democratic debate, this is presumably what they have in mind. But other interests involved are motivated mostly by their own material interests: corporations and industry associations concerned with maximizing profit and avoiding environmental controls on their operations, or labor unions concerned with the income and employment of their members, even if that means employment in unsustainable practices such as clear-cutting of ancient forests. The pluralist aspect of democratic pragmatism treats all such interests and concerns as equally legitimate (see Williams and Matheny, 1995: 19–24). The mere fact of participation in liberal democratic settings does not lead actors to discard their motivations as consumers and producers in favor of more public-spirited citizen preferences, or to conclude that pursuit of their economic interests should be confined to the market place rather than allowed to enter politics.

More insidious still are special interests that masquerade as general principles. So, for example, the "Wise Use" movement in the American West has a name that connotes commitment to sensible use of resources, but in practice it features visceral hostility to environmentalism, seeking subsidized access for local communities and corporations to minerals, grazing rights, and timber located on public lands in the region.

Political rationality in democratic pragmatism means that all actors have to be mollified, pretty much in proportion to their ability to create difficulties for government officials, irrespective of whether they are motivated by conceptions of the public interest or more selfish material interests. This does not necessarily coincide with ecological rationality, which is concerned with the integrity of natural life-support systems (see Dryzek, 1987: 118–20). So in 1993 the Clinton administration took a small step toward ecological rationality when Secretary of the Interior Bruce Babbit proposed reforming grazing law to end subsidized access for cattle ranchers to public land. It soon became evident that the politically rational thing to do was back off on these reforms for fear of the electoral weight of the western states where these reforms would take effect, and where welfare ranchers and their sympathizers could tip the balance come election day.

Democratic pragmatism in some respects merits a similar summary judgment to administrative rationalism: plenty of achievements to look back on, but limits to effectiveness increasingly apparent. This similarity applies mostly at the level of specific policies and institutions inspired or justified by the two discourses. But as a discourse, democratic pragmatism has one striking advantage: it is more conducive to an awareness of the limitations of its own institutional manifestations, and so to efforts to overcome these limits.

....

NOTES

1. See <http://www.gmnation.org.uk>

2. There are numerous case studies of this kind of process in the political science literature. Classics may be found in the work of Aaron Wildavsky (Wildavsky, 1988; Pressman and Wildavsky, 1973).

6

Leave it to the Market: Economic Rationalism

When it comes to theories to guide public policies, democratic pragmatists are quite agnostic. The only test they are inclined to apply is the pragmatic one of whether the policy inspired by the theory works out in reality. Politics of the sort pragmatists favor is home to believers in different theories and perspectives. In the last three decades, one very prominent perspective on policy in general has been market economics. This perspective goes by different names in different places: market liberalism, classical liberalism, neoliberalism, and free-market conservatism. Sometimes it was even personalized, and becomes Thatcherism in the UK, Reagonomics in the United States, Salinastroika in Mexico (after President Salinas de Gotari), or Rogernomics in New Zealand (for finance minister Roger Douglas). For a while the global financial crisis of 2008 seemed to have killed such market fundamentalism, but it made a remarkable comeback in short order (for no good reason except the sheer power of discourse).

Now, many market fundamentalists are Prometheans, who believe that government in environmental affairs should leave markets well alone, to give human ingenuity full rein. Yet there are others just as committed to market principles who recognize that, whatever the case in other areas, markets in environmental goods do not always exist, and so often need to be created and managed, sometimes even by taxation. Thus their discourse is rationalistic, entailing substantial cogitation, calculation, and design on the part of policy makers.

Economic rationalism may be defined by its commitment to the intelligent deployment of market mechanisms to achieve public ends. It differs from administrative rationalism in its hostility to environmental management by government administrators—except, of course, in establishing the basic parameters of designed markets. In this one key aspect economic rationalism turns out to depend on the administrative rationalism it otherwise so despises. The commitment to markets might imply that economic rationalism's natural political home is on the political right. In the United States, "free market environmentalists" (such as Stroup, 2003) revel in this connection, almost certainly to the detriment of the policies they favor. Yet some people with green credentials are also attracted by the use of markets in an environmental context (for example, Daly, 1992; Roodman, 1996). As Fred Krupp of the Environmental Defense Fund puts it, "harnessing the power of the market is often the best way to achieve the greatest environmental benefit at the least cost" (Krupp, 2007). Countries with governments organized along more social democratic lines (for example, Germany, the Netherlands, and France) have pioneered economic rationalist environmental policy instruments. One particular instrument (the congestion charge) is associated with socialist London Mayor Ken Livingstone.

William Reilly, Administrator of the EPA under President George Bush the elder and before that head of the Conservation Foundation, declared that "The forces of the marketplace are powerful tools for changing individual and institutional behavior. If set up correctly, they can achieve or surpass environmental objectives at less costs and with less opposition than traditional regulatory approaches" (quoted in Yandle, 1993: 188). Changes of president did not dampen this enthusiasm: in 1992 president-elect Bill Clinton spoke of "harnessing market forces" to induce companies to incorporate "environmental incentives into daily production decisions" (quoted in Nelson, 1993: 1). In 2003 George W. Bush's EPA Administrator Mike Leavitt proclaimed his belief in "markets before mandates," as "market-based approaches and economic incentives often result in more efficiency at less cost." There was perhaps some retreat in the Obama administration. In 2010 Secretary of the Interior Ken Salazar said cap and trade (the main market instrument for pollution control, which I will discuss shortly) was no longer in the "lexicon"—though this retreat had more to do with placating opponents of any government action on pollution (especially greenhouse gases).

Market-type policy instruments have been promoted by the Organization for Economic Cooperation and Development, the rich man's club of the world's developed countries (see OECD, 2010), and the European Union. The European Environment Agency (2000: 397) has even proposed a comprehensive regime of environmental taxes to replace income taxation as a main source of government revenue. Economic instruments were endorsed by the 1987 Brundtland Report, *Our Common Future,* which launched the era of sustainable development on the international stage.

My discussion of economic rationalism begins with its purest strain, emphasizing the conversion of environmental resources to private property. I then move to less radical strands that stress market incentives but not necessarily private property.

Privatizing everything if you can

Markets are systems in which goods, services, and financial instruments are exchanged for each other. Markets work smoothly to the extent that participants in transactions can be confident that they do in fact have a right to sell or buy the goods in question—in other words, they have property rights, be it to a car, a can of beans, a company, a bond, or a piece of land. If we are to have markets in environmental goods, then we need private property rights here too. According to economic rationalism, specification and enforcement of these rights is the main task of government, when it comes to natural resources and the environment no less than elsewhere (Kaplowitz, 2004). Why are private property rights and markets so desirable? Because people tend to care more for what they hold privately than for what they hold in common with others. This is why (for example) there is more litter in public parks than in private yards, or why public grazing land in the American West is more degraded than private land. Economic rationalism has a clear solution to the tragedy of the commons (introduced in Chapter 2): divide it into chunks of private property. Once the commons is divided, these chunks can be bought and sold according to who is prepared to pay the most. Economic rationalists tell us that, given a few assumptions, markets maximize social welfare; and markets in environmental goods should be no exception. The private property right to the good in question will be bought by whoever values it most, and can make the most profitable use of it.

It is easy to see how this logic of property and markets works for ordinary material goods, services, education, even human labor power; less easy to see how it applies to the environment. But economic rationalists see no real difficulties in applying the same logic here. Meiners and Yandle (1993: viii) believe that "environmental controversies seem to boil down to arguments about property rights." Of itself, this interpretation does not imply that it is going to be easy to specify, enforce, and adjudicate an appropriate set of rights. Yet economic rationalists are adamant that failure to do so lies at the heart of environmental problems; as Mitchell and Simmons (1994: 148) put it, "environmental problems must be understood more as failures by government to specify property rights than as offshoots of private profit-seeking."

What, then does an appropriate set of property rights look like? When it comes to land, the answer is easy, as systems of private property are well established, and only need extending to all land. This is really only a political issue in countries with large amounts of land in public ownership, such as the United States. American free-market environmentalists are obsessed with the public lands issue (see for example Fretwell, 2009). Much of this land is in the Western states, and most of it is controlled by agencies of the federal government, especially the National Park Service, Defense Department, Forest Service, and Bureau of Land Management. With the exception of the Pentagon, these are notionally professional land management agencies. In practice, as economic rationalists argue, these agencies often act as conduits for the abuse of land at the hands of special interests (see Anderson and Leal, 1991: 51–9, for a catalog). Ranchers can graze their cattle on public land at below-market prices, and have little incentive to care for this land, because they do not own it. Logging companies gain heavily subsidized access to national forests, as the Forest Service constructs roads at public expense. Often, the Forest Service receives less money for a timber lease than it pays to construct roads into the lease area. This amounts to publicly subsidized wilderness destruction. Wilderness lovers for their part get free and often subsidized access to the back country, leading to overuse and degradation. Tourists get heavily subsidized roads and facilities in the more accessible parts of national parks, which again become overused and abused. Mining companies can make use of antiquated nineteenth-century laws that allow them to stake claims to minerals on public lands while paying virtually nothing.

According to economic rationalists, none of these abuses would occur if the land were privately owned. Ranchers would have every incentive not to overgraze, and to invest in soil and vegetation conservation. Owners of forests that could not be logged economically would keep them as wilderness areas, or invest in wildlife conservation in order to attract hunters or photographers, who would be charged admission to provide income for these conservation investments. If mineral rights were privatized, there would be a more orderly and efficient market in mines, rather than an inefficient scramble to make (subsidized) claims. If parks were privatized, tourists and backpackers alike would have to pay the market price for access, and private owners would again have every incentive to use the income to enhance the recreational value of the park. If anyone wanted to preserve wilderness for its own sake or for the sake of the species that inhabit it rather than for recreational opportunities, then they could buy it and do so. This is exactly what the Nature Conservancy, a private organization, does. The Nature Conservancy's wholehearted acceptance of market logic and an associated corporate model eventually led it to allow oil drilling and logging on some of its lands, to sell land to supporters for the construction of large houses, and to sell land to developers for luxury vacation houses (on Martha's Vineyard island, Massachusetts). These actions could be justified on the grounds they raised money to buy more land to protect, though they hardly looked like nature conservation.

Privatization of land is a major issue only in North America, because in most other developed countries most land is already private. Not so air and water, and here a little more ingenuity in the specification of private property rights is called for. The argument becomes applicable to more countries, because all of them have polluted air and water.

Air is hard to privatize because, of course, it moves around in the way land does not (barring the occasional earthquake, landslide, or soil erosion). But the useful properties of air can have private property rights attached to them, normally in conjunction with a parcel of land. So a right to breathe clean air can be attached to ownership or occupation of a piece of residential or commercial land. Anyone violating that right by emitting pollutants into the atmosphere can be pursued through the courts to either secure compensation or prevent violation of the property right to clean air. The legal system would play an expanded role in any such regime.

The immediate problem involves identifying polluters and tracing the effects of pollution on human health. This can be extraordinarily difficult, especially when there are multiple polluters. The air in my garden may not be clean, but am I coughing because of the methane given off by the nearby landfill, the heavy metals emitted from a local toxic waste incinerator, smog coming from car exhausts, or sulfur dioxide from the city's coal-burning power station? Or is it because my neighbor is burning her garbage? Clearly needed here are vast improvements in monitoring technology, and until that technology arrives, it is not surprising that property rights in air have made little headway. Market zealots such as Anderson and Leal (1991: 165–6) recognize this problem, which is why they fantasize about adding tracers to all pollution sources, and about advances in lasimetrics and satellite tracking of atmospheric chemicals.

Some of the same problems apply when it comes to water, though private property rights to clean water have been established in some cases. In Britain the private recreational fishing rights attached to a stretch of river or lakeside come with a right to water clean enough for fish to flourish. So any polluter, upstream or elsewhere in the lake, can be sued by the individual or fishing club holding the fishing rights. The Angling Trust (formerly the Anglers' Conservation Association) has been zealous in bringing cases against polluters. The result is that British waterways, while rarely pristine, are much cleaner than they would be otherwise. Those benefiting include not just the fish and the anglers, but also the (very few, given the climate) people who swim in rivers and lakes, the (more numerous) people who rely on rivers as sources of drinking water, and the plants and animals of aquatic communities.

In arid regions, the main water issue concerns not pollution, but supply. Again the Western US offers the most contentious and troubled cases. Water rights to stream flows generally went to the first person to claim them. Thereafter, the "use it or lose it" doctrine applies, which means that users must waste water when they do not need it, for fear of losing their right to it. It does not require an economic genius to realize it would be more efficient to allow individuals and corporations to buy and sell rights to particular portions of the flow of a river or creek. Water policy in the US is also blasted by free marketeers for its enormous public subsidy for questionable schemes that build dams and canals to supply agribusiness corporations and a few other wealthy interests. The main villain here is the Bureau of Reclamation, long regarded as one of the more powerful empires in the US government (see Reisner, 1993). The Bureau's aim is to create agriculture in the desert. The massive ecological costs include elimination of stream flows, siltation behind dams, and soil salination. None of these public subsidies and ecological costs would apply if western agribusiness, cities, and industries had to pay market prices for the water they consumed. Welfare irrigation in this light is no more defensible than welfare logging, welfare ranching, welfare backpacking, welfare tourism, and welfare mining. All are costly and environmentally devastating.

Land, air, and water together cover a lot of what we normally mean by "environment," so if all can be privatized then we would, according to the marketeers, be well on the way to solving all environmental problems. We could go still further by privatizing species, wildlife, and fish. Species might be privatized through property rights to their genes. For example, rights to rare plants in endangered tropical forest ecosystems are claimed by pharmaceutical companies for the sake of their actual or potential in producing new drugs. Wildlife might be privatized in conjunction with land, or, when animals wander across property boundaries, tracked by means of radio collars. Anderson and Leal (1991: 34) suggest that whales should be converted to private property: "Whales also can be 'branded' by genetic prints and tracked by satellite." Conservationists wanting to save the whales could buy them, as could whalers wanting to hunt them. The market would determine the most appropriate balance. But note that whalers would not hunt to extinction, for once they had private property rights they would have every incentive to invest in the health of the whale stock, just as farmers invest in the health of their animals.

A market zealot would insist that solutions to environmental problems begin and end with the establishment of private property rights. As Coase (1960) demonstrated for the case of pollution, it does not even matter who has the right, the polluter or the sufferer from pollution, so long as it is legally clear. For if there is a legally unrestricted right to pollute, then market solutions to pollution can be generated by the sufferers banding together and offering to pay the polluter to cut back on emissions. Depending on what the sufferers are willing to pay, and whether this is larger or smaller than the profit the polluter is making from the activity, cutback will or will not occur in a fashion optimal in market efficiency terms. The fact that nowhere in the world can we observe sufferers offering to pay polluters to stop polluting does not stop Coase's article being regarded as a classic by economists.[1] (Scandinavian governments offered to pay Poland to stop polluting their atmosphere, but this is governmental action, not citizen-sufferers approaching polluters with an offer.)

Those who believe that if it moves you should privatize it, and if it doesn't move you should privatize it, represent the radical fringe of economic rationalism. Its stronghold is in US-based think tanks such as the

Foundation for Research on Economics and the Environment (FREE), the Property and Environment Research Center (PERC) in Bozeman, Montana, the Pacific Research Institute in San Francisco, the Independent Institute in Oakland, California, the Cato Institute in Washington, DC, and to a lesser extent mainstream conservative operations such as the American Enterprise Institute. There is a British counterpart in the Institute of Economic Affairs (London) and an Australian one in the Institute of Public Affairs (Melbourne) (see Beder, 2001, for a survey of such think tanks).

More influential have been economic rationalists who advocate not wholesale privatization and private property rights, but rather market-type mechanisms and economic incentives to induce environmentally appropriate behavior, and to these I now turn.

If you can't privatize it, market it anyway

The hard-line economic rationalist position is that private property rights in air and water need to be established and enforced, nothing more. However, given the substantial difficulties with this hard-line position, economic rationalists have often turned to the next best thing: government-managed markets and, failing that, quasi-market incentives. The most popular proposals for managed markets in the environmental realm involve pollution rights. Government defines an airshed or watershed, determines the maximum level of pollution that should be allowed (a cap), divides that level into a number of rights, then auctions off those rights to the highest bidder. After the initial auction has been held, polluters can buy and sell rights from one another. So "cap and trade" is sometimes used to describe this approach. Polluters for whom it is easy and cheap to reduce emissions will cut back rather than pay for pollution rights, whereas polluters for whom emissions reduction is expensive will purchase rights to pollute. Thus the government-specified level of abatement will be achieved in the most cost-effective manner. Environmentalists who believe abatement should be greater still can always purchase quotas themselves and leave them unused (for arguments in favor of tradeable quotas, see Anderson and Leal, 1991: 145–7; Yandle, 1993).

Tradeable quotas have been introduced to a limited extent in the United States, where in 1979 the federal EPA began by sponsoring the "bubble" concept in a few localities. However, in practice bubbles covered only a particular plant, and so the emissions "trades" occur only within a company (that is, allowing the company to decide in which part of the plant it can most cheaply reduce emissions, rather than have government regulators instruct the company in what standards and technologies to use in particular parts of the factory). The 1990 US Clean Air Act Amendments allow for emissions trading on a larger scale for sulfur dioxide from coal-burning power plants. Under this Act, pollution credits beginning in 1995 were granted to 110 of the country's dirtiest coal-burning power plants, representing between 30 and 50 percent of the sulfur dioxide currently emitted by them. The Chicago Board of Trade held auctions for additional credits. This cap and trade scheme is widely hailed as a success. In 2010 the EPA reported that sulfur dioxide emissions from power plants in the United States were 64 percent below their 1990 level. On a yet larger scale, the 1987 Montreal Protocol for the protection of the ozone layer provided for trades between countries in quotas for the emission of chlorofluorocarbons.

The 1997 Kyoto Protocol provided for international emissions trading in greenhouse gas emissions. In 2003 the European Union adopted an emissions trading scheme for carbon dioxide emissions (Jordan et al., 2010), which was widely applauded as a success—until the price of emissions permits crashed in the wake of the 2008 global financial crisis, which slowed industrial production and so produced a drop in demand for permits. This crash meant that the scheme lost its ability to curb emissions, indicating perhaps that if the scheme could be derailed so easily, it meant it was not stringent enough in terms of the total quantity of permits it allowed to begin with. In the United States, for several years carbon dioxide emissions trading was organized on a voluntary basis by the Chicago Climate Exchange, which began in 2000, but by 2011 had closed. These problems notwithstanding, a number of countries such as New Zealand have adopted emissions trading schemes at the national level. A subnational scheme exists in New South Wales in Australia, and in 2008 ten states in the Northeastern United States set up a Regional Greenhouse Gas Initiative. International financial institutions have started to develop a strong interest in making money from carbon trading.

The idea of climate marketization has come to dominate the international politics of climate change (Paterson, 2011). Aside from emissions trading, emissions offsets have become popular. The basic idea of an offset is that the emitter can pay someone, somewhere to do something that absorbs an equivalent quantity of carbon dioxide—for example, by planting trees—or forsakes doing something dirty, such as building a more efficient alternative to a polluting power station. The Clean Development Mechanism (CDM) established under the 1997 Kyoto Protocol provides especially for developing countries to sell offsets to companies, governments and (ultimately) consumers in wealthier countries (though initially the CDM largely excluded forests). More recently, the idea of offsets has been applied to biodiversity, especially in Australia: destruction of nature in one location can be offset by the destroyer paying for conservation in another location.

Tradeable quotas can also be established in resources such as fish (Stavins, 2003). The quota would refer to an allowable catch for a particular fishery for a specified time. Some government agency is needed to establish the quotas, but once established the quotas can be bought and sold on the market. Australia pioneered this system for its southern bluefin tuna fishery, and by 2004 had schemes in place for twenty-one fisheries. Tradeable quotas were introduced in Alaska's Pacific halibut fishery in 1995. Fisheries throughout the world have been notoriously subject to the tragedy of the commons, resulting in overfishing, depletion, and overcapitalization as fishers rushed to beat their competitors to the catch. Tradeable quotas have been less widely used than other forms of regulation (such as restrictions on numbers of boats, fishing seasons, equipment, and total allowable catch for the fishery as a whole).

Quasi-market incentives for their part involve setting standards and charges for pollution control, or "green taxes" as they are sometimes known. Government sets an ambient environmental standard (for example, level of carbon monoxide in urban air), and then imposes taxes or charges on the activities which threaten that standard. The taxes in question can be levied on the goods whose production causes pollution, or directly on the pollution itself. Examples of the former are rare, though the European Community applies a tax on cadmium batteries, and several years ago the UK government mooted a proposal to impose an environmental tax on walking boots, on the grounds of the damage caused by the boots to footpaths in National Parks and other scenic areas of Britain. Examples of levies on pollution itself include charges per kilogram of sulfur dioxide emitted by smokestacks, or per kilogram of BOD (biological oxygen demand) for organic pollutants in rivers.

The economic rationalist's argument for a regime of green taxes is that they leave discretion in the hands of the polluter in terms of how much to reduce pollution and what kind of technology to use. If the polluter chooses to pursue abatement, then it has every incentive to find the most cost-effective means. Polluters for whom abatement is expensive will prefer to pay the charge and continue to pollute. All polluters have an incentive to search for less-polluting methods of production, for that will always save money. Government should set the charge per unit of pollution at a level sufficient to induce the required degree of abatement (for arguments in favor of green taxes, see Anderson et al., 1977; Kneese and Schultze, 1975; Moran, 1995; for a comparison of green taxes and emissions trading, see Nordhaus, 2007b).

Green taxes are not especially popular at the federal level in the United States (though hundreds exist at state and local levels; see Beck et al., 1998). Presidential candidate Al Gore renounced his previous commitment to green taxes in his 2000 presidential campaign. The idea of green taxes captured policy discourse in Britain in the late 1980s and early 1990s, when an upsurge in environmentalism coincided with a national government committed to market values. Prime Minister Thatcher remembered that she had studied chemistry long ago at Oxford University, and so could recognize chemical pollution when she saw it. The key document was produced by the environmental economist David Pearce for the Department of the Environment in 1989, entitled *Blueprint for a Green Economy* (Pearce et al., 1989), which advocated a comprehensive regime of green taxes (see Pearce and Barbier, 2000 for an update). In 1992 the government announced that "In future, there will be a general presumption in favour of economic instruments" (quoted in Jacobs, 1995: 114). This presumption was slow to influence policy content. Part of the problem in Britain is that the Treasury interprets green taxes in revenue-raising terms, and would want to set levels without reference to environmental departments of government. This worries industry, which foresees charges rising and falling, most likely rising, in response to government's revenue needs. And it worries environmentalists, for it gives government a vested interest in pollution, for the more pollution that occurs, the more revenues does government receive (see Jacobs, 1995: 124). Because it sees green taxes in revenue-raising terms, the Treasury has generally opposed the use of the tax system for environmental purposes. In 1996 a tax was introduced on solid waste destined for landfills. The most prominent green tax in the United Kingdom is the congestion charge levied on vehicles entering central London, introduced in 2003. The charge has successfully reduced both congestion and air pollution. Mayor Ken

Livingstone staked his political future on the charge—and won re-election in 2004.

In Denmark and the Netherlands, green taxes account for around 10 percent of all tax revenue. France, Germany, and the Netherlands pioneered per-unit pollution charges. In the Netherlands, charges are successful and widely supported by environmentalists. In Germany, green taxes play only a secondary role within a more traditional regulatory system. German municipalities retain substantial control over policy implementation, and so happily dump pollution downstream. In all three countries revenue raised is earmarked for projects to improve water quality. As Hahn (1995: 146–7) notes, "charges and marketable permits schemes... are rarely, if ever, introduced in their textbook form." The same might be said of most policies inspired by economic rationalism: the textbook explication is crystal clear, the real-world implementation murky.

Denmark, Finland, the Netherlands, Norway, and Sweden were the first countries to introduce a carbon tax, levied per tonne of fossil fuel burned. Other European countries followed. In 2001 the United Kingdom introduced a climate change levy on fossil fuels burned by industries and government bodies with high emissions, though the coverage was restricted and accompanied by a complex system of exemptions. Australia introduced a carbon tax in 2012 amid bitter political conflict. China plans to introduce a carbon tax in 2015.

Before leaving green taxes, it should be noted that radical free-market zealots oppose them on the grounds that such taxes require competent and benign administrators to set and change tax rates (for example, Mitchell and Simmons, 1994: 148). Such zealots, recall, believe that the real cause of environmental problems is inadequate or inappropriate government specification of private property rights, and until that situation is rectified, policy actions are useless or counterproductive, and that includes green taxes.

Green taxes levied on goods are designed to induce consumers to make purchases that are less environmentally damaging. An alternative market-based means to the same end is provision of information about the environmental impact of a good, to facilitate green consumerism. For example, those concerned about climate change can buy goods with low carbon footprints such as hybrid cars or fluorescent lightbulbs (Szasz, 2011). The idea of "eco-labeling" goods began in Germany in 1977, though arguably the most successful scheme is "Nordic Swan" certification that has operated in the

Nordic countries since 1989. Eco-labeling now ranges from forest products (which can be certified as free from destruction of tropical hardwoods) to organic food. Critics of green consumerism point out that it does not affect the total quantity of goods consumed by individuals, and that it is an easy symbolic alternative to confronting the structural causes of ecological destruction (Maniates, 2001). Yet confronting consumption seriously could in principle have a massive impact, because the pattern of consumption drives most economic activity (Conca et al., 2001). The problem is that the individual choices of green consumers are no match for the forces of corporate capitalism pushing environmentally irresponsible consumption—including "greenwashed" products.

Analysis of economic rationalism discourse

Basic entities whose existence is recognized or constructed

Economic rationalism's world is populated by economic actors. *Homo economicus* can appear as a consumer or producer; and if producers are organized into firms, the firm still behaves like an individual. Markets, prices, and property have real existence. At some level government exists too as something more than a collection of economic individuals. However, economic rationalist discourse is ambiguous and troubled on this point. Some economic rationalists treat government as staffed entirely by *Homo economicus* individuals, all concerned only with their own material interest, exploiting the public for personal benefit. This is why they always prefer markets to politics (see for example Mitchell and Simmons, 1994). But even these die-hard economic rationalists require someone, somewhere to be steering the system in the public interest, otherwise who is going to enact the appropriate arrangement of private property rights they seek?

Notably missing from economic rationalism are citizens (of the sort populating democratic pragmatism). Also, environments do not exist in any strong sense. At most, "the environment" is only a pathway for some human decisions to have effects on other people—for example, through pollution. The existence of ecosystems, let alone ecosystems that often defy understanding, cut across chunks of private property, and impose constraints on human activity, is not perceived. There is no such thing as wilderness, only wilderness experiences (that is, human perceptions of wilderness amenity). There is an odd affinity here with postmodernists, for whom "nature" is a human social construction. This lack of recognition of nature is driven home by Anderson and Leal's (2001: 27) comment on migratory bison that stray from Yellowstone National Park onto cattle ranches, potentially spreading brucellosis: "The migration of the Yellowstone bison is like other cases of pollution in which the actions of one party, in this case the National Park Service, affect another, in this case Montana cattle ranchers." So the bison are not recognized as part of the Yellowstone ecosystem, but instead demeaned as pollutants, at most the medium for one set of people (National Park Service officials) to affect another set of people (ranchers).

Unlike Prometheans, economic rationalists recognize the existence of natural resources, which is why it is crucial to establish the right kinds of property rights to these resources. In further contrast to Prometheans, economic rationalists would not necessarily dismiss the existence of limits to human activity imposed by finite resources.

Assumptions about natural relationships

Economic rationalism assumes that the basic relationship across individuals and collective actors (such as firms) is competitive. The cooperative problem solving sought by democratic pragmatists is ruled out. Corresponding to its thoroughly ambiguous attitude toward the existence of government as anything more than an assemblage (or sometimes tool) of rational egoists out to plunder the public purse, economic rationalism is confused about the existence of hierarchy within government. Administrative rationalism, as seen in Chapter 4, happily accepts hierarchy based on expertise. When it comes down to it, economic rationalists have to do the same, because some experts must be in a position of authority to implement appropriate private property rights, or to design green taxes. Of course, the experts themselves must be economic rationalists; but they cannot be economic *actors,* for if they were they would devise schemes in their own personal interest, not in the public interest.

The other kind of hierarchy implicit in economic rationalism is between humans and the natural world. Economic rationalism is thoroughly anthropocentric: nature exists only to provide inputs to the socioeconomic machine, to satisfy human wants and needs. The appropriate expertise to manipulate these environmental inputs is taken for granted. Once appropriate property rights and incentives are in place, individual actors have no problem in deploying expertise to produce good results for society as a whole.

Agents and their motives

The main agents for economic rationalists are *Homo economicus* ones, motivated by material self-interest, and pursuing it rationally. But, as I have just noted, exemption is granted for a few agents in governmental positions, who are allowed to be motivated by concern for the public interest, albeit defined in economic rationalist terms. Fretwell (2009) is explicit: wise managers concerned with the long term should take precedence over politicians. Of course, the governmental actors who populate horror stories are not allowed any such public interested motivation; they are treated as rational egoists, whose interaction produces all kinds of perverse outcomes (Higgs and Close, 2005). Missing from economic rationalism is any notion of active citizenship; economic rationalism abolishes citizenship. When I received a circular from the economic rationalist government of the state of Victoria, where I used to live, it was addressed "Dear Customer." There were no citizens in Victoria.

Key metaphors and other rhetorical devices

Like the Promethean discourse analyzed in Chapter 3, the basic metaphor of economic rationalism is mechanistic. The social world is treated as a machine whose products meet human needs and wants, which can be understood through reference to its components and their functions. Unlike Private citizens, economic rationalists believe the machine may need to be reassembled, through, for example, redefinitions of property rights. Once we get the property rights in order, the machine will work smoothly. Environmental resources are treated as inputs to the social machine, be they raw materials for production or amenities such as wilderness and clean air.

Economic rationalists are skilled rhetoricians. Intervention by government administrators in the environmental affairs of industry and commerce used to be known, accurately and simply enough, as "regulation." Economic rationalists oppose regulation, so succeeded in stigmatizing it as "command as control." As John Baden, Chairman of FREE puts it, "There is wide agreement that FME [free market environmentalism] is intellectually dominant: no responsible scholar still supports the old command-and-control resource management of the Progressive Era" (Baden, 2012). Little command and control actually occurs in environmental administration; there is much more in the way of informal cooperative relationships between government officials and polluters (see Chapter 4). So as a description of the real world, the term is laughable; but as a rhetorical ploy, it is brilliant. Following the collapse of Soviet-style systems which really did work by command and control, who could possibly favor such a system (except perhaps the military)?

An equally clever rhetorical ploy involves use of the adjective "free," especially to describe markets. A market is a market is a market; so why does it need to be called a free market, especially given that markets can only operate if government supplies a supportive legal context? Relatedly, why are capitalist corporations styled free enterprise? The answer is that the standard set of freedoms in liberal democratic societies is very popular. In free markets and free enterprise, coercion is abolished if not in fact, then in rhetoric.

A third pervasive rhetorical strategy in economic rationalism is the horror story involving governmental action that produces perverse, inefficient, and costly results (for good selections, see Nelson, 1993; Stroup and Shaw, 1993). In the United States, one of the most widely circulated environmental horror stories picks up on the analysis of the 1977 Clean Air Act Amendments carried out by Ackerman and Hassler (1981) (who ironically are not themselves economic rationalists). Ackerman and Hassler demonstrate the disastrous results of a particular episode in legislation for environmental regulation. Eastern producers of high-sulfur coal combined with environmentalists to persuade Congress to mandate that all new coal-burning power plants install scrubbers to remove sulfur dioxide from their emissions, irrespective of how low the sulfur content of the coal was being burned, and so how much sulfur dioxide was being emitted. This measure effectively discriminated against western low-sulfur coal producers, and ensured that the ambient air quality targets would be met at a cost billions of dollars greater than could have been achieved with a switch to low-sulfur coal. Moreover, the legislation allowed existing coal-burning plants to operate with no additional controls, thus ensuring that old and dirty plants would gain a competitive edge over new plants, and so stay in use longer, thus actually encouraging increased pollution.

BOX 6.1   Discourse analysis of economic rationalism

1. **Basic entities recognized or constructed**
   - *Homo economicus*
   - Markets
   - Prices
   - Property
   - Governments (not citizens)
2. **Assumptions about Natural Relationships**
   - Competition
   - Hierarchy based on expertise
   - Subordination of nature
3. **Agents and their Motives**
   - *Homo economicus*: self-interested
   - Some government officials must be motivated by public interest
4. **Key Metaphors and other Rhetorical Devices**
   - Mechanistic
   - Stigmatizing regulation as "command and control"
   - Connection with freedom
   - Horror stories

Other good horror stories include the Superfund, seen to shuffle toxic waste around at enormous expense to little benefit (Stroup and Meiners, 2000); water policy that, bizarrely, promotes water-intensive crops such as rice and cotton in the desert; and timber policy, which heavily subsidizes otherwise uneconomic logging. Most of these horror stories are true. Their rhetorical weight comes with the economic rationalists' generalization from these stories, nearly all of which are about the United States government, to all the environmental activities of all governments. Perhaps the fault lies with the US federal government in particular, rather than government in general.

Box 6.1 provides a summary of the discourse analysis of economic rationalism.

An assessment of economic rationalism

Economic rationalism in environmental affairs has been around a long time now. Analysis and advocacy of quasi-market incentive systems has been the staple of environmental economics since the 1960s, and more radical market-oriented arguments gained ground in the 1980s. (So it is odd that such old policies were later recruited to the category of "new environmental policy instruments"; see Jordan et al., 2003.) These arguments were quite consistent with the dominant political discourse of the 1980s, at least in the Anglo-American world, which since then has expanded to dominate international economic affairs. The US delegation at the 1997 Kyoto negotiations on climate change pushed international tradeable quotas in carbon dioxide emissions. International bodies such as the OECD and European Environment Agency have been pushing such policies for a long time. Yet the pace of diffusion of economic rationalism into environmental policy practice has been slow. Regulatory policy instruments still dominate antipollution policy, tradeable quotas in access to resources are still rare, and there has been little privatization of resources and environmental goods. Even when policy instruments are adopted, there is no wholesale institutional change such as that sought by economic rationalists. Regulatory agencies are still with us and, far from being replaced by regimes of property rights or by economistic calculators of green taxes, they end up administering such schemes (as Anderson and Libecap, 2012 lament, to potentially disastrous effect). When it comes to institutions, economic rationalism has had less impact than administrative rationalism and democratic pragmatism which, as we saw in the two previous chapters, have been major factors in the evolution of environmental institutions in the last forty years. Economic rationalism's lack of influence at the policy level may reflect its failure at the institutional level, for the policy prescriptions have not been able to find a hospitable institutional home. Less commodious homes provide only for piecemeal and sometimes distorted adoption of economic policy advice.

No doubt part of the explanation for the limited progress of economic rationalism in environmental affairs lies in simple inertia, and the resistance of established routines. Another explanation might note that proposals for economic instruments can never enter in the clean and straightforward fashion of the economics textbooks. Instead, their entry and so their design is heavily dependent on the configuration of political forces and the prevailing political-economic context. We have seen in the case of Britain, for example, how the Treasury treated green taxes in terms of their revenue-raising potential, but in doing so made both industry and environmentalists nervous. More generally, businesses may oppose green taxes because they have to pay both abatement costs and the tax itself (Daugbjerg and

Svendsen, 2003). So long as green taxes and tradeable permits are applied only sporadically, firms may not reorganize themselves to respond to the cost-saving incentives these instruments offer. In addition, regulatory standards may have been designed with input from existing firms in order to discriminate against newcomers—perhaps specifying more stringent standards for new pollution sources—and so existing firms may oppose market-based alternatives (Stavins, 2002). Even when those alternatives are adopted, powerful polluters can bend them to their own liking. They can lobby government to be allocated free permits when emissions trading for carbon dioxide is introduced, profiting when they sell those permits to other firms (Spash, 2010). Green taxes are also vulnerable: the carbon tax introduced in Australia in 2012 exempted agriculture entirely, gave compensation to the coal and steel industries, with further breaks for any industry claiming exposure to international competition (on such problems more generally, see Stavins, 2009).

The fairyland of neoclassical microeconomics in which economic rationalist argument for market-oriented policy instruments is rooted is very different from the real world. The good fairies are not in charge of policy design and implementation. In the United States, economic rationalists blame the collapse in the price of sulfur dioxide permits between 2005 and 2012 on EPA regulators who did not treat the permits with the respect true property rights demanded. In particular, the EPA decided not to allow "banked" (unused) permits from previous years to be traded; and reduced the quantity of emissions a given permit allowed (Anderson and Libecap, 2012). Stavins (2002) points out that in the United States, environmental laws are written by a Congress full of lawyers who do not understand economics, and who are attracted by the symbolic politics that can please all sides by combining stringent standards with lax enforcement. Perhaps surprisingly, the rightward shift of Congressional Republicans following the 2008 election of President Obama proved to be bad news for economic rationalism in environmental policy. These Republicans started to refer to "cap and trade" as "cap and tax," attacking the system of tradeable permits for carbon dioxide emissions that had been on Congress's climate change agenda for some time (though never adopted). Republicans carried over their hostility to the idea of doing anything at all about climate change to the main instrument on the table, which just happened to be a centerpiece of economic rationalism.

A gap between theory and practice is also evident in markets for offsets for greenhouse gas emissions. If the offsets involve forestry, there is no guarantee the promised trees will actually be planted, or that they will not be sold to more than one buyer. Even if they are planted, the trees may displace land use that is both sustainable and crucial to the livelihoods of local people. The trees in question will one day die, be cut down, or burn—and when that happens, the carbon they stored will re-enter the atmosphere. Depending on their price, offsets may also look like an easy option to polluters—who might even increase their pollution as a result of the availability of offsets.

To get at deeper reasons for resistance to economic rationalism we need to treat it as a discourse rather than just a set of proposals for policies and institutions. Recall that the basic agents and motives recognized by economic rationalism treat people only as *Homo economicus* consumers and producers. There are no citizens in economic rationalism. Dobson (2004: 1–5) suggests that economic incentives alone are unlikely to yield the substantive and multifaceted changes in behavior that a sustainable society requires. More seriously, such incentives may actually undercut ecological citizenship. Sagoff (2008) argues that all individuals have both consumer preferences and citizen preferences, and that these point in different directions. As a consumer, I may want to make use of freeways to get to work more quickly; as a citizen, I may demonstrate against construction of the freeways because they destroy communities and natural areas. We would normally put our citizen preferences first, though only if given the chance to express them in political settings. But economic rationalists count only consumer preferences, repressing citizen preferences. Theirs is a world unlikely to please environmental citizen-activists, which may be why environmentalists have often opposed economic rationalist schemes. When we visit a national park, we do so as citizens. Part of the experience of being there is that it is indeed a *national* park, emblematic of what it means to be a Canadian, an American, a Costa Rican, or a Japanese; a repository of common trust and community pride. And visiting national parks in other nations can also involve recognition of and respect for the identity and citizenship of others. These are experiences that Walt Disney could never provide.

Opposition may also arise as a result of the way economic rationalism treats or, rather, does not treat the environment. Recall that in economic rationalist discourse, the environment exists only as a medium for the effects of some human actions on other humans, and as a source of inputs for the socioeconomic machine. It is in this light that Anderson and Leal (2001: 27) can refer to migrating buffalo as "pollution" because they may carry diseases that affect cattle. Thus the environment has no intrinsic value, and chunks of it can be bought or sold at will, depending only on the most profitable human use. When it comes to pollution, economic rationalism attaches no stigma: rights to pollute are just like any other commodity, to be bought or sold. As Kelman (1981) notes, this failure to stigmatize pollution in moral terms makes many environmentalists uneasy. Goodin (1994) compares this selling of pieces of the environment by governments to the selling of indulgences by the medieval Catholic Church. In both cases, individuals can have their sins forgiven if they can afford to pay. But just as places in heaven were not the church's to sell (only for God or St Peter to decide), so pieces of the environment are not government's to sell. Martin Luther (who attacked indulgences) and opponents of green taxes have much in common.

In short, no matter how attractive economic prescriptions may be in instrumental terms, even to committed environmentalists, they help constitute a discourse, and a world, which those according higher priority to citizenship, democratic, and ecological values find unattractive (see Dryzek, 1995). This is especially the case when prescriptions are tied to a general right-wing market agenda, as they are in the United States by "free market environmentalists," who thereby undermine the political prospects for the policies they favor. Paradoxically, some of these policies have been more easily implemented in social democratic North European countries, precisely because they do not attract right-wing ideological baggage there. The paradox is heightened inasmuch as the tie is increasingly rejected by right-wing Republicans, who reject any policy for the environment, especially if it involves climate change. Styling policy "free-market environmentalism" apparently makes no difference. With the loss of this right-wing constituency, the prospects for economic rationalist environmental policy in the United States look bleak. In the United Kingdom and Australia too, right-wing think tanks that once backed free-market environmentalism become increasingly Promethean, attacking green taxes and emissions trading as unnecessary governmental actions. Ironically it is international institutions such as the European Union and the United Nations Framework Convention on Climate Change, and states such as China, where these policy instruments are now more welcome.

A further limitation of economic rationalism arises from its basically mechanistic metaphorical structure. The idea that the world may be full of complex ecological and social systems interacting in variable and uncertain ways is implicitly denied by economic rationalism. Economic rationalists have no way to deal with such interactions, which may violate the boundaries of private property rights, no matter how carefully drawn. For example, proposals for tradeable quotas in ocean fisheries inevitably treat species in isolation. But rational management of a single species is impossible. Whether the species survives or flourishes depends not just on how many tons of it are caught per year, but on what is happening to other species that are predators, prey, or competitors for the same ecological niche. Moreover, other factors such as pollution or development may affect the habitat of the species.

Finally, economic rationalism as a discourse gets into all kinds of tangles in its treatment of government. Its attitude to government is thoroughly ambiguous: at one level government is populated by rational egoists feeding at the public trough, plundering the public purse, and thoroughly indifferent to environmental values. At another level public-spirited government action is needed in order to put economic rationalist prescriptions into institutional and policy practice, and so economic rationalism depends crucially on administrative rationalism. The "public choice" school of economic rationalists has thrived on horror stories about government in theory and practice; in fact, without quite realizing it, the public choice school has demonstrated that political order is impossible if everyone is a rational egoist (see Dryzek, 1992*b*). When it comes to environmental affairs, if everyone is a rational egoist, then the commons will always be abused, polluters will continue to generate externalities, and government will do absolutely nothing to remedy the situation. The obvious inference is that economic rationalism is inadequate as an orientation to environmental affairs (see Dryzek, 1996*b*). In this light, economic rationalism's real usefulness may come in detailing very precisely the destructive effects of *Homo economicus,* and the need for his or her proclivities to be controlled by more socially, politically, and ecologically benign human motivations. Economic rationalism, unlike democratic pragmatism and green radicalism, has had nothing to say about these alternative wellsprings of human action.

This concludes my discussion of the three discourses of environmental problem solving. While all three have their problems, it is fair to say that the real-world achievements of administrative rationalism and democratic pragmatism remain more substantial than those of economic rationalism, though the latter is gaining ground in some places. This conclusion will not necessarily dismay die-hard economic rationalists, who argue that the problem is precisely that their proposals have not been tested fairly. Partisans of each one of these three discourses often make their case through reference to the deficiencies of the other two, while remaining within the basic parameters of problem solving within the political-economic status quo of liberal capitalism. But the manifest difficulties of all three discourses lead others to be a bit more creative in looking for alternatives. Let me turn now to emerging discourses which remain reformist in their orientation to industrialism, but are more imaginative in seeking to dissolve familiar dilemmas and impasses.

....

NOTES

1. There are good economic reasons why they do not. As Mancur Olson (1965) pointed out in his classic analysis of the logic of collective action, the fact that individuals share an interest does not mean they will act upon it. Each person has an incentive to take a "free ride" on the efforts of others. This logic parallels that of the tragedy of the commons introduced in Chapter 2, in that rational individual decisions lead to collectively bad outcomes.

PART IV

THE QUEST FOR SUSTAINABILITY

....

The apocalyptic horizons of environmental concern were set in the early 1970s by survivalists who argued that economic growth and population expansion would have to yield to global environmental limits, sooner rather than later. Private Prometheans denied the existence of limits. The problem-solving discourses surveyed in Part III are essentially agnostic about global limits, focusing instead on the work to be done in the here and now. Yet problem solving is energized by the need to achieve some kind of resolution to conflicts between ecological values and economic values.

Life would certainly be less troublesome if such conflicts did not exist, or, failing that, could be dissolved. The unresolved dispute between the limits discourse and Prometheans could be put behind us, and environmental problem solving could proceed with renewed vigor in the knowledge that solutions are available that can respond effectively to a range of key ecological and economic concerns. Throw in commitments to global justice through the eradication of poverty and to the wellbeing of future generations, and the prospect would surely be irresistible. But what could possibly combine ecological protection, economic growth, social justice, and intergenerational equity, not just locally and immediately, but globally and in perpetuity? The answer is sustainable development, which specifies that we can have them all.

Since the early 1980s, sustainable development has become hugely popular as an integrating discourse covering environmental issues from the local to the global, as well as a host of economic and development concerns. Just what sustainable development means in practice is a matter of some dispute, as is the question of whether it can actually deliver on some, most, or all of its promises.

The notion of sustainability receives greater precision in the second discourse covered in Part IV: ecological modernization. Ecological modernization addresses the restructuring of the capitalist political economy along more environmentally defensible lines. The key is that there is money to be made in this restructuring and transition. At one level ecological modernization is about the search for green production technology, and especially clean energy. But this search also opens the door to intriguing possibilities for more thoroughgoing transformation, involving political change as well as technological change. So although at first sight ecological modernization looks like a rescue mission for industrial society, albeit an imaginative one, it also points to political and economic possibilities beyond industrial society.

7

Greener Growth: Sustainable Development

What is sustainable development?

Sustainable development refers not to any accomplishment, still less to a precise set of structures and measures to achieve collectively desirable outcomes. Rather, it is a discourse. Since the publication of the report of the Brundtland Commission in 1987 (World Commission on Environment and Development, 1987), it is arguably the dominant global discourse of ecological concern. As Torgerson (1995: 10) put it, "public discussion concerning the environment has become primarily a discourse of sustainability." But just what is sustainable development? The most widely quoted definition is Brundtland's: "Humanity has the ability to make development sustainable—to ensure that it meets the needs of the present without compromising the ability of future generations to meet their own needs" (World Commission on Environment and Development, 1987: 8). Later in the report Brundtland declares that "In essence, sustainable development is a process of change in which the exploitation of resources, the direction of investments, the orientation of technological development, and institutional change are all in harmony and enhance both current and future potential to meet human needs and aspirations" (p. 46). Beyond reiterating Brundtland, the organizers of the 2012 United Nations Conference on Sustainable Development in Rio say "Sustainable development emphasizes a holistic, equitable and far-sighted approach to decision-making at all levels. It emphasizes not just strong economic performance but intragenerational and intergenerational equity. It rests on integration and a balanced consideration of economic and environmental goals and objectives in both public and private decision making."[1] The economic, environmental, and social dimensions are sometimes referred to as the three pillars of the concept.

Sustainable development did not begin with Brundtland. The two words have been joined occasionally since the early 1970s, originally in a radical discourse for the Third World. The concept has a deeper history in the renewable resource management concept of maximum sustainable yield (perhaps deeper still in the ability of indigenous peoples to use local resources that are replenished). Maximum sustainable yield is the maximum catch from a fishery, or cut from a forest, or kill of game animals, that can be sustained indefinitely. But the maximum sustainable yield concept says nothing about growth in resource use (indeed, rules out growth), or about how management of different resources might interact, or what to do with nonrenewable resources. Sustainable development is much more ambitious in that it refers to the ensemble of life-support systems, and seeks perpetual growth in the sum of human needs that might be satisfied not through simple resource garnering, but rather through intelligent operation of natural systems and human systems in combination.

Brundtland's definition did not satisfy everyone, and other definitions of sustainable development proliferated. Opinions differ as to what human needs count, what is to be sustained, for how long, for whom, and in what terms. Attempts to take an analytical razor to the concept (e.g., Dobson, 1998) are only partially successful because they soon leave the ambiguities of the real-world discourse behind. In the early 1990s the Transportation Research Board of the United States National Academy of Sciences spent a million dollars trying to come up with a definition, but failed to do anything more than simply aggregate the concerns of its members. By 1996 the United Nations Educational, Scientific, and Cultural Organization (UNESCO) was sponsoring a project to clarify the meaning of the concept in a number of disciplines, with a view to making the concept a scientifically usable one— implying that it was not yet a scientific concept.[2] The passing decades still do not yield convergence on any precise definition (Lipschutz, 2009: 136). But the proliferation of definitions is not just a matter of analysts trying to add conceptual precision; it is also an issue of different interests trying to stake their claims in the territory. For if sustainable development is indeed a dominant discourse, astute actors recognize that its terms should be cast in terms favorable to them. Environmentalists might try to build in respect for intrinsic values in nature that is conspicuously missing in Brundtland. So Rockwood et al. (2008) stress the protection of nature as central to sustainability. Third World advocates would stress the need for global redistribution, and highlight the needs of the poor to which Brundtland pointed. Business groups equate development with economic growth, such that sustainable development mainly means continued economic growth, even if it is styled "green growth." Partisans of the limits discourse can use the language of sustainability. After endorsing Brundtland, Meadows et al. (1992: 209) go on to say that "From a systems point of view a sustainable society is one that has in place informational, social, and institutional mechanisms to keep in check the positive feedback loops that cause exponential population and capital growth." For Meadows and colleagues sustainability means an end to economic growth; for the World Business Council for Sustainable Development, sustainability requires perpetuation of economic growth. As the Council declared in its foundational document, "Economic growth in all parts of the world is essential to improve the livelihoods of the poor, to sustain growing populations, and eventually to stabilize population levels" (Schmidheiny, 1992: xi).

Does this variety of meanings mean we should dismiss sustainable development as an empty vessel that can be filled with whatever one likes? Not at all. For it is not unusual for important concepts to be contested politically. Think, for example, of the word "democracy," which has at least as many meanings and definitions as does sustainable development. Part of what makes democracy interesting is this very contestation over its essence. Democracy is doubly interesting because just about everyone who matters in today's political world claims to believe in it. The parallels with sustainable development are quite precise. Just as democracy is the main game in town when it comes to political organization, so sustainable development became the main game (though not the only game) in environmental affairs, at least global ones. Sustainable development, like democracy, is a discourse rather than a concept which can be defined with any precision. The discourse itself does, though, have boundaries. Sustainable development is different from limits and boundaries because while it recognizes that ecological limits should be respected, they can also be stretched if the right policies are chosen, so that economic growth can continue indefinitely. Langhelle (2000: 310–11) suggests that for Brundtland, at least, the limits in question were energy supply and climate change; though he also recognizes lingering ambiguities in the discourse on the question. Sustainable development is different from Promethean discourse because it requires coordinated collective efforts to achieve goals, rather than relying on human spontaneity and ingenuity. And it is different from the varieties of environmental problem solving surveyed in the previous three chapters because it is much more imaginative in its reconceptualization of the terms of environmental dispute and in its dissolution of some long-standing conflicts.

The career of the concept

Prior to the 1980s, sustainable development was part of the environmentalist lexicon, especially in a Third World development context. The concept was an alternative to mainstream interpretations of development as economic growth, which had failed to deliver. Impetus was received through contention by the emerging limits discourse that the Earth could not withstand a Third World that duplicated Western levels of affluence (Carruthers, 2001). Advocates were interested in the potential of appropriate technologies or intermediate technologies, which were low-cost, low in the environmental stress they imposed, and consistent with local cultures (see Schumacher, 1973). They preferred energy generation from cattle dung over nuclear power stations or large dams, small workshops over large factories.

The concept's prominence grew, and its meaning began to change in 1980 with the publication of the International Union for the Conservation of Nature's *World Conservation Strategy*. But the real transformation into the contemporary discourse of sustainable development can be dated to 1983, when Gro Harlem Brundtland, Prime Minister of Norway, was asked by the Secretary-General of the United Nations to chair an inquiry into interrelated global problems of environment and development. Brundtland's World Commission on Environment and Development published its report, *Our Common Future,* in 1987. The report contains analyses and recommendations pertaining to the international economy, population, food, energy, manufacturing, cities, and institutional change. Its main accomplishment was to combine systematically a number of issues that have often been treated in isolation, or at least as competitors: development, global environmental issues, population, peace and security, and social justice both within and across generations. Brundtland developed a vision of the simultaneous and mutually reinforcing pursuit of economic growth, environmental improvement, population stabilization, peace, and global equity, which could be maintained in the long term. Such a vision was seductive, though Brundtland did not demonstrate its feasibility, or indicate the practical steps that would be required.

Since 1987 the discourse of sustainable development has flourished at the international level. The United Nations Conference on Environment and Development (UNCED), held in Rio de Janeiro in 1992, was a high point. The 171 national government delegations, many with heads of government present, gave sustainable development their stamps of approval (though the various delegations may have held to different meanings of the term). The Conference endorsed *Agenda 21*, a lengthy and detailed follow-up to Brundtland's efforts, which argued that global environmental problems had arisen mainly as a result of the profligate consumption and production of the richer countries, but also recommended more economic growth for all to finance solutions. After the Conference the United Nations established a Commission on Sustainable Development to implement *Agenda 21*, with special reference to how national and local governments might act. Sustainable development advanced as a discourse for all, North and South, rich and poor; though the rich eventually lost sight of the global equity aspect that was central to Brundtland and her more radical predecessors (Meadowcroft, 2000: 379).

In 2002 Johannesburg hosted the World Summit on Sustainable Development (WSSD), then the world's largest-ever international conference. The WSSD endorsed a "Plan of Implementation" for *Agenda 21*. The plan was a little short on concrete measures, how they should be accomplished, and who exactly should do it (von Frantzius, 2004: 470), with the partial exception of targets and dates for improved access to clean water and sanitation for the world's poor. Thus sustainable development remained very much a discourse, rather than a plan of action. The WSSD saw some major repositioning in relation to the discourse. Wealthy states, long the champions of environmental concern at such gatherings, now seemed more interested in pushing the benefits of development that could be achieved through globalization and free trade (this was somewhat less true for the European Union than the United States). And Third World governments, once skeptical about environmental concern as a luxury for the rich, now recognized the severity of their own environmental problems

(Wapner, 2003: 4–6). Perhaps the most successful discursive reposition-ing was accompanied by the corporations present, which confirmed the status of business as a major participant in sustainable development, not a source of problems to be overcome. This role was solidified in partnerships involving business, governments, and NGOs, several hundred of which were established at the WSSD.

In 2012 sustainable development returned to Rio with the United Nations Conference on Sustainable Development (Rio+20), which produced much less in the way of tangible agreements, commitments, and plans than did the 1992 version. While widely seen as disappointing by environmentalists, perhaps the 2012 conference simply confirmed that the day of comprehen-sive global agreements was over, with the discourse of sustainable develop-ment now to make itself felt in a multiplicity of locations.

Outside summits, sustainable development has infused the discourse of international institutions. The World Bank, long castigated by environ-mentalists for its complicity in ecologically disastrous development projects (such as large dams and high-technology agriculture), established an Envi-ronment Department, appointing a Vice-President for Sustainable Develop-ment, and sponsors a series of publications on environmentally sustainable development. Its 2002 *World Development Report* was organized around the idea of sustainable development, though it lost sight of the global equity aspect of the discourse, recommending that the rich countries could best help the poor by becoming still richer and providing bigger markets for poor countries' products. In 2012 the Bank declared "inclusive green growth is *the* pathway to sustainable development" (World Bank, 2012: xi), the "inclusive" modifier recognizing that growth had not always meant poverty reduction, still less environmental protection. The Bank has also sponsored research on the development of indicators of sustainable development as alternatives to more established measures of national wellbeing such as gross national product. Such indicators include "comprehensive wealth" that covers natural capital (World Bank, 2012). The European Union has incorporated sustainable development in some of its constituent treaties, has adopted a Sustainable Development Strategy, and saw the WSSD as an opportunity to distinguish itself from the more skeptical position of US negotiators. The European Union proved the lone champion of renewable energy against the United States and Third World countries pushing expanded fossil fuel use (von Frantzius, 2004: 472).

While the sustainability discourse is most evident at this international level, it has made major inroads within states (see Meadowcroft, 2000 for a catalog). In 1990 Japan established a sustainable development program, with an eye to maximizing Japanese opportunities in the emerging sustainable eco-economy (opportunities which are not hurt by the energy-efficiency of the Japanese economy). China has in recent years added sustainable development ideas to its earlier emphasis on economic growth at all costs, and there exists a China Business Council for Sustainable Development. In Australia, the federal government in 1990 set up an ecologically sustainable development process, with working groups on agriculture, energy, fisheries, forestry, manufacturing, mining, transport, and tourism. Symbolizing sustainable development's positive-sum approach to economy and environment, each working group contained representatives of both industry and environmental groups (along with government and trade-union officials). The working groups reported in 1992, and their efforts were incorporated into a National Ecologically Sustainable Development Strategy, though for domestic political reasons the process and the strategy subsequently languished (see Christoff, 1995).

In the United States, the sustainable development torch was carried in the Clinton administration by the President's Council on Sustainable Development, which could draw support from Vice-President Al Gore's personal views (Gore, 1992). The Obama administration embraced the language of sustainability in its interagency Partnership for Sustainable Communities created in 2009, which pushed the idea of "smart growth." However, the dominant US approach to sustainable development is captured succinctly by Bryner (2000): "Sorry, not our problem," with little support in Congress, and no resonance for any broader public. Indifference has however been broken by right-wing Republicans. In one of the stranger episodes in the life and times of sustainable development, in 2012 the Republican National Committee passed a motion equating *Agenda 21*'s commitment to social justice with "socialist/communist redistribution of wealth," and referring to *Agenda 21* as "a comprehensive plan of extreme environmentalism, social engineering, and global political control." One could ask why, if *Agenda 21* represents such a danger, it took twenty years for the Republican National Committee to notice it existed.

Sustainable development has received at least lip service from most governments in the developed world (Lafferty and Meadowcroft, 2000), though none has addressed their own over-consumption of resources and stress on global ecosystems (Meadowcroft, 2000: 374). In Britain, the government initially endorsed Brundtland's stress on sustainable development but—astonishingly—asserted that existing British economic policy met these principles, further proof of just how far the concept can be stretched (Department of the Environment, 1988; see also Jacobs, 1991: 59). After 1997 Tony Blair's Labour government set up a Sustainable Development Unit to examine the practices of all government departments. In 2011 Conservative Prime Minister David Cameron's government published *Mainstreaming Sustainable Development*, in keeping with Cameron's promise to lead the greenest UK government ever.

International business is increasingly prominent. The International Chamber of Commerce and World Business Council for Sustainable Development (WBCSD), chaired by Stephan Schmidheiny of the Swiss company UNOTEC, were active at the 1992 Rio Summit. The Business Council was formed in 1990 at the invitation of Maurice Strong, secretary-general of the Summit. The Council is committed to economic growth, but with an environmentally sensitive face. Its component corporations such as 3M, Rio Tinto, Du Pont, Shell, Mitsubishi, and ALCOA can point to success stories in their own operations of environmentally aware practices such as recycling, efficiency benefits achieved by waste reduction, sustainable forestry, and energy-efficient production (see Holliday et al., 2002 for a compilation). By 2012 the Council was composed of 201 of the world's largest corporations, mostly from the manufacturing, mining, and energy sectors (membership is by invitation only). Not all of these 201 companies have exemplary environmental records. They once included Enron, the energy supply corporation linked to President George W. Bush, before it went bankrupt in 2002. At the 2012 Rio+20 conference the Council styled itself "the representative of progressive business."

Under the banner of "Business Action for Sustainable Development," the WBCSD was highly visible at the 2002 WSSD, where it mounted a concerted effort to publicize and embed the business view. The major statement launched at the WSSD by Holliday et al. (2002) argued that economic growth produced by free trade was the only hope for the world's poor. However, the Council did not propose growth at all costs, proclaimed commitment to corporate social responsibility, and joined with Greenpeace to criticize the United States' withdrawal from the Kyoto Protocol on climate change. The Council succeeded in establishing partnerships with business as the dominant tool for pursuing sustainable development. Cynics saw this as "the privatization of sustainable development" (von Frantzius, 2004: 469), threatening to reduce the discourse to a series of commercial projects (Wapner, 2003: 4). At Rio ten years later the Council reiterated its commitment to partnerships. Reacting to the lack of action agreement on the part of the governments assembled at Rio in 2012, WBCSD President Peter Bakker declared it was now up to business to take the lead. Breaking with the moderation of his predecessors, he accepted that "if you add up all the CSR [corporate social responsibility] programmes across the world and all the 200 plus commitments from this week [in Rio], we are not nearly going to save the world." Referring to obstructive businesses, he said "the 20% of really bad guys we need to regulate out of existence." (interview in *Guardian*, London, June 22, 2012: "Rio+20: WBCSD president says the future of the planet rests on business").

Where are the environmentalists in these developments? After all, sustainable development began life long ago as one of their concepts. Environmental groups have become less visible with time. But some environmentalists, such as Friends of the Earth Europe, have tried to keep up with the discourse, to remind everyone that sustainable development requires wholesale reductions in the stress that economic activity imposes on the environment, and respect for intrinsic values in nature. It is a struggle to sustain the idea that sustainable development might point to transformation to a different kind of world (Hopwood et al., 2005) in the face of all the forces trying to assimilate it to the status quo (Parr, 2009).

Discourse analysis of sustainable development

The core story line of sustainable development once began with recognition that the legitimate developmental aspirations of the world's peoples cannot be met by all countries following the growth path already taken by the industrialized countries, for such action would over-burden the world's ecosystems. Yet economic growth is necessary to satisfy the legitimate needs of the world's poor. The alleviation of poverty will ameliorate what is one of the basic causes of environmental degradation, for poor people are forced to abuse their local environment just to survive.

Economic growth should therefore be promoted, but guided in ways that are both environmentally benign and socially just. Justice here refers not only to distribution within the present generation, but also across future generations. Sustainable development is not just a strategy for the future of developing societies, but also for industrialized societies, which must reduce the excessive stress their past economic growth has imposed upon the Earth.

Basic entities whose existence is recognized or constructed

Sustainable development's purview is global; its justification rests in present stresses imposed on global ecosystems. But unlike the discourse of limits and boundaries, it does not stay at that global level. Sustainability is an issue at regional and local levels too, for that is where solutions will have to be found (as made clear in *Local Agenda 21*, whose principles have been adopted by local governments around the world). Thus the basic entities stressed in sustainable development are nested systems, ranging from the global to the local. The systems in question are both social and biological. Natural systems are not separate from humanity: as Brundtland put it: "The environment does not exist as a sphere separate from humans ambitions, actions, and needs...the 'environment' is where we all live" (World Commission on Environment and Development, 1987: xi). The biological components of systems are treated with more respect than the brute matter that Prometheans see in nature. But rather than seeing problems in terms of global limits and solutions in terms of global management, sustainable development takes a more disaggregated approach. Particular resources and systems can be used and developed more or less wisely, imposing more or less environmental stress.

The Brundtland Report itself is a bit ambiguous on the existence of limits. A statement that "Growth has no set limits in terms of population or resource use beyond which lies ecological disaster" in part because "accumulation of knowledge and the development of technology can enhance the carrying capacity of the resource base" is followed immediately by a recognition that "But ultimate limits there are" (World Commission on Environment and Development, 1987: 45). These ultimate limits too prove capable of being stretched by technology. As Brundtland herself later put the point, "The commission found no absolute limits to growth. Limits are indeed imposed by the impact of present technologies and social organization on the biosphere, but we have the ingenuity to change" (quoted in Hardin, 1993: 205). Ecological constraints should be respected, but once this is done economic growth can proceed indefinitely. Some commentators have tried to resolve the ambiguity here by distinguishing between "strong" and "weak" versions of sustainable development, the former explicitly recognizing limits, the latter denying them (see Hay, 2002: 214–17). Another way of putting it is that weak sustainability believes human-made capital can substitute for natural capital (Barbier, 2007). But any such resolution leaves most sustainable development discourse somewhere between the two poles; the zone of ambiguity is much larger than the polar regions.

When it comes to social systems, sustainable development now takes the capitalist economy pretty much for granted (this was not true in the more radical discourse of the 1970s). However, the structure of political systems is not taken as given. The reorientation in problem solving that sustainable development prescribes may require shifts in power between different levels to meet more effectively the challenge of sustainability. The frequent appeals to coordinated international action and grassroots participation suggest that these shifts would be away from the nation-state as presently constituted to both higher (transnational) and lower (local) levels of political organization, as well as sideways to partnerships with business. Networked governance as an alternative to top-down administration (see Chapters 4 and 5) fits well here.

Assumptions about natural relationships

The most important relationship regarded as if not exactly natural then at least attainable is the positive-sum one: economic growth, environmental protection, distributive justice, and long-term sustainability are mutually reinforcing. In the contemporary world of sustainable development there are few hierarchies recognized in human affairs. Instead, there is cooperation. However, there is a hierarchy which puts human beings above the natural world. In keeping with its integration of a range of agendas, sustainable development can take the protection of nature on board. For example, Brechin et al. (2003) argue that the basic needs of the world's poor can be met while protecting biodiversity in the ecosystems on which they depend. But for the most part sustainable development remains anthropocentric. It is sustainability of human populations and their well-being which is at issue, rather than that of nature. Relationships of competition are de-emphasized, though it exists in the background capitalist economy. Sustainable development is to be achieved through cooperative rather than competitive effort (witness the partnerships that dominated the 2002 WSSD), distancing the discourse from both economic rationalists and Prometheans.

Agents and their motives

Sustainable development's key agents are not the global managers of limits and survival or the experts with a managerial hierarchy at their disposal of the administrative rationalists. Instead, the relevant actors can exist at many levels, consistent with basic notions about the existence of nested social and biological systems. In practice, sustainable development marginally de-emphasizes national governments (one reason perhaps for the Republican opposition to the concept in the United States, discussed earlier). However, states are still needed to construct international agreements and work with NGOs and business. In the 1980s sustainable development was established as a discourse of international society, especially as that society is populated by intergovernmental organizations (IGOs) (such as the United Nations and the World Bank) and NGOs (such as global environmental groups). There is a role for the grassroots too: the green radical slogan "think globally, act locally" can be adopted here. *Agenda 21* calls for more citizen participation in environment and development decisions. And corporations have clambered on board the bandwagon to show that business too can play a constructive role. Sustainable development has been cast as a discourse of and for global civil society (see Conca, 1994; Lafferty, 1996; Wapner, 1996), though the ever-growing role of global business does perhaps attenuate that association. And more traditional areas of national government are not excluded.

Key metaphors and other rhetorical devices

Prometheans and economic rationalists alike rely on mechanistic metaphors, treating the world as a machine whose bits can be arranged to better meet human needs. In contrast, sustainable development's metaphorical structure is organic. Organisms grow and develop; so can societies. Growth here is not just physical maturation that happens automatically, for sustainable development also stipulates self-conscious improvement. As such, it is consistent with notions of personal human growth that stress education and growing awareness, enabling the individual to negotiate his or her social environment in more effective fashion. The image is of an increasingly sensitive, caring, and intelligent human being—only, of course, it is sensitive, caring, and intelligent political-economic systems which are at issue, and the environment to be negotiated is not just a social one, but also a natural one. Just as in models that portray human development in terms of lifetime learning, the growth in political-economic capacities is seen as open-ended. The difference is that individual humans eventually die, whereas for sustainable development growth in political-economic capacities can go on in perpetuity.

The discourse does respect nature—to a point. But nature is treated mainly as something that provides useful services to humans. The "natural capital" metaphor is sometimes invoked (Dobson, 1998: 41–7; Sachs, 1999: 33). That is, nature's capital stock deserves respect and should be sustained because it is imperfectly substitutable by man-made capital. This way of thinking about nature is very economistic, especially when the stock of natural capital is valued for the "ecosystem services" it provides to humans (Kareiva et al., 2011).

Sustainable development in its very name links itself to the idea of progress, and progress is one of the most powerful notions in the modern world. Whatever their other differences, Victorian industrialists, Marxists, social democrats, liberal democrats, and market liberals have all believed in the essential idea of history moving in the direction of social improvement. Sustainable development carries this idea into an environmental era.

Sustainable development also involves a rhetoric of reassurance. We *can* have it all: economic growth, environmental conservation, social justice; and not just for the moment, but in perpetuity. No painful changes are necessary. This rhetoric of reassurance is far from the images of doom and redemption found in survivalism, or the horror stories beloved of economic rationalists. Advocates of sustainable development are more likely to highlight local success stories of sustainability than they are to dwell on instances of unsustainability (Holliday et al., 2002; Schmidheiny, 1992: 181–333; UN Department of Economic and Social Affairs, 2008).

Box 7.1 provides a summary of the discourse analysis of sustainable development.

Whither sustainable development?

If we were to look for sustainable development, where would we find it? As discourse, there is a lot of it about (see Zaccai, 2012). But can we identify any practices and policies inspired by, committed to, and achieving sustainable development?

This question may not be quite the right one to ask, if we conceptualize sustainable development as a discourse rather than a target. But the same might be said of "democracy," yet this does not stop political scientists producing comparative studies of the quality of different democracies. However, such comparisons are rough and contested. It is easy to conclude that (say) contemporary Canada is more democratic than Russia under the Tsars, very hard to say which of Canada and Japan is today more democratic, harder still to conclude that Canada is a true democracy. The same applies to sustainable development. Yale and Columbia researchers working for the World Economic Forum (WEF) between 1999 and 2005 ranked 142 countries according to a sustainability index, and Finland, Sweden, and Norway initially occupied the top three places. But Finland's number one ranking did not mean it had

---

BOX 7.1	Discourse analysis of sustainable development

1. **Basic entities recognized or constructed**
   - Nested and networked social and ecological systems
   - Capitalist economy
   - Ambiguity concerning existence of limits
2. **Assumptions about natural relationships**
   - Cooperation
   - Nature subordinate
   - Economic growth, environmental protection, distributive justice, and long-term sustainability go together
3. **Agents and their motives**
   - Many agents at different levels, transnational and local as well as the state; motivated by the public good
4. **Key metaphors and other rhetorical devices**
   - Organic growth
   - Nature as natural capital
   - Connection to progress
   - Reassurance

achieved an adequate level of sustainability, and environmental groups were quick to point out Finnish shortcomings in forest management. The WEF index was controversial, and really just compiled measures of environmental performance rather than sustainability per se. As such, it missed the "development" part of the equation. This was perhaps recognized when in 2006 the sustainability index was abandoned in favor of an environmental performance index, which in 2012 put Switzerland at the top.[3] The development question becomes especially perplexing in light of sustainable development's core story line, which specifies that poor countries cannot follow the growth path already taken by wealthy countries such as Finland or Switzerland without overstressing the world's ecosystems.

Thus it is better to think of sustainable development not as a path taken by countries such as Finland and Switzerland, but as at most a discourse that will inspire experimentation with what sustainable development can mean in practice. Sustainability, like democracy, is largely about social learning, involving decentralized, exploratory, and variable approaches to its pursuit. Sustainable development (unlike survivalism) can be a multilayered and multifaceted enterprise. Rather than try to impose a common definition replete with an associated set of precise goals (which is what administrative rationalists would do), a "decentered" approach would stress pluralistic and local experimentation (Brooks, 1992; Torgerson, 1994; 1995). In this search, the very fact that agreement on the essence of sustainable development has been elusive proves to be a help rather than a hindrance, for no avenues are ruled out by stipulation, and so all kinds of new possibilities might be unearthed (Torgerson, 1994: 310–13; see also Thompson, 1993).

But if the pursuit of sustainability is to be decentered and piecemeal, what would actually harness all these efforts to the common good? The answer lies in the necessity for widespread commitment to the discourse itself, the only conceivable glue to hold these various efforts together. In this light, the sought-after restructuring of power relationships becomes understandable. Sustainable development is a discourse of and for global civil society, not just states. Luke (1997: chap. 6) interprets this feature quite cynically as simply serving the interests of managerial "ecocrats" employed in IGOs and NGOs, not to mention rhetorical cover for failure to achieve anything substantive (Luke, 2005). Luke's argument would be plausible if sustainable development did indeed constitute a unified approach. But with the decentered, piecemeal twist, the role played by global civil society can become democratic rather than managerial, an antidote to governments increasingly under the sway of market liberal ideas and committed to reducing environmental controls, expanding trade, and promoting economic growth at all costs (Lafferty, 1996). The problem is that market liberalism is now a powerful discourse in the international system itself, furthered by the same corporations now so active in the international politics of sustainable development.

There is no guarantee that widespread commitment to and pursuit of sustainable development in piecemeal fashion will deliver the goods. Economic rationalists see the whole enterprise as just the latest in a long line of futile attempts to replace markets by political management, trying to impose a discipline on people's decisions which is properly exercised by the market's price system (see Anderson and Leal, 1991: 167–71).[4] Prometheans see a lingering stress on limits poisoning the discourse (for example, Beckerman, 2002). Radical environmentalists deny that development (interpreted as economic growth) can ever be sustainable, and denounce the anthropocentric arrogance implicit in the discourse (for example, Merchant, 1992; Richardson, 1994). Radicals also argue that in an age of market liberalism, sustainable development's promise of social justice is hollow, as inequalities between rich and poor expanded in the 1990s within and across nations (Carruthers, 2001: 103). Even moderate environmentalists might wonder whether sustainable development diverts their energies by asking them to take on all the problems of the world, poverty and economic development as well as environmental protection (Wapner, 2003: 10). Survivalists attack any denial of limits and carrying capacity explicit in the discourse; so Garrett Hardin (1993: 204–6) takes Brundtland to task for failing even to ask whether the population growth she sees as inevitable and the economic growth she sees as desirable can be accommodated by the Earth's resources (see also Milbrath, 1989: 320–3). Similarly, Herman Daly (1993) believes that Brundtland's vision of a world economy five to ten times larger than its 1987 size is impossible given that the present human economy already appropriates 25 percent or more of the world's "net primary product of photosynthesis." Criticizing the declaration of the 2012 UN Conference on Sustainable Development, a spokesperson for the Climate Action Network and other NGOs stated "You cannot have a document titled *The Future we Want* without any mention of planetary boundaries, tipping points, or carrying capacity" (*Guardian*, London, June 20, 2012: "Rio+20 Earth summit talks turn into rubber-stamp job").

Such criticisms notwithstanding, Lafferty (1996) argues that there is simply no better vehicle than sustainable development for environmentalists to pursue their various goals. The different strategic choices made by some eminent survivalists are noteworthy in this context. Meadows et al. (1992) disguise their survivalism in the words of sustainable development, and praise Brundtland; Hardin (1993) rubbishes sustainable development, and berates Brundtland.

The success or failure of sustainable development rests on dissemination and acceptance of the discourse at a variety of levels, followed by action on and experimentation with its tenets. Yet the thirty years that have seen sustainable development establish itself as the leading transnational discourse of environmental concern have seen much less in the way of wholesale movements in policies, practices, and institutions at global, regional, national, and local levels. Those same thirty years have seen a more effective global movement in a very different direction about which sustainable development is sometimes silent, sometimes (in its business-friendly variant) accepting. That direction involves the increasing trans-nationalization of capitalism, especially following establishment of the World Trade Organization (WTO) in 1994. The WTO joined the International Monetary Fund and World Bank in policing international economic regimes. Free trade, capital mobility, and governments all over the world committed to market liberalization and ordinary (unsustainable) economic growth as their first imperatives threaten to override sustainable development (though lip service to sustainable development could be found in the agreement that established the WTO). At the WSSD there were no serious suggestions that the WTO could be made to submit to sustainable development, but plenty of arguments from developed countries' national delegations that on trade issues the WSSD had to proceed in the context set by the WTO.

In a world dominated by market liberalism, sustainable development's prospects are poor unless it can be demonstrated that environmental conservation is obviously good for business profitability and economic growth everywhere, not just that these competing values can be reconciled. As we shall see in the next chapter, this is exactly the claim advanced by ecological modernization.

NOTES

1. <**http://www.uncsd2012.org/rio20/ index.php?menu=62**> (accessed June 8, 2012).

2. This project was under the auspices of UNESCO's Management of Social Transformation Program, and organized through the Institute for Social-Ecological Research in Frankfurt, Germany.

3. <**http://epi.yale.edu/**> (accessed June 9, 2012).

4. Anderson and Leal regard sustainable development as sufficiently important for its contrast with their free-market environmentalism to form the conclusion of their book, which is widely regarded as the definitive statement of economic rationalism applied to environmental affairs. However, they wrongly assert that sustainable development involves a globally administered regime of zero economic growth and zero use of nonrenewable natural resources. In other words, they mistake sustainable development for an extreme form of limits and survival.

8

Industrial Society and Beyond: Ecological Modernization

Cleanest and greenest

Mirror, mirror on the wall, who is the greenest of them all? Which countries have turned in the most successful environmental policy performance in recent decades? Among developed nations, consensus picks include (in alphabetical order):

- Finland
- Germany
- Japan
- The Netherlands
- Norway
- Sweden
- Switzerland

Of course, different indicators of environmental policy success produce different rankings, and some dimensions of environmental conservation (such as biodiversity protection) are not easily measured. So any ranking is likely to be controversial, especially from the point of view of those not near the top of the list. As noted in the previous chapter, the World Economic Forum's (WEF) sustainability index by 2005 had Finland, Sweden, and Norway at the top; the successor environmental performance index (summarizing twenty-two measures) in 2012 had Switzerland in first place, with Norway third, Germany eleventh, the Netherlands sixteenth, Finland nineteenth, Japan twenty-third, all out of 132 countries.[1] Focusing more narrowly on changes in pollution levels over time, Scruggs (2001) identifies Germany as the top performer across sixteen developed countries in the 1980s and 1990s. Emphasizing level of as well as change in pollution, Jahn (1998) has the Netherlands as the top performer. Japan is not so clearly at the top of any league table, though it could claim leadership in energy efficiency (the amount of energy required to produce national income), and in its development of pollution control technology (Revell, 2003: 24–48). Poloni-Staudinger (2008) finds that consensual democracies (of which these seven countries are examples) do better on a variety of pollution control measures than their more adversarial counterparts. These seven countries have also been very supportive of international initiatives for environmental protection.

Comparative statistics tell only part of the story. If we dig a little deeper, we find the seven countries have adopted innovative and advanced procedures, policies, and institutions for dealing with environmental issues. Around 1970, environmental policy innovations mostly began in the United States, and were then copied elsewhere. But since the 1980s, the United States has fallen behind, stuck in a standoff between supporters and opponents of the laws and regulations established around 1970 (Bryner, 2000: 277). In 2012 it came only forty-ninth of 132 countries in the WEF's environmental performance index. Let us take a look at what others have been doing in the meantime.

In 1989 the Netherlands adopted a National Environmental Policy Plan designed to integrate environmental criteria into the operations of all departments of government. The plan was oriented by a set of environmental quality targets along with a timetable for achieving them, and grounded in a sophisticated theory of how pollutants are generated in and travel through human social systems. Rather than control pollutants at the end of the pipe, the Dutch plan seeks to identify and change activities that cause pollution in the first place. The changes are identified in consultation with the relevant industry, citizen groups, and responsible government officials, especially those from departments dealing with industry, agriculture, and transport. Under the plan, which relies on collaboration, not rules and penalties, 250,000 businesses made agreements with government. The plan encourages energy-efficient manufacturing and transport, agriculture that can achieve good yields while minimizing use of herbicides and pesticides, conservation of biodiversity, and so forth. The 2001 plan began to address the international dimension of Dutch environmental issues. None of this is done piecemeal, but rather in the context of the targets of the plan as a whole. The driving idea is that economic growth should be delinked from rising environmental stress, though this has yet to be achieved in practice. Environmental concerns are woven into all the relevant areas of government. The National Environmental Policy Plan had its political ups and downs, and there have been inevitable disappointments in its implementation. However, as a process for "turning government green" as Weale (1992: 122–53) puts it, the plan remains a landmark. More recently, the Dutch government speaks of "transition management" to move the country to sustainable, renewable energy (Kern and Howlett, 2009). Transition extending to the entire economy has a 2030 target date.

In Germany, concern over the implementation deficit associated with earlier environmental policies led in the 1980s to the adoption of the *vorsorgeprinzip*, or precautionary principle. The principle specifies that scientific uncertainty is no excuse for inaction on an environmental problem. Thus if there are good reasons for thinking a problem may be serious, it will be addressed, even in the absence of scientific proof. Dealing with a problem immediately and cheaply is better than waiting for it to get worse, by which time the amount of money required to fix the problem may have multiplied many times over.

The precautionary principle was strongly resisted—indeed, barely comprehended—by the national governments of Britain and the United States in the 1980s. In the US, the administrations of Reagan and Bush the elder used scientific uncertainty as an excuse for inaction on acid rain, especially over claims that sulfur emissions in the United States caused acid rain that damaged lakes and forests in Canada. This sort of excuse could also be found in the George W. Bush administration when it comes to climate change. In Britain, the absence of conclusive science was long the standard governmental excuse for inaction on every major regional and global pollution issue: acid rain, carbon dioxide, chlorofluorocarbons, coastal pollution, and sludge dumping in the North Sea, among others (matters began to change in the late 1990s). Germany moved ahead in tackling all the pollution problems that Britain had denied. By the mid-1990s environmental protection was established as a goal in the German constitution (which in a legalistic state really matters), along with a comprehensive and complex set of environmental laws (Jänicke and Weidner, 1997). Germany has done better than almost any other country in reducing greenhouse gas emissions (Widner and Mez, 2008), with 2005 emissions 18 percent below the 1990 level. Its commitment to conservation and renewable energy persists across governments of the left and right.

Japan stands out largely because of the energy-efficiency of its economy. This efficiency may be explained to a degree by the extent to which Japan depends on imported oil, and so was shaken by the energy crises of the 1970s. We find in Japan environmental policy made with a minimum of fuss and a maximum of consensus. As in Japanese policy making on all major issues, the key players are government officials and business executives. Like the Netherlands, Japan has aimed to decouple economic growth from environmental stress (Barrett and Fisher, 2005). Japanese politicians have recognized economic possibilities in the export of green technologies, together with "green" public work projects as an alternative to the traditional approach to dispensing money to regions that involves covering Japan with concrete structures nobody needs.[2]

Norway has its environmental blemishes, most notably its continued support for commercial whaling. But, as befits the home of Gro Harlem Brundtland (the Sultana of Sustainable Development), Norway has made strenuous efforts to incorporate environmental values into policy making. It has pioneered policy instruments such as green taxes. The policy-making structure of Norway is corporatist in that economic and social policies are made behind closed doors by a small number of leaders from government, the labor-union federation, the business sector—and environmental groups. The Norwegian Society for the Conservation of Nature, also known as Friends of the Earth Norway, is largely funded by government through operating grants, and is represented on key policy-making committees. The society also helps implement government policy through receiving project grants (Dryzek et al., 2003: 22–7). This situation is very different from that in the United States and Britain, where Friends of the Earth is a campaigning group that tries to influence government from the outside.

Sweden pioneered integrated pollution control (see Weale, 1992: 97–100). In most countries, antipollution policy is organized around single-medium and single-substance legislation and regulation. The result is that one pollutant may be reduced, but another pollutant increased as a result. For example, a pollutant discharged into a watercourse may be eliminated by collecting it as a toxic sludge, which might then be dried and burned, leading to air pollution. In Sweden, licenses for new manufacturing plants are issued only after a consideration of the total emissions of the plant, and what might be done to reduce that total to an acceptable level. Along with the Netherlands, Sweden has led in integrating environmental principles across all departments of government, coordinated by key cabinet ministers serving on a Delegation for Ecologically Sustainable Development (Lundqvist, 2004). In 2006, Sweden announced a plan to eliminate oil as an energy source by 2020.

Finland adopted the world's first carbon tax in 1990. Despite the cold climate, carbon dioxide emissions are relatively low. Finland has pioneered other environmental policy instruments (Sairinen, 2003), and has made substantial progress in reducing pollution levels. Finnish industry sees environmental performance as a competitive advantage, so reforms can draw on consensus spanning industry and environmental groups.

Switzerland, ranked first in the 2012 environmental performance index, implements policy on recycling, land use regulation, energy conservation, and efficient public transport with minimal controversy.

What do Germany, Japan, the Netherlands, Norway, Sweden, Finland, and Switzerland have in common that might explain their apparently superior environmental performance? The environmental movements are not any stronger in these countries than comparable others. Indeed, in Norway the movement's numbers are tiny compared to similar countries (Dryzek et al., 2003: 24). The Green Party has played a key role in German policy development, partly by forcing other parties to adopt green positions for fear of losing votes to the Greens. But the other six countries lack a green party of comparable force (though Greens have participated in the national government in Finland, and in 2010 became the third largest party in the Swedish parliament). Japan and Norway have no green party of any consequence.

What these countries have in common is a political-economic system where consensual relationships among key actors prevail. In discussing Norway, I introduced the idea of corporatism. They are all, to greater or lesser degrees, corporatist systems. Japan can be described as "corporatism without labor," leaving only government officials and business leaders to cooperate in policy formation (Lehmbruch, 1984). Thus the seven countries all eschew both adversarial policy making and unbridled capitalist competition. Their polar opposites in these respects are the English-speaking developed countries: Britain, the United States, Canada, Australia, and New Zealand. Scruggs

(2003) finds a clear positive relationship between degree of corporatism and environmental policy success. Until the 1970s, corporatist systems were all organized to emphasize issues of economic growth and income distribution. Yet once environmental values were taken on board, corporatism eventually enabled these values to be addressed in a particular fashion: that of ecological modernization (see Mol, Sonnenfeld, and Spaargaren, 2009 for a survey). Here lies the key to apparently superior performance.

The idea of ecological modernization

Ecological modernization was first identified in the early 1980s by the German social scientists Joseph Huber (1982) and Martin Jänicke (1985), who observed and interpreted its development in Germany. Ecological modernization refers to a restructuring of the capitalist political economy along more environmentally sound lines, but not in a way that requires an altogether different kind of political-economic system (Hajer, 1995: 25). Environmental criteria must be built into the redesign of the system, as in the Dutch transition management.

Conscious and coordinated intervention is needed to bring the required changes about. Public support is crucial too: people must identify with new technologies such as renewable energy (Toke, 2011). It is no good relying on any supposed "invisible hand" operating in market systems to promote good environmental outcomes (of the sort Prometheans stress). Industry itself ideally cooperates in the design and implementation of policy. The key to ecological modernization is that there is money in it for business. Thus business has every incentive to embrace rather than resist ecological modernization, provided only that business is sufficiently far-sighted, rather than interested only in quick profits. The resistance of recalcitrant economic interests such as coal-burning electricity generators may need to be overcome (Szarka, 2012).

What exactly is in it for business? First, "pollution prevention pays," as a popular slogan has it. Pollution is a sign of waste. Less pollution means more efficient production. Second, if a problem is not solved in the present, solving it in the future may be vastly more expensive for both business and government. For example, poorly managed toxic waste dumps become a stew of dangerous chemicals leaking into ground water, soil, and the air. To clean them up is extraordinarily expensive (as the experience of the Superfund in the United States demonstrates). Far better and far cheaper not to let such problems develop in the first place. Third, an unpolluted and aesthetically pleasing environment means healthier, happier, and more productive workers, who may even willingly sacrifice wages and salaries for these environmental rewards. Fourth, there is money to be made in selling green goods and services. Consumers increasingly demand products that are not excessively packaged, that do not contain artificial and toxic ingredients, and that are not produced in environmentally damaging ways. Fifth, there are profits to be had in making and selling pollution prevention and abatement products.

Traditionally, increased national income per head has gone hand-in-hand with increased stress on the environment. As an old Yorkshire saying has it, "where there's muck there's brass." Successful ecological modernization would decouple muck and brass, such that income per head could go on increasing without additional strain on the environment. This possibility would, it seems, dispel the darkest fears of the survivalists. A qualitatively different kind of growth would not have to hit ecological limits, even if those limits did have real existence. Reconciliation with the overarching need for governments to promote economic growth means that environmental values now support economic ones, which in turn allows (moderate) environmentalists to be included in the core of policy making (Dryzek et al., 2003: 64–5). This inclusion has been most successful in corporatist political systems, with Norway the very best example.

Ecological modernization is sometimes treated as a merely technical concept, referring to the retooling of industry and agriculture along more environmentally sensitive but still profitable lines. Yet if this is the case, there is nothing truly "ecological" about it, for it would say little about human interactions with ecosystems (see Christoff, 1996a). There really has to be more to the discourse than narrow engineering and technical concerns. For ecological modernization is not something that can be accomplished by business managers and engineers operating voluntarily and independently on their own products and processes. It requires political commitment, to the enlightened long term rather than the narrow-minded short term, and to a holistic analysis of economic and environmental processes rather than piecemeal focus on particular environmental abuses. Its subject matter encompasses nothing less than how capitalist society shall be guided into an environmentally enlightened era, and so involves commitments on the part of the entire society, not just industry. These commitments include foresight, attacking problems at their origins, holism, greater valuation of scarce nature, and the precautionary principle. There is a role for government in setting standards and providing incentives to industry, which helps explain why ecological modernization has flourished in countries with interventionist governments that work closely with business.

Ecological modernization bears a family resemblance to sustainable development. In his seminal book on the subject Hajer even categorizes the Brundtland Report as a key ecological modernization document (Hajer, 1995: 26). But ecological modernization has a much sharper focus than does sustainable development on exactly what needs to be done with the capitalist political economy.[3] Ecological modernization originated in wealthy countries. More recently it has found application in developing countries such as China, Brazil, South Africa, and Vietnam (Sonnenfeld and Rock, 2009), though in the context of specific industries or localities rather than as a whole of economy strategy. So for example Oelofse et al. (2006) refer to "pockets of innovation" in South Africa as presaging "the Africanization of ecological modernization," though the country's seemingly impressive national environmental legislation struggles to achieve implementation. The Chinese government in 2007 published *China Modernization Report 2007: Study on Ecological Modernization* which advocated a technocratic approach to severe environmental problems (Zhang et al., 2007). Since then China has made massive advances in renewable energy, but has seen still more massive increases in coal-fired energy.

At the global level, ecological modernization has achieved prominence in climate governance, as part of an alternative to the stalled quest for comprehensive global agreement on greenhouse gas emission reductions. A lot of the activity in the side-events at the annual Conference of the Parties to the UN Framework Convention on Climate Change revolves around the business opportunities associated with low-emission technologies, and how "green growth" can be sought in all kinds of countries. This discourse is still more evident at gatherings such as the 2009 World Business Summit on Climate Change. In this light, ecological modernization can be pursued in partnerships between government, business, and nongovernmental organizations, joining where necessary into regional or even global networks to exchange information about best practice and to make pledges for both emissions control and technology introduction (Bäckstrand and Lövbrand, 2012). Prominent players include Goldman Sachs, BP, Swiss Re, the China National Oil Corporation, and Greenpeace.

Discourse analysis of ecological modernization

The story line of ecological modernization is that the capitalist political economy needs conscious reconfiguring and far-sighted action so that economic development and environmental protection can proceed hand-in-hand and reinforce one another.[4] This story line is constructed from the following discourse elements.

Basic entities whose existence is recognized or constructed

Ecological modernization entails a systems approach that takes seriously the complex pathways by which consumption, production, resource depletion, and pollution are interrelated. This is most explicit in the Dutch National Environmental Policy Plan. The key to effective action is therefore to anticipate and prevent unwanted environmental ramifications of production and consumption decisions. This orientation is very different from the atomistic underpinnings of Promethean and economic rationalist discourse, which have little time for system complexity. However, ecological modernization's embrace of the system concept is incomplete, for it can still view natural systems in limited terms, as mere adjuncts to the human economy. Nature is treated as a source of resources and a recycler of pollutants—a giant waste treatment plant, whose capacities and balance should not be overburdened. Denied are any notion that nature might spring surprises on us, defy human management, have its own intrinsic value, and its own open-ended developmental pathways. This limited view of nature warrants green radical suspicion of ecological modernization.

Like sustainable development, ecological modernization pushes limits to growth into the background. This displacement of the limits discourse is symbolized by the 1997 report to the Club of Rome, *Factor Four,* which argued the compatibility of doubling wealth while halving resource use (von Weizsäcker et al., 1997). In 1972 it was the Club of Rome that commissioned *The Limits to Growth.* In ecological modernization discourse, limits are not so much explicitly denied as ignored. Certainly the idea of limits becomes fuzzier once economic growth is decoupled from growth in environmental stress, which seems to be happening in the seven countries I identified at the beginning of this chapter. The existence of the capitalist political economy is taken for granted. Unlike sustainable development, economic redirection does not necessarily require a de-emphasis of the state and concomitant promotion of international society and the political grassroots. Finland, Germany, Japan, the Netherlands, Norway, and Sweden are strong states which if anything become stronger as a result of their promotion of ecological modernization (but see Mol, 1996: 314–15 for an argument that ecological modernization can allow a more participatory and decentralized state).

Assumptions about natural relationships

Ecological modernization implies a partnership in which governments, businesses, moderate environmentalists, and scientists cooperate in the restructuring of the capitalist political economy along more environmentally defensible lines. This partnership is an anthropocentric one, in that the natural world is subordinate to human desires and calculations. Whether or not there are necessary hierarchies in human affairs is an open question. Certainly, there are those who would want to make ecological modernization into a doctrine for managers of the political economy; on the other hand, there is room for more egalitarian political relationships across different actors. There is also a crucial natural relationship between environmental protection and economic prosperity, in that the two are seen as properly proceeding hand-in-hand.

Agents and their motives

The key agents in ecological modernization are the partners I have just identified: governments, businesses, reform-oriented environmentalists, and scientists. Their motivations have to do with the common good or the public interest, defined in broad terms to encompass economic efficiency and environmental conservation. Ecological modernization requires widespread commitment to and action upon its principles. If it is resisted by key actors, as in the United States, then ecological modernization simply will not happen.

The question of agency under ecological modernization does, on closer inspection, provide a doorway into a potentially more far-reaching change in the way developed societies organize their economic and—especially— political systems. For the partnership is in a major enterprise: the ecological restructuring of capitalism. But the partnership itself might prove to constitute a major restructuring of political life, because its scope will be extended to questions of economic organization that have traditionally been placed off-limits to collective political control. Shortly, I will turn to the radical ramifications of this possibility.

Key metaphors and other rhetorical devices

The words "economics" and "ecology" both derive from the Greek *oikos*, meaning household. In a sense, ecological modernization returns both ecology and economics to their household root, and re-establishes their commonality. For the implicit metaphor in ecological modernization, helping to explain its widespread appeal, is that of a tidy household. This household is concerned with maximizing its wellbeing, but at the same time realizes that minimizing waste also means meeting its needs efficiently, and that commodious surroundings contribute to the household's sense of wellbeing. In this light, perhaps it is not surprising that ecological modernization has prospered in countries noted for the tidiness, prudence, and far-sightedness of their households.

The word "modernization," like the word "development," connotes progress, and so ecological modernization is linked with the ever-popular notion of social progress. Again like sustainable development, ecological modernization is a discourse of reassurance, at least for residents of relatively prosperous developed societies. No tough choices need to be made between economic growth and environmental protection, or between the present and the long-term future. Unlike sustainable development, it is rarely claimed that this happy coincidence of values extends to social justice, still less justice across the rich and poor nations of the world. However, Hawken et al. (1999: 1–2) say that justice too will follow if the technological changes they advocate are adopted. Ecological modernization was long silent about what might be the appropriate developmental path for Third World societies. To get to the point where they can now choose ecological modernization, countries like the cleaner and greener seven spent a lot of time in a modernization mode that was decidedly anti-ecological. The same might be said for wealthy societies such as Hong Kong and Singapore, which adopted technocratic, state-led ecological modernization after a substantial history of prioritizing unsustainable development (Wong, 2012). If followed by the world's poor, then that developmental path would surely impose intolerable stress on the world's ecosystems. However, as noted earlier, ecological modernization was eventually joined to the idea of green growth that stresses the opportunities for developing societies to choose profitable low-carbon technologies.

Box 8.1 provides a summary of the discourse analysis of ecological modernization.

Radicalizing ecological modernization?

In its limited technical sense, ecological modernization looks like a discourse for engineers and accountants. However, ecological modernization can also be treated as a restructuring of political and economic life, rather than a mere retooling of industry.

At one extreme can be found what Hajer (1995) refers to as "techno-corporatist" ecological modernization, which treats the issues in technical terms, and seeks a managerial structure for their implementation. Management is supplied by the existing administrative organization of the corporatist state, open to the findings and recommendations of environmental scientists and engineers. Relatedly, Christoff (1996a) refers to "weak" ecological modernization, characterized by:

- an emphasis on technological solutions to environmental problems;

- a technocratic/corporatist style of policy making monopolized by scientific, economic, and political elites;

- restriction of the analysis to privileged developed nations, who can use ecological modernization to consolidate their economic advantages and so distance themselves still further from the miserable economic and environmental conditions of the poorer nations of the world.

Christoff's "strong" ecological modernization would feature in contrast:

- consideration of broad-ranging changes to society's institutional structure and economic system, with a view to making them more responsive to ecological concerns;

BOX 8.1   Discourse analysis of ecological modernization

1. **Basic entities recognized or constructed**
   - Complex systems
   - Nature as waste treatment plant
   - Capitalist economy
   - The state
2. **Assumptions about natural relationships**
   - Partnership encompassing government, business, environmentalists, scientists
   - Subordination of nature
   - Environmental protection and economic prosperity go together
3. **Agents and their motives**
   - Partners; motivated by public good
4. **Key metaphors and other rhetorical devices**
   - Tidy household
   - Connection to progress
   - Reassurance

- open, democratic decision making maximizing not only participatory opportunities for citizens, but also authentic and competent communication about environmental affairs;

- concern with the international dimensions of environment and development.

An excellent illustration of the contrast between weak and strong ecological modernization, especially when it comes to the difference between technical and structural solutions, can be found in González's (2001*b*) analysis of air pollution policy in California. California has long pursued a policy of forcing technical changes to car engines in order to reduce emissions. However, total emissions continue to rise because the benefits of these changes are more than offset by increases in the number of cars on the road and average per-year distance traveled. Planning to reduce reliance on private cars and control urban sprawl is not on the agenda. Such planning would be central to strong ecological modernization, which would have to question the very idea of car culture (González, 2009). In this light, the success of Germany and Japan in responding to ecological modernization by producing cars that are far less polluting than their American counterparts (Mikler, 2009) is not enough.

Consistent with Christoff 's "strong" viewpoint, Hajer (1995) speaks of the possibility of "reflexive" ecological modernization. By reflexive, Hajer means political and economic development that proceed on the basis of a critical self-awareness. Modernization was long treated in nonreflexive terms as just a matter of hitching a ride on the ineluctable progress from "traditional" to "modern" society. Reflexive modernization still recognizes that the ride must be taken, but introduces a host of anxieties about the quality and trajectory of the ride which must be subject to continued monitoring and control. No longer can experts and governments be trusted to know what is best for the rest of us; no longer should we regard economic growth of whatever composition as automatically a good thing; no longer should we place economic affairs and the organization of the economic system as off-limits to public scrutiny and democratic control. Experts and elites would have to justify their policies to citizens, in comprehensible language, and with no recourse to the privilege of rank or expertise. Reflexive ecological modernization is for everybody (see Wong, 2012 on the need for greater civil society participation in ecological modernization in Singapore).

Clearly it matters a great deal to which of these two versions of ecological modernization a society commits itself. Weak or techno-corporatist ecological modernization might, as Hajer (1995: 32–4) recognizes, involve just a rhetorical rescue operation for a capitalist economy confounded by ecological crises. Much more is at stake in the strong version, which points to the exit from industrial society. Ulrich Beck (1992) has argued that issues of environmental risk, especially risk related to chemical pollution, toxic wastes, nuclear energy, and biotechnology, call into question the very foundations of industrial society. In industrial society, Beck argues, we happily put issues of economic organization and technological change off-limits to conscious and collective human control. For this reason, Beck believes that industrial society was only "semi-modern," in that it only partially fulfilled modernity's promise of rational social development. Beck's emerging "risk society," in contrast, puts these issues firmly on the agenda. To Beck, the politics of industrial society was mostly about conflict between social classes, and redistributive issues reflecting this conflict between capitalists and workers. In contrast, the politics of the emerging risk society is organized around the environmental risks which industrial society has generated, but with which it has shown itself incapable of dealing. Unlike industrial society's main hazard of poverty, the rich have no immunity from the hazards of risk society. As Beck (1992: 36) puts it, "smog is democratic."

The prospects for strong or reflexive ecological modernization are improved to the extent that environmental affairs can be joined to the risk drama portrayed by Beck. But so long as these affairs are treated in more mundane terms of pollution control and management of material flows, weak or techno-corporatist ecological modernization will prevail. Blowers (1997) believes this mundane character is inescapable, and so excludes ecological modernization from any contribution to a reflexive modernity. Langhelle (2000) and Pepper (1999) both see more radical potential in sustainable development discourse, for all its faults. However, sustainable development for Langhelle comes in its Nordic version, true to the spirit of Brundtland rather than the World Business Council for Sustainable Development version. For Pepper, a now-marginalized conception of "strong sustainability" is the key.

In the weak or techno-corporatist version of ecological modernization, government, corporate capitalism, and the scientific establishment manage the transition to a more environmentally sensitive economic system. But in Beck's risk society, these three institutions warrant skepticism for their complicity in the production of risks. Thus the dominant institutions of industrial society lose their legitimacy in the eyes of the public. Risk society is in fact conducive to the insurgency of a whole new set of interlinked democratic institutions. Experts would lose their privilege, and science would be reformed such that "research will fundamentally take account of the public's questions and be addressed to them" (Beck, 1999: 70), enabling citizens to reach their own judgments on technical issues. Authority in general would be reconstituted in networks that would cross traditional boundaries of the state, economy, and society, the institutions of a reflexive modernity (see also Beck et al., 1994). They could resemble a radicalized version of the governance networks discussed in Chapters 4 and 5.

Ecological modernization in the balance

If ecological modernization does prevail, which kind will it be? Will we get environmentally sensitive management of technological change? Or will we see instead wholesale transformation of the capitalist political economy, the doorway to a reflexive ecological modernity in which the latent human potential for full control of our destiny comes into view for the first time in history? The jury is still out. When it comes to the prospects for this strong or reflexive version of ecological modernization, Beck overstates his case that the transition from industrial society to risk society has occurred. Politics is still mostly about the distribution of material rewards rather than about the production, allocation, amelioration, and distribution of risks, even though the occasional risk issue, such as mad cow disease (BSE) in Britain in the late 1990s or genetically modified organisms, occasionally rises to the top of the political agenda. Moreover, if and when risk society does arrive, it will not necessarily be as conducive to broad-ranging democratization as Beck hopes. For risks can be distributed along class lines. Toxic waste dumps and other noxious facilities are normally located in the vicinity of the poor and ethnic minorities. The rich can escape the risks of mad cow disease and genetically modified food by buying organic food. Weak ecological modernization in the wealthy countries could be bought by transferring risks to poor countries—by locating polluting industries in poor countries, or exporting wastes to them, or exploiting their resources in unsustainable fashion. Japan's ecological footprint is very large, but the negative effects are felt mostly outside Japan, in destroyed tropical forests in Southeast Asia, in Pacific islands covered in golf courses, in depleted ocean fisheries, in polluting industries relocated to other countries.

Of the seven countries I have emphasized, glimpses of strong ecological modernization can be seen mainly in Germany, where consensual elite-level politics confronts strong oppositional social movements. Ecological research institutes such as the Institute for Applied Ecology (and more than eighty others) supply Beck's "counter-expertise" for the public, and raise structural questions in their influence upon public policy. The Green Party in the federal governing coalition negotiated a planned phaseout of nuclear power, which in 2011 was confirmed by Angela Merkel's conservative government that did not involve the Greens. German environmentalists have become major players without having to suppress radicalism (the increasing moderation of the Green Party notwithstanding), which has been the price of inclusion elsewhere (Dryzek et al., 2003: 185–91).

I argued at the end of the previous chapter that sustainable development fits uneasily in a world seemingly committed to free trade and the deregulation of markets (unless the discourse is bent heavily in the direction of market liberalism). Ecological modernization faces even greater problems here, given its commitment to conscious collective control of the political economy in the ecological restructuring of capitalism. However, states that operate along these lines might find that they can obtain a competitive edge in the emerging world economic order, if there is money to be made in environmental conservation. Transnational partnerships and networks promoting (for example) low-carbon technologies for economic development may also find profitable niches.

Concerted pursuit of ecological modernization requires a consensual and interventionist policy style consistent with corporatism. This style is, however, anathema to governments under the sway of market liberal doctrines, which helps explain why ecological modernization faces an uphill struggle in the English-speaking industrialized nations. However, González (2002) points out that at least one element of ecological modernization has been present in the United States since the late nineteenth century, as local economic elites have sought to control pollution for the sake of local economic advantage. Similarly, Scheinberg (2003) suggests looking at the local level, for example at recycling. More far-reaching ideas appeared in former Vice-President Al Gore's book, *Earth in the Balance* (1992), whose proposals are essentially consistent with ecological modernization (though he never uses the term). Gore the Vice-President proved a pale shadow of Gore the author, and none of the book's prescriptions found any place in policy making, still less his 2000 presidential campaign. The disillusioned environmentalists who greeted his public appearances with a chant of "Read your book!" had a point. Ideas about green growth and the profitability of emissions reduction re-appear with Gore's subsequent role as a leading advocate for action on climate change, globally as well as in the United States. In Gore's 2006 *An Inconvenient Truth* documentary and associated lecture tour (for which he won both a Nobel Peace Prize and an Academy Award), the stress is on consumers demanding products with low associated emissions, though there is also a role for activists to pressure government and business to adopt low-carbon practices. US businesses such as the big Interface carpet company and Wal-Mart have begun to heed this lesson (Schlosberg and Rinfret, 2008: 260). Ecological modernization in the United States can also be linked to national security, because a more energy-efficient economy would depend less on oil from unstable and authoritarian parts of the world (Schlosberg and Rinfret, 2008: 261–5). High fashion green consumerism can also play a part (Schlosberg and Rinfret, 2008: 266–8).

The United Kingdom for its part did eventually begin to consider some aspects of ecological modernization in the late 1990s. Fabian Society

Director Michael Jacobs (1999) sketched the idea of "environmental modernisation," and tried to link it to the general modernization agenda of Tony Blair's Labour government. In 2000 Blair responded, speaking of "a new coalition for the environment… that harnesses consumer demand for a better environment, and encourages business to see the profit of new technologies." As Barry (2003: 199) points out, Blair's "new coalition" apparently did not contain environmentalists. In 1998 the UK's Royal Commission on Environmental Pollution published a report, *Setting Environmental Standards*, which remarkably (for a British report) recommended abandoning the established secretive and informal approach to regulation in favor of a more participatory process involving citizens with conscious scrutiny of public values (Weale, 2001: 362–8). This report is actually consistent with strong ecological modernization, but the response from government was tepid, and its recommendations were not implemented. In 2010 new Conservative Prime Minister David Cameron announced that he wanted to lead "the greenest government ever," going on to say "We've got a real opportunity to drive the green economy to have green jobs, and make sure we have our share of the industries of the future,"[5] suggesting all the major parties in the UK had now accepted ecological modernization. Yet this commitment struggles against the market liberalism that looms so large in the UK, no less than other Anglo-American industrial countries.

The idea that capitalism's future might be green and corporatist is ridiculed by Prometheans. They regard ecological modernization's precautionary principle as tantamount to lunacy (see, for example, Wildavsky, 1995: 427–33), as guaranteeing only that the wealth which is the real key to environmental health will be dissipated by excessive and costly regulations. Economic rationalists see in corporatism only opportunities for special interests to conspire against the public good. However, policy instruments developed by economic rationalists, notably quasi-market incentive mechanisms (as discussed in Chapter 6), have often found favor among ecological modernizers, who paradoxically find it much easier to implement them because they can strip the instruments of their "free market environmentalism" ideological baggage.

Green radicals are uneasy with ecological modernization because it threatens to deflect their critiques of industrial society. Ecological modernization might pave the way for the inclusion of green groups in policy making, but at the price of their moderation (Barry, 2003: 204–6). The strong reflexive version of ecological modernization could be stretched to encompass green radical views, though some more romantic green notions would have to be jettisoned to fit this very rationalistic discourse. However far it is stretched, ecological modernization does not easily admit the idea that nature might have intrinsic value beyond its material uses, or green desires for living simply upon the Earth in convivial fashion. Human life on Earth for ecological modernizers is always going to be a complicated affair, and will never be for living simply.

Those subscribing to a limits discourse, Prometheans, economic rationalists, and green romantics are probably never going to accommodate themselves to ecological modernization. Governments that have always resisted consensual and corporatist policy making will probably also continue to resist ecological modernization. Despite some inroads, the discourse still cannot offer poorer countries a comprehensive developmental alternative.

Still, in its weak and techno-corporatist senses, ecological modernization has already proved itself in the cleanest and greenest developed nations. Long silent on what to do at the global level, it has increasingly made its presence felt in global climate governance. Strong ecological modernization linked to a reflexive modernity is both more intriguing and more speculative. Alone among the discourses surveyed here, it offers a plausible strategy for transforming industrial society into a radically different and more environmentally defensible (but still capitalist) alternative.

....

NOTES

1. <http://epi.yale.edu/epi2012/rankings>

2. "Green Dreams: Japan," *The Economist* 362 (January 12, 2002): 40–1.

3. Ecological modernization can also be treated as a social science theory for the analysis of environmental developments (Mol and Spaargaren, 2000). In this chapter I confine the discussion to ecological modernization as a discourse, not a theory.

4. Hajer (1995: 65) defines the "credible and attractive story-lines" of ecological modernization as "the regulation of the environmental problem appears as a positive-sum game; pollution is a matter of inefficiency; nature has a balance that should be respected; anticipation is better than cure; and sustainable development is the alternative to the previous path of defiling growth."

5. "Cameron: I want coalition to be the 'greenest government ever,'" *Guardian*, May 14, 2010.

PART V
GREEN RADICALISM

....

As befits its imaginative and radical leanings, the world of green discourse is a diverse and lively place, home to a wide variety of ideologies, parties, movements, groups, and thinkers. Found here are green parties and their factions, bioregionalists, ecofeminists, deep ecologists, social ecologists, eco-Marxists, eco-socialists, eco-anarchists, ecological Christians, Buddhists, Taoists, pagans, environmental and climate justice advocates, green economists, new materialists, critical theorists, postmodernists, and many others. This variety makes classification difficult. However, green radicalism can be divided into two categories: one that focuses on changed consciousness, another that looks more explicitly to green politics. A stress on green consciousness means that the way people experience and regard the world in which they live, and each other, is the key to green change. Once consciousness has changed in an appropriate direction, then policies, social structures, institutions, and economic systems are expected to fall into place. This prioritization of consciousness is widespread in the green movement, among deep ecologists, bioregionalists, ecofeminists, ecotheologists, and lifestyle greens, among others. Other greens are more attuned to the need to target recalcitrant social, economic, and political structures and practices more directly. They include green parties, social ecologists, eco-Marxists, and transition towns, environmental justice, Third World, and antiglobalization activists. Sometimes the difference between green consciousness and green politics is just a matter of emphasis, and the two join to constitute a green public sphere. Some greens endeavor to combine consciousness change and political change. At other times some contrasts come into play.

These two aspects of green radicalism represent the main options for any social movement. Movements aim to change both the way people think and so behave on the one hand, and social institutions and collective decisions on the other. These institutions and decisions include governments and their policies, though social movements can also target international organizations and corporations, and even help create alternatives to the formal structures of government.

PART V

GREEN RADICALISM

9

Changing People: Green Consciousness

One route to changing the world is through the way people think. In an environmental context, this change would involve the way people experience the world, and new kinds of ecological sensibility. The precise content of this sensibility is contested. In some cases it is radically new, looking to innovative notions of ecological citizenship. In other cases it is radically old, looking back to primal human society before the rise of agriculture. Sometimes, the radically new and radically old are combined in creative fashion.

The varieties of green consciousness

Deep ecology

Deep ecology as a movement and a label is most prevalent in the United States, though its origins are Norwegian, and it has adherents in Canada, Australia, New Zealand, and elsewhere. Deep ecology was given its name and its initial content by the Norwegian philosopher Arne Naess (1973), who drew a contrast with the "shallow" ecology movement that only wanted to reform some of the practices of industrial society (see also Naess, 1989). Subsequent development occurred largely in the United States, especially the Western states (see especially Devall and Sessions, 1985), where it became associated with the radical wilderness defense group Earth First!, and with nature writers such as Edward Abbey and Barry Lopez.

According to Devall and Sessions (1985: 67), deep ecology's two basic principles are self-realization and biocentric equality. Self-realization means identification with a larger organic "Self" beyond the individual person; or "self-in-Self," as they put it. The idea is to cultivate a deep consciousness and awareness of organic unity, of the holistic nature of the ecological webs in which every individual is enmeshed. Along these lines, Warwick Fox (1990) describes a "transpersonal ecology," a psychological condition of identification and care for other beings, ecosystems, and nature in its entirety. Deep ecologists value species, populations, and ecosystems, not just individual creatures. Biocentric equality means that no species, including the human species, is regarded as more valuable or in any sense higher than any other species. The opposite of biocentric equality is anthropocentric arrogance.

Devall and Sessions (1985: 70) elaborate on these two basic principles to argue that nature and its diversity have intrinsic value irrespective of human uses and interests. Given current excessive ecological stress imposed by humans, respect for nature and its diversity requires a reduction in human populations. Unlike some other deep ecologists, Devall and Sessions are not misanthropic, and indeed allow that nature's diversity can be legitimately depleted in order to satisfy "vital" human needs. It is probably fair to say that their conception of vital human needs does not extend to sports utility vehicles, speedboats, vacation homes, or home entertainment systems.

More misanthropic deep ecologists, most notoriously the pseudonymous columnist in the Earth First! Journal, Miss Ann Thropy, deny the legitimacy of special human interests.[1] In a 1987 article Miss Ann Thropy welcomed famine and disease (such as AIDS) as useful checks on human numbers. The splinter group VHEMT (pronounced vehement), the Voluntary Human Extinction Movement, sounds misanthropic, but its slogan, "May we live long and die out," implies only that people voluntarily stop breeding so that the biosphere can recover from us.[2]

Many deep ecologists take pains to distance themselves from the misanthropes. All seek a major reduction in human arrogance when it comes to dealing with the natural world. Most would probably agree with Eckersley (1992: 46), who in defining ecocentrism (roughly synonymous with biocentrism) specifies that it "recognises the full range of human interests in the nonhuman world" as well as "the interests of the nonhuman community."

The question of how to balance human and nonhuman interests is perhaps more easily answered in particular cases rather than at the level of philosophical abstraction. Philosophical dispute about the relative worth of human beings and the smallpox virus does not get in the way of the recognized need to protect the remnant ancient forests of California, Oregon, Washington, and British Columbia against logging; to keep uranium mines out of national parks; and to return the Colorado River to its free-flowing state.

Deep ecologists are quite clear on what to do when it comes to wilderness: preserve, expand, and protect it. As Earth First! co-founder Dave Foreman (2000: 38) put it, "Big wilderness areas are not only necessary for inspiration and a true wilderness experience, but they are absolutely necessary for the preservation and restoration of ecological integrity, native species diversity, and evolution." Foreman went on in 2003 to co-found the Rewilding Institute to promote this agenda. Against social constructionist approaches to nature (see Chapter 1), deep ecologists are adamant that wilderness has real existence that predates human appropriation, and represents the only authentic essence of nature (Foreman, 1998). Deep ecologists have much less to say on other environmental issues, such as air and water pollution in urban areas. Urban agglomerations are by definition outside the bounds of defensible human–nature interactions, and thus of no concern. In Edward Abbey's wonderful deep ecological novel *The Monkey Wrench Gang (1975)*, one of the heroes, Hayduke, measures road distances in terms of six-packs of beer the driver needs to consume. Hayduke throws the empty cans out of the window: if the environment has already been trashed by a road, a few beer cans make no essential difference.

Ecofeminism

Ecofeminism is a deep philosophy in the sense that it seeks radical changes in ecological consciousness. But ecofeminists attack deep ecologists for consorting with macho mountain men such as the fictional Hayduke and the real-world Dave Foreman, co-founder of Earth First! In this light, deep ecology is a doctrine for redneck male adventurers. Worse, its basic diagnosis is wrong. The root of all environmental problems, according to ecofeminists, is not anthropocentrism (human domination of nature), but rather androcentrism (male domination of everything). According to ecofeminists, things begin to go drastically wrong in the way humans treat each other and the natural world with the rise of patriarchy, which dominates women and nature alike. Thus the liberation of women is tied up with liberation of nature (Diamond and Orenstein, 1990; Plant, 1989). Patriarchy is seen as cultural rather than natural, and ecofeminists look back to egalitarian and matriarchal societies, some complete with goddesses, prior to the rise of cities, kingdoms, and empires.

Ecofeminism differs further from deep ecology in its sympathy with animal liberation (Kheel, 2008). Deep ecologists, in contrast, show no concern for animals once they are out of nature—for example, in factory farms or laboratories. Even animals in nature are seen as (literally) fair game for deep ecologists, to be hunted and eaten as an expression of the proper human place in ecosystems. Only organic wholes such as ecosystems are to be preserved, not individual creatures. Another point of divergence is on population control. Deep ecologists see a reduction in human population as essential. Ecofeminists believe such a reduction is likely to be accomplished only by further repression and control of women's fertility by the male power structure and its technology (Diamond, 1994).

For all their differences, deep ecologists and ecofeminists alike believe in cultivation of radically different human sensibilities, involving a noninstrumental and nondominating, more empathetic and intuitive relationship to nature. Both camps are also home to those who advocate a nature-based spirituality, with divinity located in this world, rather than in (male) figures located off the planet (for deep ecology, see Devall and Sessions, 1985: 8, 90–1, 100–1; and Fox, 1984: 203–4; but note that Foreman, 1991: 46 is an atheist. For ecofeminism, see Christ, 2003). Spiritual ecofeminists often look to pagan religions, and are attracted to goddess imagery (for ecofeminist witchcraft, see Starhawk, 1987).

Ecofeminism began in France in 1972 with the formation of Ecologie-Féminisme by Françoise d'Eaubonne, and flourished in the United States in the 1980s. Its Third World dimension is well represented by arguably the world's most prominent ecofeminist, Vandana Shiva, who writes from India. The root of most contemporary social and ecological evils is, according to Shiva, the Enlightenment commitment to science and economic growth, which together destroy life's diversity and sanctity (Shiva, 2000). Shiva is especially concerned by the degree to which imported agricultural and industrial technologies driven by globalization (most recently, genetically modified organisms) further disadvantage Third World women (for example, by denigrating their traditional knowledge of the land and its workings). She points to the leading role played by women in Third World environmental movements, notably the Chipko tree-protection movement in India.

Women are often seen as closer than men to nature by the fact of their ability to give birth and nurture children (though see Biehl, 1991 for a critique of this dualism). It is the female virtues related to care, empathy, intuition, connection, and cooperation that are crucial. As Plumwood (1993: 9) puts it, many ecofeminists cultivate the myth of a female "angel in the ecosystem" (Plumwood herself renounces this myth). Men might be able to reason their way toward ecofeminism, but they could never *feel* it. And it is a one-sided emphasis on reason that helped get humanity into such ecological trouble in the first place, by making men so arrogant as to think they could use reason to control nature.

Most ecofeminism is "cultural" in that it begins with condemnation of one kind of human sensibility and ends with advocacy of another. A more "social" ecofeminism attends to how society is organized (Carlassare, 1994). The work of Shiva combines cultural and social aspects. Social analysis can also be found in feminist activism on climate change—associated for example with the global network *Gender CC-Women for Climate Justice*. Another good example of this kind of analysis can be found in Plumwood's (1995) scrutiny of alternative models of democracy. Plumwood argues that so long as it remains under the sway of liberalism, democracy can never extend itself in a truly ecological direction. For inherent in liberalism are assumptions about the degree to which individuals are properly isolated from one another, rational in a narrowly instrumental and egoistic sense, and unequal in both material wealth and the capacity to exercise power and reason. The consequences are both socially unjust and environmentally destructive. Plumwood's proposed ecofeminist democracy would involve social and ecological citizenship more attuned to an ethic of care and responsibility, together with a more egalitarian political order extending to equality across humanity and nature. However, cultural change still matters for Plumwood (2002).

Bioregionalism

Bioregionalists seek the reinhabitation of places in which people live (McGinnis, 1998). Bioregions can be defined in different ways: by water-shed, or by predominant vegetation type. Examples of bioregions would be Pacific Cascadia, covering the coastal forests west of the Cascade Crest from southern British Columbia to northern California; and the Murray–Darling River Basin in Australia. As a movement, bioregionalism is strongest in North America (Sale, 1985), where it is propounded by the Planet Drum Foundation. Central to bioregionalism is cultivation of a sense of place. People who live in a bioregion need to adopt it as their true home, to be respected and sustained so that the region in turn can sustain human health and life (Dodge, 1981). They need to become aware of the kind of ecosystem they inhabit, and regard themselves as a part of it, rather than identify with ethnic groups or nations or other human groupings that transcend ecological boundaries. Bioregional consciousness is, then, very different from the kind of consciousness inculcated by the capitalist economy and cultural globalization, which are destroying regional identity of any kind. Both deep ecological consciousness and ecofeminist consciousness could fit quite easily into a bioregional setting.

Ultimately bioregionalists want to replace local, state, and national political institutions with governments organized along bioregional lines, foreshadowed by existing river basin authorities, which normally, however, lack the right consciousness. Bioregionalists point to the inability of bureaucracies organized on non-bioregional bases to cope with complex ecosystems. A standard example concerns the number of jurisdictions through which salmon in the Columbia River Basin must swim between the ocean and their spawning grounds. Proposals for reorganized governments include the "Europe of the regions" advocated by European greens, which would dissolve existing national boundaries. In North America, Pacific Cascadia might govern what is now Western British Columbia, Oregon, and Washington, and a portion of northwestern California (Todd, 2008). Ecological concerns would be by definition at the forefront of the agenda of such governments, addressed and deliberated across all policy areas (Evanoff, 2011).

Societies whose focus is provided by the ecosystems which they inhabit, and upon which they must rely for their sustenance, would have to care for those ecosystems very carefully. This assumes that trade across regions would be regulated, presumably by agreement or confederation across bioregions. The basic questions of how exactly to draw boundaries and how large bioregions should be remain unresolved. In terms of size, bioregions may be nested within one another. In terms of where to draw boundaries, vegetation type, terrain, human culture, and watersheds may give different answers, and compromises may be necessary across these principles. For example, Pacific Cascadia is a bioregion defined by temperate Douglas Fir forests. But parts of this bioregion fall within the Columbia River Basin— which also contains mid-continent deserts. Many bioregionalists would say such issues are secondary, and that solutions would fall into place once the necessary consciousness were disseminated widely enough.

Ecological citizenship

Bioregional consciousness implies a kind of ecological citizenship, in which individuals learn to become respectful citizens of a place, rather than transforming the place to suit themselves. Such citizenship involves awareness of how the ecosystem supports life, and of life's vulnerabilities. It involves meeting one's material as well as spiritual needs from the resources available locally. However, ecological citizenship does not have to be linked to bioregionalism and obligations to place. For Christoff (1996b), such citizenship is equally a matter of commitment to a stewardship ethic and obligations to future generations and other species, irrespective of where they live. Against economic rationalists, Dobson (2004) insists that a sustainable society can be built only by ecologically motivated citizens, and not by consumers and producers responding to the carrots and sticks of economic incentives. Dobson stresses the obligations of the wealthy, who have already imposed excessive demands upon "ecological space," to the poor who have little ecological space. Such space extends to wherever the impact of one's consumption is felt. So ecological citizenship refers also to the sustainability of one's ecological footprint upon the Earth. Ethics of compassion and care for other humans help, and point to an affinity between ecological citizenship and ecofeminism (MacGregor, 2006).

Jagers (2009) finds that at least in Sweden, 12–20 percent of respondents to a survey seemed willing to practice some aspects of ecological citizenship, especially in supporting environmental responsibilities across borders. In a very different context, ecological citizenship has political force in the Brazilian state of Acre, where *florestania* refers both to sustainable citizens' forestry and citizenship within the forest itself.

Lifestyle greens

Green lifestyles can begin with consumer decisions: buying Body Shop or Aveda cosmetics whose constituent chemicals are not tested on animals, eating vegetables grown organically, boycotting genetically modified organisms, buying biodegradable cleaning products, using toilet paper made from recycled fibers, and resisting the blandishments of corporate advertisers (especially when they attempt to "greenwash" their products). Recycling, composting, and bicycling as opposed to driving a car all play their parts. The green lifestyle is often vegetarian, for the vegetarian's caloric intake imposes much less stress on agricultural land than does flesh-eating. Between 14 percent and 22 percent of global greenhouse gas emissions come from meat production (Fiala, 2009).

Such decisions can be instrumentally good for the environment, and may even make good economic sense. So local governments throughout the world have adopted recycling for both environmental and economic reasons. Yet lifestyle greens are concerned with much more than the immediate piecemeal effects of such decisions. It is not just a matter of doing green things, it is a matter of being green in doing them, of using these actions to cultivate a post-industrial way of experiencing and relating to the world, perhaps a way-station on the road to political activism (Szasz, 2011: 595).

Ecotheology

I have already noted that deep ecologists and ecofeminists alike are often attracted by some kind of nature-based spirituality (see also La Chapelle, 1978; Spretnack, 1986). However, these two movements do not exhaust the range of ecotheology (for comprehensive catalogs, see Gottlieb, 1996; Hay, 2002: 94–119; and, for updates, the journal *Ecotheology*). Ecotheologians diagnose the root of environmental problems in spiritual terms, and if the root of the problem is spiritual, then so too must be the cure. The classic argument here is that of the historian Lynn White (1967), who argues that environmental crisis is the product of Judeo-Christian religious tradition, which places God outside of and above nature, and then proclaims that man is made in God's image. This placement provides justification for unlimited human manipulation and abuse of nature for purely human ends. White does see in the Judeo-Christian tradition an alternative possibility, associated most prominently with St Francis of Assisi, who White proposes as the patron saint of ecology. The idea of "creation care" has gained ground among US evangelical Christians (an Evangelical Environmental Network was founded in 1993). Creation care urges Christians to make "godly, just, and sustainable choices" (The Evangelical Declaration of Creation Care, quoted in Kearns, 2011: 421). Sally McFague (2008) goes much further in proposing a Christian ecotheology based on a metaphor of the Earth as the body of God.

Other ecotheologists are more inclined to give up on Judaism and Christianity in favor of Taoism, Buddhism, and Hinduism, all of which cast humanity in far more humble terms, adopting a contemplative and reverential attitude toward nature. E. F. Schumacher's (1973) "Buddhist economics" would be built on individuals who seek to maximize wellbeing at a minimum level of consumption. Critics point out that the societies in which these religions flourish are no less prone to ecological destruction than Western societies. Moreover, they also seem to go hand-in-hand with mass political passivity, which might severely hinder any attempt to reorient society in a more environmentally sound direction through grassroots action.

Ecotheology can also enter the analyses and prescriptions of movements and thinkers interested primarily in political change. In 1991, the First National People of Color Environmental Leadership Summit in the United States declared that "environmental justice affirms the sacredness of Mother Earth." Two of the prominent survivalists discussed in Chapter 2, Robert Heilbroner and William Ophuls, both argue that the wholesale political transformations they advocate must be accompanied by some kind of spiritual transformation. So Heilbroner (1991: 176–7) speaks of governments of the future that will be "monastic" in their form, combining "religious orientation with a military discipline." Ophuls (1977: 243) for his part believes in the necessity of "metanoia...tantamount to religious conversion." For Heilbroner, religion's main value is instrumental rather than intrinsic: it is just a way of keeping people in line, to stop them abusing the environment. For Ophuls, it is helpful in making the transition to a different kind of political economy more palatable to the population at large. Along these lines, leading British Green Jonathon Porritt (2005) stresses the "spiritual capital" needed for the pursuit of sustainability.

The romantic disposition and its critics

For romantics, politics is not about devising strategies to achieve tangible goals; rather, it is an arena in which different kinds of experiences can be sought and developed. Historically, the term romanticism was attached to an intellectual movement in the eighteenth and nineteenth centuries that opposed the rise of modern science and liberal politics and positioned itself against the Enlightenment. Enlightenment is the name for the eighteenth-century movement that renounced religion, myth, and traditional social order in the name of reason. Reason in turn meant liberal politics and human rights of the sort established in the English, American, and French Revolutions of 1689, 1776, and 1789 respectively. Reason also meant that modern science became the route to secure knowledge, which enabled in turn the growth of modern technology and the manipulation of nature on a large scale. The defining feature of modern society is that it embodies the principles of the Enlightenment. The original romantics favored instead an artistic and aesthetic orientation to life and politics. To romantic poets such as Coleridge, Wordsworth, and Shelley, nature and humanity belonged in an organic relationship best understood and developed through feeling and insight. In the United States, the romantic disposition was developed in the nineteenth century by Ralph Waldo Emerson and Henry David Thoreau.

Just like the romantics of the eighteenth and nineteenth centuries, green romanticism rejects core Enlightenment principles, pointing to the environmental destruction caused by modern science and technology wielded in human arrogance (Hay, 2002: 4–11). Green romanticism seeks to save the world through cultivation of more empathetic and less manipulative orientations toward nature and other people. It is heir to the older romantic rejection of the Enlightenment's emphasis on rationality and progress. This kind of disposition can be found among deep ecologists, though Foreman (2000: 38) rejects "airy-fairy flights of romantic fantasy." It is shared by some ecofeminists, especially those who subscribe to what Plumwood criticizes as "the angel in the ecosystem" image; by those bioregionalists who place intuitive experience of place above all else; and by spiritual greens attuned to oneness with nature.

Other greens caution against abandoning Enlightenment values (Hayward, 1995). Hari (2009) refers scathingly to "cause-discrediting voodoo." Enlightenment does have a dark side, in the form of instrumental reason in the service of anthropocentric arrogance, underwriting uncontrolled economic growth, oblivious to the constraints imposed by the natural world, and to the damage done to conviviality in the social world. The brighter side of Enlightenment involves hostility to unquestioned hierarchy, a corresponding commitment to equality (at least among humans), basic human rights, and the possibility of free dialogue as the essence of rational social relationships. For Enlightenment rationality is not just a matter of manipulating the world on behalf of the mind's desires, as green romantics would have it. Rationality is also a matter of open-ended and critical questioning of values, principles, and ways of life—which opens the door to critical ecological questioning. As Plumwood (1993: 4) puts it: "critiquing the dominant forms of reason which embody the master identity and oppose themselves to the sphere of nature does not imply abandoning all forms of reason, science, and individuality. Rather, it involves their redefinition or reconstruction in less oppositional and hierarchical ways." Hay (2002: 10–11) points out that contemporary green radicalism is rooted in science as well as aesthetics, an ecosystemic view rather than romantic individualism, and progress to a better future, not a return to some golden past. On the other hand, as Martin Palmer, Secretary-General of the Alliance of Religions and Conservation, put it in a 2009 interview, "Nobody was ever moved to change the way they live by a pie chart" (quoted in Kearns, 2011: 414).

Discourse analysis of green consciousness

The essential story line of green consciousness change is that industrial society induces a warped conception of persons and their place in the world. Required to remedy this situation are new kinds of human sensibilities, less destructive to nature. While the precise content of the required sensibilities varies, they would generally involve a less manipulative and more humble human attitude to the natural world and to each other. Digging a little deeper, the story line is constructed from the following elements.

Basic entities whose existence is recognized or constructed

In the background of green radicalism are global ecological limits of the sort that energize survivalists: the existence and proximity of these limits impart a sense of urgency. As Dobson (1990: 73) puts it: "the foundation stone of Green politics is the belief that our finite Earth places limits on our industrial growth." Green radicals would not, however, share the authoritarian political prescriptions once favored by some survivalists. Green cultural change would still be coherent and defensible (though less urgent) in the absence of limits.

The basic entity whose existence is recognized and constructed, and which forms the real foundation for the discourse, is nature. Both inner nature (that is, of the mind, body, and spirit) and outer nature are at issue here. Green cultural change would bring these two into closer harmony by operating on human sensibilities and obligations. Such harmony is the essence of deep ecological notions of "self-in-Self," and of cultural ecofeminist principles concerning a more intuitive and empathetic human orientation to the natural world—and to other humans. Opposed to these conceptions of nature and the natural are notions of the unnatural. Included here would be the core practices and—still more important—the core sensibilities that industrial society has inculcated in people. Such unnatural acts and orientations would include the anthropocentric arrogance of Prometheans, the relentless quest for more and better consumer goods, and the instrumental calculation emphasized by economic rationalism. Ecofeminists would add patriarchy to this list.

An emphasis on consciousness change means that social structures, institutions, and policies are seen as having no independent life of their own, but instead as ultimately reducible to the underlying sensibilities of the members of society. Thus does green consciousness fall squarely in the philosophical tradition of idealism (as opposed to materialism, which stresses the causal influence of economic forces in shaping society). It is ideas, not material forces, that move history: so the key to changing the world is to change ideas.

Assumptions about natural relationships

The natural relationships stressed by advocates of green consciousness change are often, quite simply, natural relationships. The images of nature and the kinds of relationships it contains may vary in their details. For example, deep ecologists are often quite happy with a nature "red in tooth and claw," to use an expression favored by some followers of Charles Darwin, and celebrate predation and hunting as parts of the natural order. Ecofeminists are more likely to see in the natural world harmony between creatures and species. Whatever its balance of competition and cooperation, the natural order is an egalitarian one (the deep ecologists' biocentric equality), in which there is no hierarchy, and certainly not a hierarchy that puts humans on top of everything else. Green radicals also believe that this order has been violated by humankind, be it through anthropocentric arrogance, patriarchy, or industrialist indifference.

Such violation often comes in the name of rationality. The dominant form of rationality in today's world is instrumental rationality: the capacity to devise, select, and effect good means to clarified and consistent ends. Instrumental rationality calls up a dichotomy between subject and object. Only the human mind is subject. Everything else, including the natural world and disadvantaged humans, consists of objects to be manipulated and dominated for the sake of whatever the mind desires. Thus instrumental rationality estranges us from nature and each other, with all kinds of disastrous consequences. Nature takes its revenge for our arrogance by inflicting environmental crises upon us.

Agents and their motives

The cultural aspect of green radicalism is about the cultivation of alternative kinds of ecological subjectivity. Every person can be an agent, with the capacity to craft his or her own relationships to the natural and human world. This discourse is, then, well populated by human subjects. More important, it contains only subjects. People are subject to themselves in that it is up to all of them to create an appropriate orientation to life; nobody else can do it for them. Collective actors such as governments, corporations, and other organizations are largely ignored, except to be condemned, as are elites who might have the power to impose their will on other people. However, the discourse does allow for some human subjects to be more enlightened than others, and so show the way. Thus there is scope for green education (see Dobson, 2004: 174–207).

The ascription of agency does not stop with human beings. Agency can be seen as existing in (external) nature too. This is especially true for the romantic disposition in green consciousness change. Nature does not have to be blind, unthinking, and unfeeling; instead, it can be truly alive with meaning and purpose. This applies to individual creatures, to species, to ecosystems, and perhaps even to the planet as a whole. James Lovelock's (1979) Gaia hypothesis has found a sympathetic reception among greens (though as a persistent enthusiast for nuclear power he has hardly sought such a reception). This hypothesis states that the biosphere in its totality acts collectively to maintain the conditions for life on Earth. In this light, the biosphere is a self-regulating entity that can correct for threats to its capacity to support life—threats that come, for example, through increases in the level of solar radiation, volcanic activity, or pollution. Acceptance of this hypothesis does not guarantee an environmentalist outlook. For Gaia may be quite able to correct for any abuses that we humans can dream up, be it pollution from burning fossil fuels or nuclear holocaust. We may wipe ourselves out, but Gaia will persist, just as it has outlasted the extinction of millions of species. Green radicals are more likely to regard Gaia as both vulnerable and worthy of reverence.

Key metaphors and other rhetorical devices

Green advocates of consciousness change make use of an eclectic range of biological and organic metaphors. Given the focus on the cultivation of human subjectivity, many of these metaphors are incorporated into exhortations about how to experience the world. For example, according to Robert Aitken, "Deep ecology... requires openness to the black bear, becoming truly intimate with the black bear, so that honey dribbles down your fur coat as you catch the bus to work" (quoted in Dobson, 1990: 61). To Karen Davis (1995), the key to a feminist understanding of animal liberation is "thinking like a chicken." To use a popular expression in deep ecology, the key is instead "thinking like a mountain." Dave Foreman, deep ecological founder of Earth First!, used to conclude his standard stump speech by getting his audience to howl like wolves.

Changing the way people experience the world is crucial. This can be done through argument; and there are indeed many detailed arguments, some of considerable philosophical sophistication, on behalf of the various green positions I have surveyed. But ultimately, argument may not be enough. Reasoned argument can only take us so far along the road. The rest of the path may require rhetorical strategies that reach beyond reason to passion. If the point is to convince listeners of the desirability of an intuitive and empathetic orientation to nature, then this can be done by relating personal stories, analogous to accounts of religious conversion and how it changed the life of the teller of the story. So, for example, the ecofeminist Julia Russell (1990: 224) relates how she came to the realization that the Earth is a living being through contemplation of her compost pile, which showed her that "The Earth turns everything given to it into itself." Appeals can be and are made to intuitions and emotions. Poetry, art, religious and quasi-religious ceremonies, the telling and re-telling of myths and creation stories can all play their parts. Dobson (2004: 211) suggests that "an hour's lived experience can produce more politicisation than a year in class" when it comes to inculcating a sense of ecological citizenship.

Box 9.1 provides a summary of the discourse analysis of green consciousness.

The impact of green consciousness change

For most of the discourses surveyed in earlier chapters, it makes sense to look for real-world impacts in terms of the policies of governments and international bodies, and in the reconstruction of social, economic, and political institutions and practices. But to assess green consciousness change in similar terms would be to miss its central point. For these greens want *people* to be different; and when they are, then everything else is expected to fall into place. Many social movements do in fact take effect largely through the changes in culture, ethics, and so people's behavior that the movement induces (Tesh, 1993). Feminism, for example, has successfully altered relationships of power between the sexes within the household, and in society more generally. Some of these changes have been confirmed by legislation such as family law and equal opportunity measures, but many of them have not been so compelled. Similarly, a large part of the impact of the last forty years of environmentalism is in the way people have come to think about their everyday behavior: in recycling wastes, in insulating their houses, in

BOX 9.1	Discourse analysis of green consciousness change

1. **Basic entities recognized or constructed**
   - Global limits
   - Nature
   - Unnatural practices
   - Ideas
2. **Assumptions about natural relationships**
   - Natural relationships between humans and nature that have been violated
   - Equality across people and nature
3. **Agents and their motives**
   - Human subjects, some more ecologically aware than others
   - Agency can exist in nature too
4. **Key metaphors and other rhetorical devices**
   - Wide range of biological and organic metaphors
   - Passion
   - Appeals to emotions, intuitions

paying attention to the environmental friendliness of products they purchase, in thinking about their carbon footprints, in what they tell their children about the world. Cultural change can also influence the understandings of key decision makers (Wapner, 2002a: 53–8), though by the time green ideas get taken up they have often lost much of their radical bite.

Thus it is in this cultural realm that we should seek evidence of the real impact of green ideas. The cultivation of new ways of being is done not just for the benefit of the individual so enlightened, but for the good of society, and ultimately the good of the planet.

In these terms, it is a bit ironic that the main impact so far of green consciousness change is probably at the level of changing consumer behavior, such that, of the varieties of cultural change surveyed earlier, it is the lifestyle greens who have had the most effect. In industrial societies, at least, many people do happily sort and recycle their garbage, read labels of products on the supermarket shelves, shun ozone-depleting chemicals and genetically modified organisms, compost food scraps and garden waste, force companies like McDonald's to stop using unrecyclable Styrofoam packaging, and improve the energy-efficiency of their lifestyles. Here, green cultural change provides useful and perhaps unexpected support for ecological modernization, which requires consumers to behave in exactly this fashion.

What people have not done, except in very small numbers, is adopt the kind of ecological consciousness of the kind sought by deep ecologists, ecofeminists, bioregionalists, or ecotheologians. The relevant groups and networks are often quite small, and not especially visible to a larger public. The most noteworthy such group is probably Earth First!, founded in the United States in 1980 (later with some international affiliates). Earth First! is perhaps known less for its deep ecological philosophy as for the exploits of its members. These exploits include lying down in front of bulldozers, gatecrashing the anniversary celebrations of Lake Powell reservoir on the Colorado River, occupying the tops of trees in old growth forests scheduled for clear-cutting, putting a "crack" on the face of the Glen Canyon Dam, blockading mountaintop removal for coal mining in Appalachia, and so forth. Earth First! is also associated with monkeywrenching or ecotage: that is, sabotage of environmentally damaging activities. Monkeywrenching figures large in the rhetoric of Earth First! supporters and opponents alike (for a field guide, see Foreman, 1985). The possibilities include pouring emery powder into the crank-cases of earth-moving machines, pouring syrup into fuel tanks, hammering spikes into trees to make it dangerous to cut them, pulling up survey stakes, and destroying logging roads. Since 1997, the impetus has been taken up by the Earth Liberation Front (ELF), whose supporters torched a ski lodge under construction in Vail, Colorado, in 1998, and later set fire to environmentally destructive sports utility vehicles in dealerships.

Monkeywrenching in fiction is far more thoroughgoing: the best accounts remain those of the deep ecological nature writer and novelist Edward Abbey (1975, 1990). The rhetoric and fiction have obviously influenced the United States Federal Bureau of Investigation (FBI), which devoted a great deal of effort to infiltrating Earth First! and entrapping some of its members, including Dave Foreman, in a 1989 plot to blow up power lines. The FBI eventually classified the Earth Liberation Front as the number one terrorist group in the United States, even though no person has ever been injured, let alone killed, as a result of an ELF action. So the term "ecoterrorism," successfully disseminated by anti-environmentalists, is a misnomer. "Ecotage" really is a better description (Vanderheiden, 2008).

In 2005–2006 the FBI-led "Operation Backfire" led to a number of prosecutions of ELF activists. The FBI has been far less diligent in seeking out the perpetrators of the real violence surrounding deep ecology, which comes almost entirely from the anti-ecological side. For example, when a bomb in her car injured Earth First! activist Judi Bari, the authorities initially described it as a case of the activists being blown up by their own bomb; when that account was discredited, no proper effort was made to catch the real bombers. When in 1998 Earth First!er David Chain was killed by a logger felling a tree on him in California's Headwaters Forest, no charges were laid.

Many of those who share green sensibilities do not belong to any group. Many belong to more conventional environmental interest groups. David Brower was perhaps the most visible, militant, and influential figure in conventional environmentalism in the United States from the 1950s to the 1990s, leading the Sierra Club, founding the League of Conservation Voters, Friends of the Earth, and the Earth Island Institute. Green romanticism was quite explicit in his speeches and writings. Not for nothing was he known as the Archdruid (McPhee, 1970).

Green consciousness can also be cultivated in what Torgerson (1999) calls the "carnival" aspect of green politics. Here, industrialism is opposed not just by serious political action, but also by green comedy. Such comedy might include Earth First!-style tree sitting in the United States, Canada, and Australia; the digging and inhabitation of precarious tunnels in the path of motorways by anti-roads activists in Britain; Greenpeace stunts such as installing solar panels on the roof of the house of Australian prime minister John Howard, a die-hard fossil fuel promoter; and Reclaim the Streets' events in London that shut down traffic. Torgerson's carnival would inspire creative thinking about the place of people in their world. If nothing else, green comedy would help prevent greens becoming like their opponents: constipated, serious, strategic, calculating, and gray.

Can green consciousness save the Earth?

Green radicals believe the world needs saving. But is consciousness change up to the task? There are several reasons why it may fall short. The first problem is the practical one of convincing large numbers of people to change the way they relate to the world. How exactly is the green vanguard to convince everyone else? Surveys show that most people, at least in developed countries, already consider themselves environmentalists—61 percent in the United States, according to a 2010 Gallup Poll.[3] Among people under the age of thirty in the United States, this figure is as high as 85 percent (Thiele, 1999: 211). But such commitments are often shallow. While widespread in American high schools, environmental education does not challenge entrenched industrialist worldviews, and imparts only a very thin conception of ecology (Bowers, 1999).

A further problem arises in connection with complexity in ecological affairs. The biologist and environmental activist Barry Commoner argued long ago (1972) that the first law of ecology is that "everything is connected to everything else." While this is a slight overstatement, there is no denying the inherent complexity of ecological problems (see also Dryzek, 1987: 28–9). Interventions in complex systems can produce counterintuitive results, however well intentioned the intervention. Thus good intentions and sensibilities are never sufficient as secure guides to action. For example, it was long believed that the best way to protect ecosystems in the forests of the American West was to suppress fires; ecologists later realized that these ecosystems depended for their renewal on periodic burning. Loving the Earth never guarantees that you will treat it well.

Matters here are made more difficult still once environmental affairs are recognized in terms of crisis. Crisis means that human interactions with the natural world are in severe disequilibrium. Now, improved green sensibilities might be sufficient to maintain an equilibrium in which people lived in harmony with nature, but they cannot tell us how to get from our current severe disequilibrium to this harmonious state. There is no theory of the transition, which surely requires some political program, and some kind of action at the collective level. The problem here is that social, political, and economic structure is more than just a reflection of the attitudes of society's masses or elites, and so changed sensibilities will not necessarily lead to structural change.

Why does social structure matter? The main reason is that macro consequences (in terms of policies, institutions, and events such as revolutions) are rarely if ever a simple extrapolation of micro causes. In Buddhist, Taoist, and Hindu societies, pervasive environmentally sensitive sentiments can coexist with despotic and anti-environmental social, political, and economic systems. There are major issues involved in the aggregation of individual-level preferences, attitudes, and sensibilities into macro-level results (see Coleman, 1986). Speaking as a social scientist, I note that social science only exists because societal and social-structural phenomena are not reducible to individual psychology. So even if there were large-scale conversion of individuals along the lines sought by greens, it is quite possible that nothing at all would change at the macro level. If there is no structural setting which facilitates the articulation of frustration with the old order, the construction of solidarity against that order, and action based on that solidarity, then the old order will survive. Mass psychological and cultural changes can have macro-level consequences, but they are never a simple reflection of micro-level transformations. Psychological changes can be frustrated by a host of factors: electoral systems that discriminate against new parties, market systems that reward and reinforce materialistic and egoistic behavior, social structures that isolate individuals and privatize their concerns, employment structures that make it hard to meet and organize, family structures that either keep women in the home or reinforce privatization by making both male and female income-earners too exhausted to have time for political action.

The most important such structural constraint exists in connection with a global liberal capitalist political economy that is more secure and powerful than ever before (and soon shrugged off the global financial crisis of 2008 to re-affirm its basic character). This political economy conditions not just structures and institutions, but also identities, subjectivities, and discourses. As Lindblom (1982) notes, the market imprisons government policy: there are certain things governments simply must do as a first priority, notably maintain the confidence of capitalist investors. He adds that the market also imprisons the way most people think: if there is a conflict between market imperatives and other values (including environmental ones), it is generally taken for granted that these other values must give way.

Thus the challenge to greens is: how will your proposed alternative consciousness fare in a world currently structured to guarantee its frustration, and moving in a direction that reinforces such frustration? What aspects of the world are conducive to alternative green subjectivities? What aspects get in the way? What is the relative strength of these enabling and constraining forces? How might political and economic structures be changed so as to alter the balance of these forces? Who or what would resist such changes?

It is exactly such questions that the more explicitly political strand of green radicalism seeks to answer.

··

NOTES

1. Miss Ann Thropy is actually Christopher Manes, whose own account of radical environmentalism can be found in Manes (1990).

2. See <http://www.vhemt.org>.

3. <http://www.greenchange.org/article. php?id=5766> (accessed July 1, 2012).

10

....

New Society: Green Politics

Green radicalism is about political change targeted at social structures and institutions as well as consciousness change. This more overtly political emphasis is advanced by a number of movements and schools of thought. Their degree of radicalism varies from eco-anarchists who seek a wholly new and currently very distant kind of society to "realo" greens who in several countries have achieved a share in the power of government.

The varieties of green politics

Green parties

Green radicalism finds its most conventional form of organization in political parties. Green parties have been part of the electoral landscape for over a quarter of a century, and have in several countries (including Belgium, the Czech Republic, Finland, France, Germany, Ireland, and Italy) joined governing coalitions and provided government ministers (especially environment ministers). The German Greens, *Die Grünen,* occupy a central position. The German Green Party was not the world's first—claimants for that title include the United Tasmania Group in Australia and New Zealand's Values Party, both formed in 1972. But the German Greens have long been regarded as the world's most significant, for reasons relating to their size and persisting success (Rüdig, 2012). *Die Grünen* were founded in 1980 and entered the federal *Bundestag* in 1983 with 5.6 percent of the national vote. Their electoral high point came with 10.7 percent of the vote in 2009. Previously in 1998–2005 they had been in a federal governing coalition with the Social Democratic Party. In 2011 the Greens in the German state of

Baden-Württemburg won 24.2 percent of the vote and provided their first state-level prime minister.

The deep national history with which the German Greens have had to cope is one in which romanticism looms large. The romantic reaction against modernity in the eighteenth and nineteenth centuries was stronger in Germany than elsewhere, and bound up with reactionary German nationalism. Later, this combination would gain an environmental edge in a strand within the Nazi Party, which idealized the Nordic natural environment (the Rhine, Black Forest, Alps, etc.) as well as the Nordic race, proposing a mystical connection between race and environment (Brüggemeier et al., 2005). Mindful of this history, the German Greens are wary of romanticism, and especially suspicious of green spirituality (see Capra and Spretnack, 1984: 53–6).

The German Green Party was long divided into *Realo* and *Fundi* factions (the Greens' best-known figure from the early days, Petra Kelly, was eventually reviled by both when she became a media star). *Realos* believe in action through the system, accepting the need for a "long march through the institutions" (Wiesenthal, 1993). They attend closely to vote-maximizing strategies, party organization, and parliamentary tactics, and are open to coalition with other progressive forces, notably the Social Democratic Party. Such coalitions began in government at the city and *Land* (state) levels. *Fundis,* in contrast, believe that the Greens are properly a social movement rather than a political party, and that it is the green task to confront an irrational political system rather than work within it. The most well-known *Fundi,* Rudolf Bahro, left the party noisily in 1985 in protest against its refusal to issue a blanket condemnation of animal experimentation. The dispute between the two factions was largely resolved with the victory of the *Realos* in the early 1990s, under the leadership of Joschka Fischer. But even in his ascendancy Fischer admitted publicly that his main problem was that most members of his party thought he was a jerk. This assessment was not shared by the German electorate. Fischer proved to be a popular foreign minister after the Greens joined a federal governing coalition in 1998, and is widely credited with saving the coalition at the 2002 federal election. By this time Fischer was respected internationally as a leading statesman, a far cry from the fiery radicalism of his youth.

Green *Realos* want to change the world through influence on public policy, not just individual consciousness. Claus Offe's (1990) analysis of the

German Greens treats them as a paradigm case of a new social movement. Offe believes that such movements take on historical significance as the third major wave of protest in modern societies. The first wave was liberal capitalist protest against the rigidities of a feudal society governed by aristocracy and monarchy. The second wave involved socialist protest against the victorious liberal capitalist system. And the third is that of the new social movements, encompassing not just greens but also feminists, peace activists, and various urban protests. Such movements are committed to what Offe (1985: 853) calls a "selective radicalization of modern values," notably freedom, equality, and democracy. Thus they can be located squarely within the Enlightenment emphasis on social progress. Obviously the Greens regard much of what has transpired in the name of modernity—the destruction of nature, the depletion of resources, the bureaucratization of social relationships—as undesirable. But the solution is not to be found merely in changed individual sensibilities, in any return to a preindustrial Eden, or in postmodern playfulness. Rather, it is to be found in hardheaded analysis of social, political, and economic practice and structure. This analysis in turn can best be developed and put into effect through discursive and democratic interaction within the movement.

In the United States, in 2000 the Green ticket of Ralph Nader and Winona Laduke won 2.6 percent of the vote in the presidential election, over 5 percent in eleven states. Nader was accused of denying victory to Democrat Al Gore, and enabling George W. Bush to be installed under dubious circumstances following electoral irregularities in Florida. The US electoral system discriminates against third parties, which find it almost impossible to secure representation under the single-member constituency, simple-plurality voting rule, though Greens have elected representatives in local councils and three state legislatures (Arkansas, California, and Maine). Most environmental groups in the United States therefore shun the Green Party.

Social ecology

Social ecology is associated with the American eco-anarchist Murray Bookchin, (see Biehl, 1997 for an edited collection of his writings). To Bookchin, the root of all evil, in human society and in human relationships with nature, is hierarchy. Hierarchy has arisen only in the last six thousand years or so of human civilization. Whether manifested in the domination of peasants by lords, of women by men, of the countryside by the city, of the young by the old, of workers by capitalists, of society by the state, of nature by people, or of the body by the mind, hierarchy is a profoundly undesirable and unnatural phenomenon. Relationships that humans perceive as competitive or dominating in nature are in fact subtle examples of mutual benefit. For example, herbivores benefit from predation by carnivores because it keeps their populations in check, eliminating frail and diseased members. Nature is not the violent struggle for survival of the fittest which apologists for war and capitalism portray. Instead, nature is a cooperative place, a model for harmonious human society.

Humans for Bookchin are the only bit of nature that has yet achieved self-consciousness. We should not deny this aspect of *our* nature in the name of biocentric egalitarianism. In this light, Bookchin (1986: 75) argues that "we cannot avoid the use of conventional reason, present-day modes of science, and modern technology." The alternative to the hierarchy and competition associated with modern state structures and capitalism involves small-scale, mostly self-sufficient local communities existing in harmony with their neighbors and with their local environment. Bookchin in his later work and his followers in New England have developed ideas about "radical municipalism," which involves the renewal of political institutions from the ground up, starting at the local level. Curran (2006) discerns echoes of social ecology in antiglobalization movements, though movement participants are probably unaware of the connection.

Bookchin reserves his most bitter invective not for oil companies, chemical corporations, or their servants in government, but for other environmentalists. His most frequent target in the 1980s were deep ecologists, denounced as reactionaries guilty of racism and eco-brutalism. For deep ecology, Edward Abbey responded in kind: the late 1980s saw these two sweet old men laying into one another. Abbey at one point threatened to take a quirt (horsewhip) to Bookchin if he ever showed up in Arizona; though Abbey later relented, saying that a fat old woman like Bookchin had nothing to fear from him. Come the 1990s, reconciliation was in the air: Abbey was dead, and Bookchin and Foreman (1991) showed in amicable debate just how much common ground could be found between deep and social ecology.

Bookchin's ideals are at home in the pastoral landscape of Vermont (where the Institute for Social Ecology is located), where an image of humanity and nature in productive harmony is readily envisaged. In the American

West, in contrast, the clash between humanity and nature appears violent and intractable. There, human economic activity takes the form of clear-cut forests, ravaged grazing land, mining scars upon the desert that do not heal, huge dams that destroy riverine ecosystems. Deep ecology has both its most fervent supporters and its most bitter opponents in the West, which is also home to hard-line anti-environmentalism, for which nature exists only as a challenge to be conquered.

Transition towns and new materialism

The transition towns movement is a network of local initiatives that began in 2005 in Kinsale in Ireland and Totnes in England, subsequently growing to involve 500 communities worldwide (mostly in wealthier countries). The ostensible justification is reaction to the failure of national governments and global negotiations to confront climate change and the (more dubious) imminent arrival of peak oil (after which global oil production is supposed to decline). Local governments in the "towns" in the title do not necessarily adopt the whole program, though they may adopt some aspects. Transition towns are actually more of a social movement, promoting self-sufficiency, energy conservation, greenhouse gas emissions reduction, and resilience in the face of environmental threats (Hopkins, 2011). For Barry (2012: 101–8) the movement offers therapy, an action alternative to denial and despair.

Far from embodying post-material values, transition towns manifest a new, sustainable materialism, concerned as they are with how people relate to resources and nonhuman nature, especially when it comes to flows of food, wastes, and energy. Rather than just engage in protest and advocacy, new materialism practices redesign and relocalization of production and distribution in participatory fashion. This impetus is shared by the sustainable food movement, which speaks of "food sovereignty" (Alkon and Agyeman, 2011). While these movements look tiny, they intend to offer glimpses of a feasible alternative world.

Red and green

One of the German Green slogans is "Neither left nor right, but in front." Not all greens agree, least of all in Germany, where there used to be a sizeable Marxist faction within the Greens. Of course, there is much more to the left than Marxism, and so much more to left green thinking than eco-Marxism.

In the early years of environmental resurgence in the 1970s, Marxists typically denounced environmentalism as bourgeois and concerned only with life's pleasures, a distraction from the real stuff of class struggle. Marx himself was a Promethean, who cared about nature mostly for the sake of its conquest. Matters have now changed, and many Marxists are now eco-Marxists. With capitalism's own dynamics having failed to culminate in socialist revolution as Marxists once predicted, they can now look to ecological crisis as a harbinger of a general crisis of capitalism (Foster et al., 2010). On this account, capitalism destroys the ecological base upon which all human economic activity rests. A more rational economic system would not be subject to ecological limits. Kovel and Lowy (2002: 156) speak of a "transformation of needs" that would make limits irrelevant because the economic system would be freed from pursuit of ever-greater quantities of material wealth.

Eco-Marxists see ecological issues as laying bare many of the contradictions of capitalism, and ultimately contributing to its demise, though they are a bit coy on exactly how and when this will happen. Kovel and Lowy (2002: 1) envision an "ecosocialist international" that would unify local and national struggles that currently do not recognize their links to one another, and to the Marxist critique of capitalism. Any alternative political-economic system to replace liberal capitalism would of course have to avoid the gross environmental failings of the countries of the former Soviet bloc—failings which provide plenty of ammunition to anti-Marxists (for example, Lewis, 1992: 163–6).

Eco-Marxists believe that the real explanation for ecological crisis revolves around material economic factors, not anthropocentrism. Human consciousness is relevant only to the extent it can be tied to these forces. Thus they scorn the ecocentric proposals of deep ecologists (Pepper, 1993: 221–5). Eco-Marxism's leading lights include the US sociologist James O'Connor (1988), founder of the journal *Capitalism, Nature, Socialism,* and Joel Kovel (2007).

Environmental justice

The environmental justice movement in the United States has roots in 1978, when the Love Canal Homeowners' Association was organized by residents whose houses turned out to be on top of an abandoned toxic waste dump once operated by the Hooker Chemical Corporation in Buffalo, New York. After dragging its feet, the federal Environmental Protection Agency eventually agreed that this situation was unhealthy and dangerous, and the federal government bought out the residents' homes. Love Canal catapulted Lois Gibbs to stardom; previously an unpolitical working-class housewife, she went on to organize and head the national Citizens' Clearinghouse on Hazardous Waste (later renamed the Center for Health, Environment, and Justice). The other foundational action was a 1982 struggle against plans for a dump for toxic PCBs (polychlorinated biphenyls) in Warren County, North Carolina, a predominantly African-American community. The dump was built, but the idea of "environmental racism" began to achieve prominence.

The environmental justice movement is concerned with the degree to which the environmental risks generated by industrial society fall most heavily on the poor and ethnic minorities (Bullard, 2005). Issues of class and race, traditionally ignored by a mainstream US environmental movement composed mostly of middle-class whites, are highlighted. At issue is not just the unfair distribution of risks and hazards, but also the struggle for recognition of those subject to hazards (Schlosberg, 2009). The risks in question related initially to toxic waste dumps, but concern soon broadened to encompass nuclear facilities, waste incinerators, air and water pollution, mining operations as they threatened the health of rural people (especially Native Americans), pesticide use as it threatened the health of migrant farm workers, mountaintop removal coal mining in Appalachia, and fracking of coal seams to release gas. The movement grew out of thousands of groups organized locally to fight particular environmental threats. Derided by their opponents as having only a NIMBY (Not In My Back Yard) orientation, local groups soon got in touch with each other in conscious pursuit of a goal of NIABY (Not In Anybody's Back Yard). As Lois Gibbs puts it, the idea is to "plug the toilet" on toxic wastes, and force industry to stop producing them in the first place (Dowie, 1995: 126). The movement therefore opposes the risk management paradigm discussed in Chapter 4, seeking instead to prevent the generation of risks.

The distinctive organizational form of the movement is the network (Schlosberg, 1999). Local groups relate to each other without any national leadership or bureaucratic structure. This form is very different from that of the mainstream environmental groups, such as the National Wildlife Federation, Sierra Club, and Environmental Defense Fund, criticized for their plush offices in Washington DC, highly paid chief executives, and easy access to the corridors of power (though Sierra Club Books has published several key environmental justice titles). Lois Gibbs, for one, does not even like being called an environmentalist. As she puts it, environmentalists are people who eat yoghurt, while her people drink Budweiser and smoke (Dowie, 1995: 171).

The networks of the environmental justice movement can bring together otherwise very different kinds of people: for example, white suburban housewives, inner city blacks, and Native Americans on reservations, united in opposition to a particular polluter or an interconnected set of environmental threats. Schlosberg (1999) stresses "critical pluralism," as groups with very different characteristics reach out across their differences in respectful fashion as they engage common adversaries. When it comes to tactics, the movement is eclectic. Like the mainstream, it engages in litigation and lobbying, but it is also more comfortable with confrontational tactics involving demonstrations, blockades, sit-ins, and boycotts.

With its conversion from NIMBY to NIABY strategies, environmental justice eventually raises the structural issue. The implication of "plugging the toilet" is a transformed political economy, one in which hazardous wastes are no longer conceptualized as byproducts to be dealt with as an afterthought. Rather, these wastes are evidence of fundamental irrationality in the system, demanding cure in the form of production planning to eliminate the generation of wastes. Some clear parallels with ecological modernization can be discerned here. The main difference is that ecological modernizers believe capitalist enterprises themselves can seek efficiency and profit through waste minimization, whereas the environmental justice movement believes that such changes can only be forced upon reluctant corporations through political action.

Environmental justice is perhaps only weakly ecological: that is, there is little appreciation of the role played by complex ecosystems in sustaining life on Earth. Yet this lack of appreciation is perhaps a contingent feature stemming from the movement's origins in existing community groups faced with some immediate local health hazards. The movement can only benefit from an appreciation of the ecosystemic nature of things, as this would provide further justification for the network form of social and political organization, and further support for the need radically to overhaul the industrial political economy. Schlosberg (2009) insists that environmental justice should extend to relationships between people and nonhuman nature.

Environmental justice eventually went truly global under the heading of climate justice. Justice arguments permeate global climate change negotiations. Some have nothing to do with green radicalism (or even green moderation), as for example when the United States complains about the injustice of being asked to cut back its emissions while countries like China get a free pass. Other climate justice claims are more consistent with green radicalism. Those mostly responsible for climate change are wealthy consumers who have benefitted from a long history of economic development and fossil fuel use. Those most vulnerable are the rural poor in Africa, low-lying island states, or places like Bangladesh, whose contribution to creating the problem was minimal. The radical version of climate justice involves seeking agency for the world's poor and marginalized at the expense of the large emitters and global market capitalism (Bäckstrand and Lövbrand, 2012). Justice claims are also raised on behalf of the future generations who will feel the consequences of current greenhouse gas emissions. The Climate Justice Now! Network coordinates the efforts of organizations around the world.

Environmentalism of the global poor

Only after some time did the environmental justice movement spread by that name to the developing world (see the special issue of the journal *Environmental Justice* on "Environmental Justice in Latin America," April 2012). However Guha (1997) refers to a long-established "environmentalism of the poor," who experience degraded environments very directly as a result of deforestation, falling water tables, soil erosion, physical displacement by large projects such as dams, industrialized fishing, and high-technology agriculture. One of the first protests in reaction to such assaults was the Chipko movement against logging in India in the 1970s. Other actions have opposed dams, resource reallocation to the wealthy (such as timber companies operating in tropical forests), biopiracy by corporations that steal local ecological knowledge about valuable plant products (and sometimes even try to sell the knowledge back), the privatization of common land, and the creation of debt. The repertoire of such movements now includes nonviolent civil disobedience, hunger strikes, occupations, demonstrations, media publicity, and seeking support from international NGOs. In 2004, Kenyan environmentalist Wangari Maathai won the Nobel Peace Prize. Her Green Belt movement was responsible for planting more than 30 million trees since 1977. The idea is that reforestation fights soil erosion and provides fuel sources; the movement links environmental protection and social justice.

These movements and actions are preoccupied with immediate material needs and so at first sight appear a bit distant from more ecocentric greens in the developed world. Many movements in the Third World are not solely environmental, being linked to independence struggles, anticorruption, political reform, and democracy (Haynes, 1999). *La Via Campesina* international peasants' movement fights for land rights and locally-controlled sustainable agriculture, fighting agribusiness and agrochemicals. *La Via Campesina* is visible on the sidelines of global gatherings such as the 2012 United Nations Conference on Sustainable Development in Rio. Addressing climate change, its slogan is "we peasants can cool the planet!"

To the extent that environmental degradation and economic damage flow from expansion of the global political economy into their land and lives, activists can make common cause with antiglobalization protestors (Shiva, 2005). If a Third World movement can gain the attention of international NGOs, then its cause may prosper. The Ogoni people in Nigeria, fighting both the Nigerian government and oil companies despoiling their land, have been especially successful in this respect, and the Shell corporation tried to change its ways after being embarrassed by the resulting international publicity. However, most struggles fail to make the international limelight, and the attention of NGOs is itself a scarce resource. Sometimes the "environmentalism of the poor" may conflict with environmentalists whose idea of wilderness has no people in it. Indigenous people who have lived on and with this land may even find themselves expelled from land designated as wilderness preserve, becoming what Dowie (2009) calls "conservation refugees." Particularly tragic is the case of Kenya, where Masai, Turkana, and Ndorobo people were expelled in the interests of elephant conservation in the early 1990s (Haynes, 1999: 230–2).

Antiglobalization, global justice, and Occupy

The antiglobalization movement came to public attention following street battles outside the 1999 meeting of the World Trade Organization (WTO) in Seattle. Since then, meetings of the WTO, World Economic Forum, International Monetary Fund (IMF), and G8 group of wealthy economies are normally accompanied by protests, except when they are held in places like Qatar where protestors are not admitted. The protests are the visible manifestations of a larger network of discontent. Unlike some more established social movements, the protestors do not really have a coherent program, still less an alternative to global capitalism. Even the term "antiglobalization" is really just journalistic shorthand, an over-simplification given that protest itself is globalized. The protests were initially ridiculed by the global economic establishment and its supportive media, but this establishment has been forced to notice and address a range of concerns it had previously ignored under its drive for free trade and capital mobility. The particular concerns of the protestors have included the political power of multinational corporations, the effect of marketization on the global environment, lax labor practices such as sweatshops and child labor, loss of jobs in high-wage societies, and unfair terms of trade between rich and poor countries. Only some of the concerns have an environmental aspect. With time, the various concerns begin to coalesce into a more coherent critique of global capitalism.

Given the fluidity and variety it embodies, the movement can be interpreted in several different ways. Organizationally, it resembles the kind of network pioneered earlier by the environmental justice movement, taking networks and associated respect for diverse identities and positions across national boundaries. The carnival-like atmosphere of the street protests resonates with Torgerson's (1999) proposals for a green public sphere that downplays the goal-oriented logic of environmental politics and its social movements.

The Occupy movements that began with Occupy Wall Street in 2011 are likewise multifaceted protests against the excesses of banks and corporate capitalism. Environmental concerns can be raised as part of the critique, for example in the DisruptDirtyPower.org spinoff from Occupy Wall Street.

Radical summits

International conferences on environmental and economic affairs are routinely accompanied by parallel gatherings of radical activists. Nowhere is this more evident than in the case of the annual Conference of the Parties to the UN Framework Convention on Climate Change. So for example the 2009 Conference of the Parties in Copenhagen (COP-15) was shadowed by Klimaforum09 in a different venue in the city. Around 50,000 people attended the Klimaforum over two weeks. Participants articulated a wide range of radical positions, including indigenous peoples' rights, militant vegetarianism, ecofeminism, de-growth, and climate justice. The discourse was very different to that in the official negotiations, though a few states' delegations (notably Bolivia) selectively adopted and articulated radical concerns.

The Bolivian government of President Evo Morales responded to the failure of COP-15 to secure any meaningful binding agreement by organizing and hosting a 2010 People's World Summit on Climate Change and Mother Earth Rights in the city of Cochabamba in 2010 (see Stevenson, 2011). This summit attracted 35,000 participants from 140 countries, though the majority was from Bolivia itself. Indigenous peoples organizations and *La Via Campesina* were prominent. The Cochabamba platform was avowedly anticapitalist, treating climate change as the fault of global capitalism, seeking radical solutions (though the "Peoples' Agreement" produced by the Summit also recognized the need for effective global organizations). Some of the options canvassed were local self-reliance, organic agriculture, alternative small-scale technologies, and community control. Some of these looked like a return to the pre-Brundtland 1970s roots of sustainable development, when it was an alternative developmental discourse for the Third World. The "Mother Earth" in the title of the Summit indicated a tinge of green spirituality.

Discourse analysis of green politics

The story line of radical green politics points to multifaceted social and ecological crises that can only be resolved through political action and structural change. Alternative forms of consciousness may be welcome as part of this project, but both the causes of crisis and the required approaches to solution involve a lot more. Complex social relations are at issue too, and action needs to take place both within and upon these relationships.

Basic entities whose existence is recognized or constructed

Green radicalism's urgency in the face of crisis is backed by recognition of ecological limits (though in eco-Marxism such limits are treated as applying only to capitalism, and in environmental justice and the environmentalism of the global poor limits receive little explicit attention). Nature is recognized in the form of complex ecosystems whose wellbeing requires that humans change their ways. But the necessary change is not simply cultural. Green politics emphasizes reflection and reasoning, though this does not mean that humans have to be *Homo economicus* individuals, concerned only with calculation of what is in their own immediate material interest. Human horizons can and should be much wider. In contrast to a more cultural approach, social, political, and economic structures are recognized as having an important influence that cannot be reduced to the sensibilities of the individuals inhabiting them.

Assumptions about natural relationships

Green politics assumes a natural relationship of equality across individuals, at least in terms of the capacity to engage in reasoned communication about collective ends. Hierarchy that both predates and is reinforced by modernity is recognized and condemned. The most elaborate analysis of hierarchy comes in social ecology, whose political philosophy is rooted in a demonstration of the unnaturalness of hierarchy of all kinds.

Despite its core egalitarianism, green politics can allow compromise with other kinds of relationships, such as competitive ones, especially in its contemplation of economic systems. Such competitive relationships should, however, be kept in check by more egalitarian political structures. The precise character of desirable political structures is disputed. There is a substantial gap between the quasi-anarchism of social ecology, the localism of transition towns, and the statism of *Realo* greens.

When it comes to specifying appropriate relationships linking human systems and natural systems, there is (or can be) a strong conception of complex ecological connections. Unlike deep ecology this conception does not have to reduce to any simple biocentric egalitarianism. Humans can be set apart from nature by virtue of their reasoning capacities, but this does not warrant hierarchy and domination of nature. A stewardship relationship is more likely to be posited.

Agents and their motives

Political agency is granted to a variety of actors, both individual and collective, and so encompasses movements, parties, states, and international organizations as well as persons. Collective actors are central to this side of green politics, in contrast to the more individualistic emphasis in green consciousness change. The possibility that there might be agency in nature is generally downplayed, except in social ecology (see also Dryzek, 1990a).

Green radical politics is likely to treat the essence of human motivation as multidimensional, at once competitive and cooperative, violent and peaceful, instrumental and communicative, selfish and public-spirited. Political life is mainly about promoting institutional structure and political action to evoke the more benign motivation in each of these pairs, and control the more nefarious one.

Key metaphors and other rhetorical devices

Over the last few hundred years, the modern world has been constructed in terms of mechanistic images of both human social systems and natural systems (as we have seen in earlier discussions of Promethean discourse and economic rationalism). Greens reject this imagery. Metaphors present in green radical politics are perhaps less vivid and colorful than those featured in green cultural change, though there is a shared emphasis on organic metaphors. The world is approached in terms of organic balance, where wholes cannot be understood by reduction to their component parts, and living things interact in ways that can never be understood fully. Human systems may be irrational at present (committed, for example, to blind pursuit of material riches, to economic growth at the expense of the global climate, or the generation of toxic wastes with nowhere to put them), but they are capable of a greater rationality in their interactions with natural systems. We can apply standards of ecological rationality to the analysis and redesign of these systems. Social systems, like individuals, must be treated as capable of learning.

Green politics involves argument, not just appeal to the emotions. The accompanying rhetoric is likely to appeal to ideals of progress beyond an irrational industrial order, rather than promise return to some primal Eden. Like sustainable development and ecological modernization, a belief in progress can make reference to a model of individual human development.

Box 10.1 provides a summary of the discourse analysis of green politics.

Green politics in practice

Green political action has sought to change institutions, practices, and poli-cies. Its impact should be sought not just in the tangible achievements of particular parties, networks, or other green organizations, but also in the degree to which green discourse has permeated political-economic life more generally.

Green parties have been represented in the parliaments of an increas-ing number of countries since 1981, when the Francophone Ecolo and Flemish Agalev parties won seats in the Belgian parliament. The success of green parties in winning seats depends crucially on the kind of electoral system in operation. The first-past-the-post or simple plurality system dis-advantages small parties and hinders their growth, explaining the minor electoral impact of green parties in the United States and United Kingdom. However, in 2010 the British Greens showed the barrier is not completely insuperable by winning the seat of Brighton Pavilion in the general elec-tion (with 31.3 percent of the vote). The simple plurality system was long the norm in the English-speaking world, though even here proportional

---

BOX 10.1   Discourse analysis of green politics

1. **Basic entities recognized or constructed**
   - Global limits
   - Nature as complex ecosystems
   - Humans with broad capacities
   - Social, economic, and political structures
2. **Assumptions about natural relationships**
   - Equality among people
   - Complex interconnections between humans and nature
3. **Agents and their motives**
   - Many individual and collective actors, multidimensional motivation
   - Agency in nature downplayed though not necessarily denied
4. **Key metaphors and other rhetorical devices**
   - Organic metaphors
   - Appeals to social learning
   - Link to progress

representation can be found in the Irish Republic, the Welsh and Scottish assemblies, upper houses in Australian parliaments, and the parliament of New Zealand, in all of which green parties have secured seats. Proportional representation advantages all small and emerging parties, not just green ones. Green parliamentary representation has long been important in the German *Bundestag,* and in 1998 *Die Grünen* joined a federal governing coalition for the first time.

The trajectory of green votes seats reveals growth in the number of countries with electorally significant green parties, but only gradual take-off in the strength of votes beyond single percentage points into the teens. Greens can, though, point to the degree to which voters in post-industrial societies should in principle be sympathetic to many of the values that green parties stand for (see Inglehart, 1990).

Green parties have also forced more established "gray" parties, and the political system as a whole, to craft responses to the green electoral threat. The development of the discourse of ecological modernization detailed in Chapter 8 can be interpreted as an attempt by the prevailing political order to head off the green challenge. Ecological modernization has developed in the European heartland of green party politics, and has appropriated more than a few ideas originally developed by the greens. Certainly, ecological modernization lacks the radical edge of green politics. Yet it still posits a structural transformation of capitalism. The irony is that if this transformation succeeds it will deprive green radicalism of its bite by showing that transition to a totally different political economy is unnecessary. The historical parallel here is with the rise of socialism, which in the early to mid-twentieth century forced the capitalist political economy to develop welfare states and full employment practices, thus blunting the radical edge of the socialist critique of capitalism. The difference is that socialist parties could often dominate parliamentary majorities, and sometimes formed governments by themselves.

Green parties have, however, participated in governing coalitions in city, state, and national governments in several European countries, normally alongside parties of the social democratic left. No program of wholesale political-economic transformation has yet come from any such coalition. The price of participation in government has often been a heavy one in terms of moderation of green demands, though there are exceptions. Green parties can rarely make a credible threat of defection to a coalition with larger right-wing parties, and so their social-democratic coalition partners can sometimes take their support for granted (Poguntke, 2002: 138).

The most significant achievement of a green party in power may be the planned phaseout of nuclear power secured by the German Greens after 1998. While this plan was to take effect over several decades, so it could be reversed by a subsequent government. In 2011 the Green-less conservative government of Angela Merkel confirmed the phaseout, largely in response to the public reaction to the meltdowns at Fukushima in Japan. The German Greens were actually quite successful in preventing the construction of nuclear installations in their prior days as an oppositional social movement (for example, in forcing the cancellation of a reprocessing plant at Wackensdorf in 1989). In Australia, after national elections in 2010, the Greens held the balance of power in the Senate, and as part of a deal with the Labor government secured passage of a carbon tax to control greenhouse gas emissions that came into force in 2012.

Yet to focus on the limited policy impact by green parties in government would be to miss the crucial role of green discourse in transforming the terms of political debate, and requiring other parties to adjust their positions on environmental issues and other green concerns. The German Greens have a name for this: *themenklau,* the stealing of green ideas by gray parties.

Not everyone within the green movement believes that electoral politics is the proper focus of green energies. Political life can also cover discussions in bars, coffee shops, and social media, community organizing, educational efforts, self-help groups, boycotts, demonstrations, strikes, blockades, ecotage, sit-ins, internet campaigns (such as those sponsored by Avaaz.org on climate change), and various kinds of media events. Greenpeace specializes in media events—for example, inserting a plug into the end of a pipeline discharging radioactive waste into the Irish Sea from the British Nuclear Fuels Ltd. installation at Sellafield, pulling up genetically modified crops, boarding a Shell oil exploration ship bound for the Arctic, draping banners from the smokestacks of coal-burning power stations. Sea Shepherd harasses Japanese whaling ships in the Southern Ocean. With time, the green direct action repertoire expands. In Britain (and later elsewhere), Reclaim the Streets developed the tactic of shutting down traffic on urban streets, organizing by word of mouth and the internet in order to beat the police to a site. In the British countryside, tree-sitters and tunnelers put themselves in the way of motorway construction—winning the public relations war even as each road was eventually constructed (Doherty, 1999). To avoid the grasp of government and its compliant legal system, these British activists did not organize formally. These unorganized groups were unfettered in their activism, and did not have to worry about their assets being seized or their access to government threatened. Such worries frightened off more established groups such as Friends of the Earth, which looked uncomfortable: their heart was with the protestors, but expediency meant they had to keep their distance (Rootes, 2003: 5–6). Later, week-long "climate camps" targeted coal-burning power stations and Heathrow Airport. After 2006 Plane Stupid carried out a series of airport blockades in the UK, again without any formal organization that could have its assets seized.

In Germany, antinuclear protests on a large scale continued after the Greens joined the federal governing coalition. In 2001 these protests targeted shipments of nuclear wastes for reprocessing. In 2011, antinuclear protests in many German cities following the Fukushima meltdowns helped convince the government to confirm that Germany would eventually abandon nuclear power.

Shunning the state in favor of movement politics might seem to some an abdication of ambition, even of responsibility, leading to voluntary exile in a political wasteland. But such a perception is in error. Political pressure can be exerted at a distance upon the state. Here, social movements have at their disposal a number of instruments. They include the rhetorical ability to change the terms of policy debate, creation of fear of political instability, the production of ideas, and the embarrassment of governments. Much of the success of the antiglobalization/global justice/occupy movements since 1999 can be interpreted in these terms. The movements have forced social justice and environmental issues onto the agenda of economic organizations such as the WTO and IMF.

Pressure from a distance also embodies the hopes (if not yet accomplishments) of the radical forums that accompany global environmental negotiations, such as the UN Framework Convention on Climate Change. Those in the official negotiations are certainly aware of the presence of the radicals, but this does not mean what goes on in the parallel radical forums has much impact on the negotiations. There are some means through which messages get through. Sympathetic states such as Bolivia may pick up arguments. The Climate Action Network (CAN) that coordinates nongovernmental climate activists has a presence inside the negotiating hall, conducting a colorful

"Fossil of the Day" ceremony that "honors" the country deemed to have been most obstructive in that day's negotiations (Canada is a perennial winner). The efforts of CAN do sometimes force negotiators to reflect upon and justify their positions, though rarely to change them.

When it comes to changing public ideas and attitudes, it is hard to disentangle the relative influence of more mainstream environmentalism and green radicalism, but at least in Europe the established mainstream environmental groups (such as the Council for the Protection of Rural England, the World Wildlife Fund, and *Deutsch Naturschutzring*) have been rather staid and unimaginative. They were around long before the 1970s upsurge in green politics, with very little to show in terms of value change in society at large. It is the green radicals who have made the running in instigating change in ideas and attitudes, which extends to those who do not vote for green parties, still less join more radical green actions. Aspects of this change include (dim) awareness of ecological limits, sensitivity to the risks generated by industrial society in terms of chemical, nuclear, and biotechnological hazards, and recognition of the possibilities for a more convivial way of life than the aggressively individualistic materialism of contemporary market society. Green radicalism has had less success in achieving broad acceptance of its core values relating to grassroots democracy and structural change in the political economy.

Green politics itself helps to constitute a parallel political society where at least some individuals can lead their social and political lives, an alternative to the gray mainstream of party politics (see Dryzek, 1996a: 46–53). This "green public sphere" acts as a standing reminder to industrial society of the error of its ways, a place where critiques can be generated and alternatives explored (Torgerson, 1999). This parallel polity can be oriented to the public policy debates of the day, even as a critical distance from mainstream politics is maintained. This kind of oppositional sphere was long the hallmark of green politics in Germany, especially when environmentalists lacked any points of access to government. Lack of access did not necessarily mean lack of influence, especially when it came to blocking environmentally destructive projects such as nuclear plants. And when the German government did open up in the 1990s, activists who had honed their skills and critiques in a radical public sphere sometimes succeeded in getting critical concerns onto the policy agenda, if not necessarily into policy practice (Dryzek et al., 2003: 190–1).

Green politics can also involve action oriented to the solution of particular well-defined problems in a fashion that attempts to reclaim political authority from the state. For example, in 1995 Greenpeace activists occupied the Brent Spar, an oil storage platform whose working life in the North Sea had come to an end. The Shell corporation intended to dispose of the platform by towing it into deeper water in the North Atlantic and sinking it. The publicity generated by Greenpeace, which also organized a consumer boycott of Shell throughout Europe, forced the company to change its plans and dispose of the platform on land. Shell's decision angered the British government, which was prepared to use force to evict the Greenpeace protestors. In this case at least, green activists possessed more political authority in relation to Shell than did the British government. In another case from the early 1990s, Greenpeace succeeded in persuading German paper companies to stop using chlorine to bleach paper. The key point in the campaign came when Greenpeace printed a plagiarized edition of *Der Spiegel,* the leading news weekly, on paper bleached without chlorine, with a hardly noticeable difference in quality.

Another case of such reclamation of political authority arises with the practice of "popular epidemiology," or community-based research on risk assessment. The paradigm case occurred in the community of Woburn in Massachusetts, where citizens angered by government denial that any problem existed organized a group called FACE (For a Clean Environment) which then conducted its own survey of the incidence of leukemia and birth defects which its members believed were linked to toxic waste sites. State and federal government agencies rejected this effort, arguing that the citizen risk investigators had no proper training in risk assessment, such that their findings were unreliable. Yet the results assembled by FACE were used as evidence in a lawsuit which was eventually settled out of court by one of the companies that had dumped toxics (see Brown and Mikkelsen, 1990). This case formed the basis for the 1998 film *A Civil Action,* starring John Travolta.

More recently, the transition towns movement embodies an attempt to reclaim authority from national governments and global bodies that have failed to act effectively on climate change and other environmental issues. The movement acts locally, even as it has its eye firmly on global questions.

In the United States, tangible impacts are associated with the environmental justice movement. The movement has moved on a variety of fronts, involving conventional litigation and lobbying as well as demonstrations, blockades, and boycotts. In the negative, the movement has achieved many victories, blocking plans for noxious facilities and forcing corporations and governments to compensate victims. The toilet is well and truly plugged. As yet, this plugging has not led to any real movement toward a greener economy. However, the simple presence of environmental justice and its network form of organization is itself a significant political development in green and democratic politics.

Environmental justice has permeated the highest levels of policy making in the United States, Institutionalization came in the form of the Office of Environmental Justice and the National Environmental Justice Advisory Committee, both associated with the federal EPA, as well as a Federal Interagency Working Group on Environmental Justice. The result is something like a governance network of the sort discussed in Chapters 4 and 5, linked to a social movement network. As EPA Administrator Lisa Jackson put it on the Interagency Group's web site in 2010, "Our continued success depends on close collaboration with our federal partners and strong input from the groups and individuals engaged at the community level."[1]

The environmentalism of the global poor is highly varied in its content and strategies, and so its impact defies easy summary. There have been local successes in (for example) forcing oil companies to clean up their operations, preventing the construction of large dams, and slowing deforestation. More positive projects include experiments in agroecology and community control of resources. But structural change in the political economy generally remains a remote prospect, and the reach of the globalized political economy continues to grow.

Being green in global capitalist times

In the last four decades or so green radicalism has come from nowhere to develop a comprehensive critique of the environmental, social, political, and economic shortcomings of industrial society. As such, it represents perhaps the most significant ideological development of the late twentieth century. Yet there remains a great deal of uncertainty about the best way to practice green politics in the face of a seemingly recalcitrant and secure liberal capitalist political economy, increasingly entrenched at the global level beyond the control of most national governments. This political economy is reinforced by several of the discourses analyzed in earlier chapters. Market-oriented Prometheans of course have nothing but scorn for green critiques, and when they do address green thinking completely trivialize it. The three problem-solving discourses see no need for the kind of wholesale structural change green rationalists seek. Sustainable development and ecological moderniza-tion are more likely to take these concerns seriously, but believe a structural response can be crafted that does not involve abandoning the basic param-eters of liberal capitalism, even as they are uneasy with the global spread of market liberalism.

So just what kind of alternative political economy do greens want? Is capitalism to be overthrown, transcended, or transformed? Certainly, capi-talism as it currently stands is regarded as unacceptable, but most greens remain uncertain about exactly what to do with it. Even eco-Marxists are a bit coy about whether they envisage capitalism being overthrown in favor of some socialist alternative, or even gradually transformed into such an alternative. These viewpoints perhaps make more sense as critical devices, in which socialism is raised mainly as a way of highlighting the flaws of capitalism, the real-world prospects for any kind of socialism (be it reform-ist or revolutionary) having receded rather dramatically.

But to demand a blueprint for an alternative society may be asking too much. If the twentieth century holds one political lesson, it is that we should beware of anyone peddling such blueprints, be they socialist paradises, fascist Reichs to last a thousand years, or free-market utopias popularized in the Anglo-American world in the 1980s and exported in the form of "shock therapy" to several East European countries after 1989. Whatever the leanings of their advocates and supporters, such blueprints inevitably go wrong when confronted with the complexities of the real world, and bring at best only the kind of state centralization and authoritarianism introduced in Britain by Margaret Thatcher (ironically alongside a rhetoric of freedom and choice). At worst, they bring totalitarianism and a police state. The explanation is simple: as soon as real world surprises come along, proponents of the blue-print feel they have to save it via increasingly coercive measures. The notion that the blueprint itself may be flawed never crosses their minds (for more detail on this general argument, see Popper, 1966, 1972; for an application to free-market utopias in Eastern Europe, see Pickel, 1993).

In this light, the fact that greens do not have any well-defined blueprint for a new society twinned with a coordinated strategy for achieving it is actually a point in their favor. What greens do have in abundance are ideas that can be pressed into a decentered approach to the achievement of a greener society, where there is room for a variety of experiments whose general orientation is given by green discourse, but whose specifics can vary quite substantially. Such variety is the essence of the green public sphere (Torgerson, 1999). Bioregional projects, networks of community activists, oppositional political forums, experiments in local grassroots democracy, social ecology's radical municipalism, transition towns, and attempts to radicalize democratic pragmatist initiatives of the sort discussed in Chapter 5 can all fit in here.

Such a decentralized approach fits quite nicely with green ideas about local initiative and community self-control. However, can such a loosely coordinated set of responses ever be adequate in the face of a liberal capitalist political economy which is more secure and more entrenched than ever before in history? This system is increasingly geared to free trade, economic growth, and the mobility of investment capital across national boundaries. It is this system which is the dominant political reality of our times. Almost all national, regional, and local governments now see it as their first task to accommodate themselves to the imperatives of this system, to keep investors happy by promoting a positive climate for business. A decentered program of green initiatives might appear just a minor set of irritants to this monolithic, global, transnational capitalist political economy. If in the face of this behemoth green politics is to be more than theater, then perhaps it has something to learn from other discourses of environmental concern. Some possibilities along these lines are addressed in the concluding chapter.

....

NOTE

1. <http://epa.gov/environmentaljustice/ interagency/index.html>(accessed July 4, 2012).

PART VI
CONCLUSION

11

....

Ecological Democracy

Each of the discourses analyzed in this book offers a reasonably comprehensive account of and orientation to environmental affairs at all levels, from the global to the local, and across different issue areas (pollution, resource depletion, biodiversity, climate change, and so forth). With these competing comprehensive visions in mind, any intelligent approach to environmental issues demands two things. The first is a dynamic, structural-level analysis of the liberal capitalist political economy, where it might be headed, and what realistically can be done to alter this trajectory to more ecologically benign ends. For a globally organized liberal capitalism mostly insensitive to environmental concerns is the dominant political fact of our times. Its confidence was only momentarily shaken by global financial crisis in 2008. Without an analysis of this system, we are reduced to wishful thinking about how things might be different, while in practice any collision between environmental concerns and the economic priorities of the system and its national and global institutions, environmental concerns lose. Of the discourses surveyed, only Promethean discourse and ecological modernization provide any coherent analysis of what to do with the liberal capitalist economic order (a discourse of limits wants it to be different, and green radicalism may want to replace it, but neither can explain how).

Market-committed Prometheans of course believe that the current trajectory of liberal capitalism is unproblematic, and that all we need do is leave it alone to provide abundance for humanity, in the future as in the past. Promethean environmentalists do however see a role for government in promoting and financing the transition to abundant and clean energy technologies. Ecological modernizers recognize that laissez-faire liberal capitalism is environmentally destructive. Thus they seek an ecological restructuring of capitalism. If one rejects the Promethean denial of limits, constraints, and boundaries—and I argued in Chapter 3 that there are good reasons to do so—then the second quality demanded by an intelligent approach to environmental affairs comes into play.

This second quality is the capacity to facilitate and engage in collective learning in an ecological context. Environmental issues feature high degrees of uncertainty and complexity, which are magnified as ecological systems interact with social, economic, and political systems. Thus we need institutions and discourses which are capable of learning—not least about their own shortcomings. The antithesis of learning can be found in the efforts of the organized climate change denial movement discussed in Chapter 3, whose intention is to manipulate knowledge to serve power.

Discourses do change with time; but does this connote learning? The discourse of limits and survival develops into planetary boundaries, not quite the same concept as the limits of the 1970s. Some Prometheans came to accept the reality of climate change and the need for coordinated (but high-technology) response. Sustainable development eventually adopts the language of green growth. Ecological modernization takes on the idea of transition management. Administrative rationalism yields to networked governance. Green radicalism increasingly takes on issues of social justice, including global climate justice. Not all these changes connote learning: so green growth can look like a regressive accommodation with the realities of global capitalism, pushed by large corporations, further marginalizing the sustainability and social justice concerns that once animated sustainable development. Any shift from government to governance does not necessarily yield better results if governance is dominated by the same old actors committed to the same old imperatives. Further impediments to learning can be found to the degree that particular discourses have complete confidence in the correctness of their interpretations and prescriptions; such confidence pervades limits, Promethean, administrative rationalist, and economic rationalist discourses. Yet none of these is actually monolithic, and democratic pragmatism, sustainable development, ecological modernization, and green radicalism seem to provide more possibilities for learning.

From democratic pragmatism come discursive procedures for the resolution of disputes through cooperative problem solving. Such procedures, including policy dialogue, environmental mediation, lay citizen deliberation, governance networks, and societal dialogues, are often limited in their scope and constrained by the structural context in which they operate. Critics of them rightly note that they can involve co-optation and neutralization of troublemakers by powerful government and corporate officials. The key, then, is try to break these shackles, moving such procedures in the direction of what I described long ago as discursive designs, which point to a more radical democracy. Discursive designs involve collective decision making through authentic democratic discussion, open to all interests, under which political power, money, and strategizing do not determine outcomes (see Dryzek, 1990b: 29–56). A careful search reveals an ever-growing number of cases (see also Smith, 2009).

From sustainable development comes the possibility of a decentered approach to the pursuit of sustainability. While at first glance the sheer variety of available definitions of sustainable development seems like a defect of this discourse, from the perspective of social learning it is a distinct advantage, for it does not rule out a variety of experiments in what sustainability can mean in different contexts, including the global context. A decentered approach to sustainability meshes quite nicely with discursive designs, which could find roles as the steering institutions and reflective components of experiments in sustainability—as Torgerson (1994, 1995) also recognizes.

From ecological modernization comes the possibility of a "strong" or "reflexive" version of the discourse, the essence of which goes beyond retooling of the economy with waste reduction and profitability in mind. Here it is possible to think more seriously about transition, in particular to energy systems beyond fossil fuels. Ecological modernization so radicalized can involve institutional change in the direction of democratic experimentation, and open-ended exploration of what ecological modernization itself might mean. The very idea of reflexive development is that it is self-monitoring and critically aware of itself, thus conducive to social learning. Again, this fits quite nicely with a decentered approach to sustainability and discursive designs.

From green radicalism, with support from limits and boundaries, come the reasons why democratic pragmatism, sustainable development, and ecological modernization need to be radicalized to begin with. The old survivalist flirtation with authoritarianism alienated democratic pragmatists, sustainable developers, and ecological modernizers alike, but that is (mostly) in the past. Green cultural change can also contribute here to the extent its adherents can become interested and involved in social institutions. Green radicalism can also remind us that oppositional politics in the public sphere and social movements can play a key role in social learning, which does not have to be tied to conventional politics (and may indeed proceed more readily outside the realm of conventional politics). Green politics can further bring to bear plenty of ideas about how political and economic institutions might look in an ecological future beyond industrial society. Linking these ideas to the other three discourses is a way of grounding such ideas in a more realistic analysis of how the future can actually unfold, as opposed to wishful thinking about how it should unfold.

The common thread that can be developed here is a renewed democratic politics, an ecological democracy.[1] It is the communicative aspect of democracy that proves to do most of the work—rather than the more familiar electoral aspect. This communicative aspect has been developed in both theory and practice under the banner of deliberative democracy. Deliberative democracy rests on the idea that legitimate governance depends on the right, opportunity, and capacity of those subject to a collective decision (or their representatives) to participate in consequential deliberation about that decision. Deliberation involves reaching judgments and reflecting upon preferences in the context of dialogue that is informed, respectful, and competent. Communication should be noncoercive, strive to connect any particular claims to more general concerns, and to reach others who do not share the conceptual framework of the speaker. Several specific claims can be made on behalf of deliberative democracy in an environmental context (Baber and Bartlett, 2007; Dryzek and Stevenson, 2011; Smith 2003).

The first claim is that deliberation is a particularly good way of integrating the different perspectives that inevitably attend any complex issue. The perspectives that need coordinating can be those of experts (such as ecologists and economists), representatives of people concerned with different kinds of values (such as environmental justice, biodiversity, community wellbeing), and ordinary citizens, who might be in possession of substantial local knowledge.

The second claim is that deliberation is particularly good at generating and assimilating feedback on the state of social-ecological systems, provided it is inclusive of the discourses that interpret the various aspects of those systems. Deliberation is about listening as well as speaking (Dobson, 2010)—including listening to news about the condition of vital systems. A discourse stressing environmental justice will highlight different concerns than one stressing planetary boundaries, but both can generate crucial kinds of information.

The third claim is that the kinds of values that can survive authentic democratic deliberation are those oriented to the interests of the community as a whole, rather than selfish interests within the community (or outside it). Arguments based on public goods or shared interests are more persuasive than those based on self-interest. Foremost among such common interests is the integrity of the ecological base upon which society depends. From green radicalism comes a reminder that existing liberal democracies typically frustrate such processes: the influence of power, money, and strategy need to be unmasked and countered, as does the degree to which human communities have lost any sense of their ecological foundations.

The fourth claim is that deliberation inspires people to think not just about their own interests and those of others present in the deliberative forum—but also about those not physically present. Foremost among those not physically present are future generations and nonhuman nature (Goodin, 1996).

The fifth claim is that deliberation ought to be good at generating creative solutions to problems; the evidence for this claim comes mostly from the literature on environmental conflict resolution, where the key to resolution of a dispute is often finding a new way to meet the core concerns of parties to that dispute, such as environmentalists and developers (see Chapter 5).

The sixth claim is that deliberation enables interpretation of what a general principle actually means when it comes to application to a particular case. That principle might be climate justice; or it might be sustainability.

The final claim is that deliberative processes have a self-critical aspect: they are good at identifying their own deficiencies, and if necessary correcting for them (for example, by including a broader variety of participants, or recognizing they need to give further consideration to particular sorts of issues).

Authentic communication is central to deliberative democracy. Overcoming the impediments that distort such communication is crucial. One such impediment, ignored in the history of democratic theory but now exposed by the rise of green thinking, concerns communication with the nonhuman world. It would be absurd to think of that world as having preferences, or able to "vote," which is why most models of democracy are of limited applicability in a green context. But the nonhuman world can communicate, and human decision processes can be structured so as to listen to its communications more or less well. Large bureaucracies operating according to standard procedures insensitive to local ecological contexts fail this test; bioregional authorities governed by citizens with a thorough knowledge of local circumstances are likely to do much better.

Ecological democracy should transcend the boundary between human social systems and natural systems. There is an additional sense in which ecological democracy is democracy beyond boundaries. Ecological problems and issues transcend established governmental jurisdictions, such that democratic exercises may need to be constituted in order to fit the size and scope of particular issues. When established authority in governmental jurisdictions is recalcitrant, then such forums may need to be constituted as oppositional democratic spheres, of the sort we see in radical summits in parallel to international negotiations.

This sort of ecological democracy beyond boundaries is clearly very different from the institutions established by and in industrial society whose priorities still dominate today's world. However, occasionally crises can enable environmental concerns to come into alignment with those concerns, and so advances can be made in terms of both the democratization and greening of dominant institutions. Examples here would include the legitimation crisis faced by the Nixon administration around 1970, which was defused by reaching out to environmentalists as the least radical element of the counter-culture, and led to a burst of environmental legislation as well as inclusion of (moderate) environmentalists in government. Risk-related crises in Europe related to food safety (mad cow disease and genetically modified organisms) have had less thoroughgoing but still significant impact. But there are no guarantees that crisis advances democracy. Environmental authoritarianism today has fewer proponents than in the 1970s, but has undergone recent revival in connection with the seeming ability of China to respond to crisis by taking decisive action on some fronts—especially renewable energy.

Ecological modernization allows a more persistent link with the key economic priority of governments. At the national level, the most prominent political configuration that currently looks at all feasible would feature a consensual corporatist state pursuing ecological modernization confronted by a lively green public sphere. Germany has at times seemed the best example of such a combination—though of course Germany is far from being an ecological democracy. One hazard accompanying the inclusion of greens and environmentalists in corporatist government is depletion of the public sphere, as former activists are attracted into government, and accept moderation as the price to be paid. This situation characterizes Norway, a top performer in cross-national environmental comparisons, but with no social movements or oppositional public sphere to push the country further (Dryzek et al., 2003).

Many of the more significant ecological problems do of course transcend national boundaries. Global environmental governance is underperforming, as epitomized by continuing impasse on responding to climate change. The basic ideas of ecological democracy can be applied to the global level no less than elsewhere (though that level has long been resistant to democracy of any sort). This application would envisage a more effective global deliberative system that, just like such systems within more successful states, features relatively consensual construction of public authority in combination with a lively and contestatory public sphere (see Dryzek and Stevenson, 2011 for details). Public authority need not look anything like a world government. It does not have to be universal in membership, and could involve governance networks as discussed in Chapters 4 and 5. If such public authority proves unobtainable, then the pursuit of transnational and global ecological democracy needs to rest still further on the conditions of contestation and engagement of discourses in the global public sphere—remembering that discourses can coordinate governance in the absence of formal institutions.

For discourses, including environmental ones, help to constitute and reconstitute the world just as surely as do formal institutions or material economic forces. Environmentalism already flourishes in opposition to industrialism; but much remains to be done if industrial society is ever to give way to ecological society.

....

NOTE

1. More extensive discussion of ecological democracy may be found in some of my other writings (for example, Dryzek, 1987, 1990a,).

REFERENCES

ABBEY, EDWARD (1975), *The Monkey Wrench Gang*. Philadelphia, Pa.: J. B. Lippincott.

—— (1990), *Hayduke Lives!* Boston, Mass.: Little, Brown.

ACKERMAN, BRUCE A. and HASSLER, WILLIAM T. (1981), *Clean Coal, Dirty Air: or How the Clean Air Act became a Multibillion-Dollar Bail-Out for High-Sulfur Coal Producers and What Should Be Done About It*. New Haven, Conn.: Yale University Press.

ALEXANDER, CHRISTOPHER (1964), *Notes on the Synthesis of Form*. Cambridge, Mass.: Harvard University Press.

ALKON, ALISON HOPE and AGYEMAN, JULIAN (eds.) (2011), *Cultivating Food Justice: Race, Class and Sustainability*. Cambridge, Mass.: MIT Press.

AMY, DOUGLAS J. (1987), *The Politics of Environmental Mediation*. New York: Columbia University Press.

—— (1990), 'Decision Techniques for Environmental Policy: A Critique,' pp. 59–79 in Robert Paehlke and Douglas Torgerson (eds.), *Managing Leviathan: Environmental Politics and the Administrative State*. Peterborough, Ontario: Broadview.

ANDERSON, FREDERICK L., KNEESE, ALLEN V., REED, P. D., STEVENSON, R. B., and TAYLOR, S. (1977), *Environmental Improvement Through Economic Incentives*. Baltimore, Md.: Johns Hopkins University Press for Resources for the Future.

ANDERSON, TERRY L. and LEAL, DONALD R. (1991), *Free Market Environmentalism*. Boulder, Colo.: Westview.

——, —— (2001), *Free Market Environmentalism*, revised edition. New York: Palgrave.

—— and LIBECAP, GARY (2012), 'Cap and Take,' *The Daily Caller* 15 May. <**http://dailycaller.com/2012/5/15/cap-and-take**>.

ARIAS-MALDONADO, MANUEL (2000), 'The Democratisation of Sustainability: The Search for a Green Democratic Model,' *Environmental Politics*, 9 (4): 43–58.

ARROW, K., COSTANZA, R., DASGUPTA, P., FOLKE, C., HOLLING, C. S., JANSSON, B. E., LEVIN, S., MALER, K.-G., PERRINGS, C., and PIMENTAL, D. (1995), 'Economic Growth, Carrying Capacity and the Environment,' *Science*, 268: 520–1.

ASCHER, WILLIAM, STEELMAN, TODDI, and HEALY, ROBERT (2010), *Knowledge and Environmental Policy: Re-Imagining the Boundaries of Science and Politics*. Cambridge, Mass.: MIT Press.

BABER, WALTER F. and BARTLETT, ROBERT V. (2007), *Deliberative Environmental Politics: Democracy and Ecological Rationality*. Cambridge, Mass.: MIT Press.

BÄCKSTRAND, KARIN, KHAN, JAMIL, KRONSELL, ANNICA and LÖVBRAND, EVA (eds.) (2010), *Environmental Politics and Deliberative Democracy: Examining the Promise of New Modes of Governance*. Cheltenham: Edward Elgar.

—— and LÖVBRAND, EVA (2012), 'Re-Thinking Climate Governance Post-Copenhagen: Power, Knowledge and Discourses at the Durban Summit,' paper presented at the Conference on A Planet Under Pressure, London, 26–29 March.

BADEN, JOHN (2012), 'FREE Market Environmentalism,' <**http://free-eco. org/insights/articles/free-market-environmentalism.html**>

BAILEY, RONALD (ed.) (2000), *Earth Report 2000: Revisiting the True State of the Planet*. New York: McGraw Hill.

BARBIER, EDWARD R. (2007), *Natural Resources and Economic Development*. Cambridge: Cambridge University Press.

BARNET, RICHARD J. (1980), *The Lean Years: Politics in the Age of Scarcity*. New York: Simon and Schuster.

BARNETT, HAROLD J., and MORSE, CHANDLER (1963), *Scarcity and Growth: The Economics of Natural Resource Availability*. Baltimore, Md.: Johns Hopkins University Press for Resources for the Future.

BARNOSKY, ANTHONY D. et al. (2012), 'Approaching a State Shift in the Earth's Biosphere,' *Nature*, 486: 52–8.

BARRETT, BRENDAN, and FISHER, DANA (2005), *Ecological Modernization in Japan*. London: Routledge.

BARRY, JOHN (2003), 'Ecological Modernisation,' pp. 191–213 in Edward Page and John Proops (eds.), *Environmental Thought*. Cheltenham: Edward Elgar.

—— (2012), *The Politics of Actually Existing Unsustainability: Human Flourishing in a Climate-Changed, Carbon-Constrained World*. Oxford: Oxford University Press.

BARTLETT, ROBERT V. (1990), 'Ecological Reason in Administration: Environmental Impact Assessment and Administrative Theory,' pp. 81–96 in Robert Paehlke and Douglas Torgerson (eds.), *Managing Leviathan:*

Environmental Politics and the Administrative State. Peterborough, Ontario: Broadview.

BECK, HANNO, DUNKEN, BRIAN and KRIPKE, GAWAIN (1998), *Citizens' Guide to Environmental Tax Shifting*. Washington, DC: Friends of the Earth.

BECK, ULRICH (1992), *Risk Society: Towards a New Modernity*. London: Sage.

—— (1999), *World Risk Society*. Cambridge: Polity.

——, GIDDENS, ANTHONY and LASH, SCOTT (1994), *Reflexive Modernization: Politics, Tradition and Aesthetics in the Modern Social Order*. Cambridge: Polity.

BECKERMAN, WILFRED (1974), *In Defence of Economic Growth*. London: Cape.

—— (1995), *Small is Stupid: Blowing the Whistle on the Greens*. London: Duckworth.

—— (2002), *A Poverty of Reason: Sustainable Development and Economic Growth*. Oakland, Calif.: The Independent Institute.

BEDER, SHARON (2001), 'Neoliberal Think Tanks and Free Market Environmentalism,' *Environmental Politics*, 10 (2): 128–33.

BEESON, MARK (2010), 'The Coming of Environmental Authoritarianism,' *Environmental Politics*, 19: 276–94.

BELL, STEPHEN and HINDMOOR, ANDREW (2009), *Rethinking Governance: The Centrality of the State in Modern Society*. Cambridge: Cambridge University Press.

—— and —— (2012), 'Governance without Government?, The Case of the Forest Stewardship Council,' *Public Administration*, 90: 144–59.

BENNETT, JANE, and CHALOUPKA, WILLIAM (eds.) (1993), *In the Nature of Things: Language, Politics, and the*

Environment. Minneapolis: University of Minnesota Press.

BEREJIKIAN, JEFFREY (2004), *International Relations Under Risk: Framing State Choice*. Albany: State University of New York Press.

BERGER, THOMAS (1977), *Northern Frontier, Northern Homeland: Report of the MacKenzie Valley Pipeline Inquiry*. Toronto: James Lorimer.

BHASKAR, ROY (1975), *A Realist Theory of Science*. Brighton: Harvester.

BIEHL, JANET (1991), *Rethinking Ecofeminist Politics*. Boston, Mass.: South End Press.

—— (ed.) (1997), *The Murray Bookchin Reader*. London: Cassell.

BIERMANN, FRANK et al. (2012), 'Navigating the Anthropocene: Improving Earth System Governance', *Science*, 335: 1306–7.

BLOWERS, ANDREW (1997), 'Environmental Policy: Ecological Modernisation or the Risk Society?' *Urban Studies*, 34: 845–71.

BOARDMAN, ANTHONY E., GREENBERG, DAVID H., VINING, AIDAN R., and WEINER, DAVID L. (2010), *Cost Benefit Analysis: Concepts and Practice*, 4th edition. Upper Saddle River, NJ: Prentice Hall.

BOOKCHIN, MURRAY (1986), *The Modern Crisis*. Philadelphia, Pa.: New Society.

—— and FOREMAN, DAVE (1991), *Defending the Earth*. Boston, Mass.: South End Press.

BOULDING, KENNETH R. (1966), 'The Economics of the Coming Spaceship Earth', in Henry Jarrett (ed.), *Environmental Quality in a Growing Economy*. Baltimore, Md.: Johns Hopkins University Press.

BOWERS, CHET (1999), 'The Role of Education and Ideology in the Transition from a Modern to a More Bioregionally-Oriented Culture', pp. 199–204 in Michael Vincent McGinnis (ed.), *Bioregionalism*. New York: Routledge.

BOYKOFF, MAXWELL T. and BOYKOFF, JULES M. (2004), 'Balance as Bias: Global Warming and the US Prestige Press', *Global Environmental Change*, 14: 125–36.

BRADLEY, ROBERT L. (2003), *Climate Alarmism Reconsidered*. London: Institute of Economic Affairs.

BRAITHWAITE, JOHN, and DRAHOS, PETER (2000), *Global Business Regulation*. Cambridge: Cambridge University Press.

BRECHIN, STEPHEN R., WILSHUSEN, PETER R., FORTWANGLER, CRYSTAL L., and WEST, PATRICK C. (2003), *Contested Nature: Promoting International Biodiversity with Social Justice in the Twenty-first Century*. Albany: State University of New York Press.

BROOKS, D. B. (1992), 'The Challenge of Sustainability: Is Integrating Environment and Economy Enough?', *Policy Sciences*, 26: 401–8.

BROWN, LESTER R. (1978), *The Twenty-Ninth Day: Accommodating Human Needs and Numbers to the Earth's Resources*. New York: Norton.

—— (1981), *Building a Sustainable Society*. New York: Norton.

—— (2003), *Plan B: Rescuing a Planet Under Stress and a Civilization in Trouble*. Washington, DC: Earth Policy Institute.

——, FLAVIN, CHRISTOPHER, and POSTEL, SANDRA (1992), *Saving the Planet: How to Shape an Environmentally Sustainable Global Economy*. London: Earthscan.

BROWN, PHIL, and MIKKELSEN, EDWIN J. (1990), *No Safe Place: Toxic Waste, Leukemia, and Community Action*.

Berkeley, Calif.: University of California Press.

BRÜGGEMEIER, FRANZ-JOSEF, CIOC, MARK, and ZELLER, THOMAS (2005), *How Green were the Nazis? Nature, Environment, and Nation in the Third Reich*. Athens, Ohio: Ohio University Press.

BRYNER, GARY C. (2000), 'The United States: "Sorry—Not Our Problem," ' pp. 273–302 in William M. Lafferty and James Meadowcroft (eds.), *Implementing Sustainable Development: Strategies and Initiatives from High Consumption Societies*. Oxford: Oxford University Press.

BÜHRS, TON (2009), *Environmental Integration: Our Common Challenge*. Albany: State University of New York Press.

BULLARD, ROBERT D. (ed.) (2005), *The Quest for Environmental Justice: Human Rights and the Politics of Pollution*. San Francisco: Sierra Club Books.

BURKE, TOM (2001), *Ten Pinches of Salt: A Reply to Bjørn Lomborg*. London: Green Alliance.

BURLESON, ELIZABETH, LYE, LIN-HENG, and ROBINSON, NICHOLAS A. (2012), *Comparative Environmental Law and Regulation*. Westlaw (online resource).

CALDWELL, LYNTON K. (1978), 'The Environmental Impact Statement: A Misused Tool,' in Ravinder Jain and Bruce Hutchings (eds.), *Environmental Impact Analysis*. Urbana: University of Illinois Press.

—— (1982), *Science and the National Environmental Policy Act: Redirecting Policy Through Administrative Reform*. Tuscaloosa: University of Alabama Press.

—— (1984), 'The World Environment: Reversing US Policy Commitments,' pp. 319–38 in Norman J. Vig and Michael

E. Kraft (eds.), *Environmental Policy in the 1980s: Reagan's New Agenda*. Washington, DC: Congressional Quarterly Press.

CAPRA, FRITJOF, and SPRETNACK, CHARLENE (1984), *Green Politics: The Global Promise*. New York: E. P. Dutton.

CARLASSARE, ELIZABETH (1994), 'Essentialism in Ecofeminist Discourse,' *Capitalism, Nature, Socialism*, 5 (3): 1–18.

CARRUTHERS, DAVID (2001), 'From Opposition to Orthodoxy: The Remaking of Sustainable Development,' *Journal of Third World Studies*, 18 (2): 93–112.

CASTELLS, MANUEL (1996), *The Rise of the Network Society*. Oxford: Basil Blackwell.

CATTON, WILLIAM R. (1980), *Overshoot: The Ecological Basis of Revolutionary Change*. Urbana: University of Illinois Press.

CHOCK, PHYLLIS PEASE (1995), 'Ambiguity in Policy Discourse: Congressional Talk About Immigration,' *Policy Sciences*, 28: 165–84.

CHRIST, CAROL P. (2003), *She Who Changes: Imagining the Divine in the World*. New York: Palgrave Macmillan.

CHRISTOFF, PETER (1995), 'Whatever Happened to Ecologically Sustainable Development?,' *Cappucchino Papers* (Australian Conservation Foundation), 1: 69–74.

—— (1996a), 'Ecological Modernisation, Ecological Modernities,' *Environmental Politics*, 5: 476–500.

—— (1996b), 'Ecological Citizens and Ecologically Guided Democracy,' pp. 151–69 in Brian Doherty and Marius de Geus (eds.), *Democracy and Green Political Thought*. London: Routledge.

—— and ECKERSLEY, ROBYN (2011), 'Comparing State responses,' pp. 431–8 in John S. Dryzek, Richard B. Norgaard, and David Schlosberg (eds.), *The Oxford Handbook of Climate Change and Society*. Oxford: Oxford University Press.

CLAPP, JENNIFER and DAUVERGNE, PETER (2005), *Paths to a Green World: The Political Economy of the Global Environment*. Cambridge, Mass.: MIT Press.

COASE, RONALD H. (1960), 'The Problem of Social Cost,' *Journal of Law and Economics*, 3: 1–44.

COHEN, BERNARD L. (1984), 'Statement of Dissent,' p. 556 in Julian L. Simon and Herman Kahn (eds.), *The Resourceful Earth: A Response to Global 2000*. New York: Basil Blackwell.

COLEMAN, JAMES S. (1986), 'Social Theory, Social Research, and a Theory of Action,' *American Journal of Sociology*, 91: 1309–35.

COMMONER, BARRY (1972), *The Closing Circle*. New York: Bantam.

CONCA, KEN (1994), 'Peace, Justice, and Sustainability,' *Newsletter of the Committee on the Political Economy of the Good Society*, 4 (1): 1–7.

——, PRINCEN, THOMAS, and MANIATES, MICHAEL F. (2001), 'Confronting Consumption,' *Global Environmental Politics*, 1 (3): 1–10.

CRIST, EILEEN (2004), 'Against the Social Construction of Nature and Wilderness,' *Environmental Ethics*, 26: 5–24.

CRONON, WILLIAM (1995), 'The Trouble with Wilderness; or, Getting Back to the Wrong Nature,' pp. 69–90 in William Cronon (ed.), *Uncommon Ground: Rethinking the Human Place in Nature*. New York: W.W. Norton.

CURRAN, GIOREL (2006), *21st Century Dissent: Anarchism, Anti-Globalization, Environmentalism*. Basingstoke: Palgrave Macmillan.

CZECH, BRIAN (2000), *Shoveling Fuel for a Runaway Train: Errant Economists, Shameful Spenders, and a Plan to Stop Them All*. Berkeley: University of California Press.

DALY, HERMAN E. (1977), *Steady-State Economics*. San Francisco: W. H. Freeman.

—— (1992), 'Sustainable Growth: An Impossibility Theorem,' pp. 267–73 in Herman E. Daly and Kenneth E. Townsend (eds.), *Valuing the Earth: Economics, Ecology, Ethics*. Cambridge, Mass.: MIT Press.

—— and FARLEY, JOSHUA. 2010. *Ecological Economics: Principles and Applications*, 2nd edition. Washington, DC: Island Press.

DAUGBJERG, CARSTEN, and SVENDSEN, GERT TINGGAARD (2003), 'Designing Green Taxes in a Political Context: From Optimal to Feasible Environmental Regulation,' *Environmental Politics*, 12 (4): 76–95.

DAVIS, KAREN (1995), 'Thinking Like a Chicken: Farm Animals and the Feminine Connection,' pp.192–212 in Carol J. Adams and Josephine Donovan (eds.), *Animals and Women: Feminist Theoretical Explorations*. Durham, NC: Duke University Press.

Department of the Environment (United Kingdom) (1988), *Our Common Future: A Perspective by the United Kingdom on the Report of the World Commission on Environment and Development*. London: HMSO.

DE-SHALIT, AVNER (2000), *The Environment Between Theory and Practice*. Oxford: Oxford University Press.

DEVALL, BILL, and SESSIONS, GEORGE (1985), *Deep Ecology: Living as if*

Nature Mattered. Salt Lake City, Utah: Peregrine Smith.

DIAMOND, IRENE (1994), *Fertile Ground: Women, Fertility, and the Living Earth.* Boston, Mass.: Beacon.

—— and FEMAN ORENSTEIN, GLORIA (eds) (1990), *Reweaving the World: The Emergence of Ecofeminism.* San Francisco, Calif.: Sierra Club Books.

DIAMOND, JARED (2005), *Collapse: How Societies Choose to Fail or Survive.* New York: Viking Penguin.

DIZEREGA, GUS (2000), *Persuasion, Power and Authority: A Theory of Democratic Self-Organization.* New York: Hampton Press.

DOBSON, ANDREW (1990), *Green Political Thought: An Introduction.* London: Unwin Hyman.

—— (1998), *Justice and the Environment: Conceptions of Environmental Sustainability and Social Justice.* Oxford: Oxford University Press.

—— (2004), *Citizenship and the Environment.* Oxford: Oxford University Press.

—— (2010), 'Democracy and Nature: Speaking and Listening,' *Political Studies,* 58: 752–68.

DODGE, JIM (1981), 'Living by Life: Some Bioregional Theory and Practice,' *Coevolution Quarterly,* 32: 6–12.

DOHERTY, BRIAN (1999), 'Paving the Way: The Rise of Direct Action Against Road-Building and the Changing Character of British Environmentalism,' *Political Studies,* 47: 275–91.

DOWIE, MARK (1995), *Losing Ground: American Environmentalism at the Close of the Twentieth Century.* Cambridge, Mass.: MIT Press.

—— (2009), *Conservation Refugees: The Hundred-Year Conflict Between Global Conservation and Native Peoples.* Cambridge, Mass.: MIT Press.

DRYZEK, JOHN S. (1987), *Rational Ecology: Environment and Political Economy.* New York: Basil Blackwell.

—— (1990a), 'Green Reason: Communicative Ethics for the Biosphere,' *Environmental Ethics,* 12: 195–210.

—— (1990b), *Discursive Democracy: Politics, Policy, and Political Science.* New York: Cambridge University Press.

—— (1992a), 'The Good Society versus the State: Freedom and Necessity in Political Innovation,' *Journal of Politics,* 54: 518–40.

—— (1992b), 'How far is it From Virginia and Rochester to Frankfurt? Public Choice as Critical Theory,' *British Journal of Political Science,* 22: 397–417.

—— (1995), 'The Informal Logic of Institutional Design,' pp. 103–25 in Robert E. Goodin (ed,) *The Theory of Institutional Design.* New York: Cambridge University Press.

—— (1996a), *Democracy in Capitalist Times: Ideals, Limits, and Struggles.* New York: Oxford University Press.

—— (1996b), 'Foundations for Environmental Political Economy: The Search for Homo Ecologicus?,' *New Political Economy,* 1: 27–40.

——, DOWNES, DAVID, HUNOLD, CHRISTIAN, and SCHLOSBERG, DAVID, with Hernes, Hans-Kristian (2003), *Green States and Social Movements: Environmentalism in the United States, United Kingdom, Germany, and Norway.* Oxford: Oxford University Press.

—— and STEVENSON, HAYLEY (2011), 'Global democracy and Earth System Governance,' *Ecological Economics,* 70: 1865–74.

——, TUCKER, AVIEZER, GOODIN, ROBERT E., and REBER, BERNARD (2009), 'Promethean Elites Encounter

Precautionary Publics: The Case of GM Foods,' *Science, Technology, and Human Values*, 34: 263–88.

DUNLAP, RILEY E. and MCCRIGHT, AARON M. (2011), 'Organized Climate Change Denial,' pp. 144–60 in John S. Dryzek, Richard B. Norgaard, and David Schlosberg (eds.), *The Oxford Handbook of Climate Change and Society*. Oxford: Oxford University Press.

EASTERBROOK, GREG (1995), *A Moment on the Earth: The Coming Age of Environmental Optimism*. New York: Penguin.

ECKERSLEY, ROBYN (1992), *Environmentalism and Political Theory: Toward an Ecocentric Approach*. Albany: State University of New York Press.

EDWARDS, DEREK and POTTER, JONATHAN (1992), *Discursive Psychology*. London: Sage.

EHRLICH, PAUL (1968), *The Population Bomb*. New York: Ballantine.

—— and EHRLICH, ANNE H. (1974), *The End of Affluence: A Blueprint for Your Future*. New York: Ballantine.

——, —— (2004), *One with Nineveh: Politics, Consumption, and the Human Future*. Washington, DC: Island Press.

ENGELMAN, ROBERT (2011), 'An End to Population Growth: Why Family Planning is Key to a Sustainable Future,' *Solutions*, 2 (3): 32–41.

Environment 2004 (2003), *The Bush Environmental Record: An Unprecedented Assault on America's Health and Heritage*. Washington, DC: Environment 2004.

EPSTEIN, CHARLOTTE (2008), *The Power of Words in International Relations: Birth of an Anti-Whaling Discourse*. Cambridge, Mass.: MIT Press.

European Environment Agency (2000), *Environmental Taxation: Recent Developments in Tools for Integration*. Copenhagen: European Environment Agency.

EVANOFF, RICHARD (2011), *Bioregionalism and Global Ethics: A Transactional Approach to Achieving Ecological Sustainability, Social Justice, and Human Well-being*. New York: Routledge.

FAIRCLOUGH, NORMAN (2003), *Analysing Discourse: Textual Analysis for Social Research*. London: Routledge.

—— (2006), *Language and Globalisation*. London: Routledge.

FARZIN, Y. HOSSEIN and BOND, CRAIG A. (2006), 'Democracy and Environmental Quality,' *Journal of Development Economics*, 81: 213–35.

FIALA, NATHAN (2009), 'How Meat Contributes to Global Warming,' *Scientific American*, February 4.

FIORINO, DANIEL J. (1995), *Making Environmental Policy*. Berkeley, Calif.: University of California Press.

—— (2004), 'Flexibility,' pp. 393–425 in ROBERT F. DURANT, Daniel J. Fiorino, and Rosemary O'Leary (eds.), *Environmental Governance Reconsidered*. Cambridge, Mass.: MIT Press.

—— (2006), *The New Environmental Regulation*. Cambridge, Mass.: MIT Press.

FISCHER, FRANK (1993), 'Citizen Participation and the Democratization of Policy Expertise: From Theoretical Inquiry to Practical Cases,' *Policy Sciences*, 26: 165–87.

FISCHOFF, BARUCH and KADVANY, JOHN (2011), *Risk: A Very Short Introduction*. Oxford: Oxford University Press.

FOREMAN, DAVE (1985), *Ecodefense: A Field Guide to Monkeywrenching*. Tucson, Ariz.: Ned Ludd Books.

—— (1991), Contribution to Murray Bookchin and Dave Foreman, *Defending the Earth: A Dialogue Between Murray Bookchin and Dave Foreman*. Boston, Mass.: South End Press.

—— (1998), 'Wilderness Areas for Real,' pp. 395–407 in J. Baird Callicott and Michael P. Nelson (eds.), *The Great New Wilderness Debate*. Athens, Ga: University of Georgia Press.

—— (2000), 'The Real Wilderness Idea,' *USDA Forest Service Proceedings*, RMRS-P-15-Vol-1.

FOSTER, JOHN BELLAMY, CLARK, BRETT, and YORK, RICHARD (2010), *The Ecological Rift: Capitalism's War on the Earth*. New York: Monthly Review Press.

FOUCAULT, MICHEL (1980), *Power/Knowledge: Selected Interviews and Other Writings, 1972–1977*. Brighton: Harvester.

FOX, WARWICK (1984), 'On Guiding Stars to Deep Ecology: A Reply to Naess,' *The Ecologist*, 14: 203–4.

—— (1990), *Toward a Transpersonal Ecology: Developing New Foundations for Environmentalism*. Boston, Mass.: Shambhala.

FREEMAN, CHRISTOPHER (1973), 'Malthus with a Computer,' in H. S. D. Cole, C. Freeman, M. Jahoda, and K. L. R. Pravitts (eds.), *Models of Doom: A Critique of The Limits to Growth*. New York: Universe.

FRETWELL, HOLLY LIPPKE (2009), *Who is Minding the Federal Estate? Political Management of America's Public Lands*. Lanham, Md: Lexington Books.

GAFFNEY, OWEN and HÖPPE, PETER (2012), 'Risky Business,' *Global Change*, 78: 24–7.

GARNAUT, ROSS (2008), *The Garnaut Climate Change Review*. Cambridge: Cambridge University Press.

GEORGESCU-ROEGEN, NICHOLAS (1971), *The Entropy Law and the Economic Process*. Cambridge, Mass.: Harvard University Press.

GERTH, H. H., and WRIGHT MILLS, C. (1948), *From Max Weber: Essays in Sociology*. London: Routledge and Kegan Paul.

GILMAN, NILS, RANDALL, DOUG, and SCHWARTZ, PETER (2011), 'Climate Change and 'Security,'' pp. 251–66 in John S. Dryzek, Richard B. Norgaard, and David Schlosberg (eds.), *The Oxford Handbook of Climate Change and Society*. Oxford: Oxford University Press.

GONZÁLEZ, GEORGE A. (2001*a*), *Corporate Power and the Environment: The Political Economy of US Environmental Policy*. Lanham, Md.: Rowman and Littlefield.

—— (2001*b*), 'Democratic Ethics and Ecological Modernization: The Formulation of California's Automobile Emission Standards,' *Public Integrity*, 3: 325–44.

—— (2002), 'Local Growth Coalitions and Air Pollution Controls: The Ecological Modernisation of the US in Historical Perspective,' *Environmental Politics*, 11 (3): 121–44.

—— (2009), *Urban Sprawl, Global Warming, and the Empire of Capital*. Albany: State University of New York Press.

GOODIN, ROBERT E. (1994), 'Selling Environmental Indulgences,' *Kyklos*, 47: 573–95.

—— (1996), 'Enfranchising the Earth, and its Alternatives,' *Political Studies*, 44: 835–49.

GORDON, H. SCOTT (1954), 'The Economic Theory of a Common-Property Resource: The Fishery,' *Journal of Political Economy*, 62: 124–42.

GORE, ALBERT (1992), *Earth in the Balance*. Boston, Mass.: Houghton Mifflin.

GORE, AL (2006), *An Inconvenient Truth: The Planetary Emergency of Global Warming and What We Can Do About It*. New York: Rodale.

GOTTLEIB, ROGER S. (ed.) (1996), *This Sacred Earth: Religion, Nature, Environment*. New York: Routledge.

GRAY, TIM (2000), 'A Discourse Analysis of UK Contaminated Land Policy,' paper presented at the Conference of the Political Studies Association, London, April 10–13.

GUHA, RAMACHANDRA (1997), 'The Environmentalism of the Poor,' pp. 3–21 in Ramachandra Guha and Juan Martinez-Alier (eds.), *Varieties of Environmentalism*. London: Earthscan.

GUNDERSEN, ADOLF (1995), *The Environmental Promise of Democratic Deliberation*. Madison: University of Wisconsin Press.

HAAS, PETER M. (1992), 'Banning Chlorofluorocarbons: Efforts to Protect Stratospheric Ozone,' *International Organization*, 46: 187–224.

HAHN, ROBERT W. (1995), 'Economic Prescriptions for Environmental Policy Instruments: Lessons from the United States and Continental Europe,' pp. 129–56 in Robyn Eckersley (ed.), *Markets, the State, and the Environment: Towards Integration*. Melbourne: Macmillan.

HAJER, MAARTEN A. (1995), *The Politics of Environmental Discourse: Ecological Modernization and the Policy Process*. Oxford: Oxford University Press.

—— (2003), 'A Frame in the Fields,' pp. 88–110 in Marten A. Hajer and Hendrik Wagenaar (eds.), *Deliberative Policy Analysis: Understanding Governance in the Network Society*.

Cambridge: Cambridge University Press.

—— (2011), *The Energetic Society: In Search of a Governance Philosophy for a Clean Economy*. The Hague: PBL.

—— and VERSTEEG, WYTSKE (2005), 'A Decade of Discourse Analysis of Environmental Politics: Achievements, Challenges, Perspectives,' *Journal of Environmental Policy and Planning*, 7: 175–84.

HANNAH, ELIZABETH G. (2011), 'Health Hazards,' pp. 217–31 in John S. Dryzek, Richard B. Norgaard, and David Schlosberg (eds.), *The Oxford Handbook of Climate Change and Society*. Oxford: Oxford University Press.

HARDIN, GARRETT (1968), 'The Tragedy of the Commons,' *Science*, 162: 1243–8.

—— (1977), 'Living on a Lifeboat,' pp. 261–79 in Garrett Hardin and John Baden (eds.), *Managing the Commons*. San Francisco, Calif.: W. H. Freeman.

—— (1993), *Living Within Limits: Ecology, Economics, and Population Taboos*. New York: Oxford University Press.

HARI, JOHANNA (2009), 'Move Over Thoreau: Rationalist Environmentalism Better Prevail, and Fast,' *Slate*, January 12. Online at <**http://www.slate.com**>.

HARRINGTON, WINSTON and RICHARD D. MORGENSTERN (2004), 'Economic Incentives versus Command and Control: What's the Best Approach for Solving Environmental Problems?' *Resources*, 152: 15–17.

HAWKEN, PAUL, LOVINS, AMORY B., and LOVINS, L. HUNTER (1999), *Natural Capitalism: Creating the Next Industrial Revolution*. Boston, Mass.: Little, Brown.

HAY, PETER (2002), *Main Currents in Western Environmental Thought*. Sydney: University of New South Wales Press.

HAYEK, FRIEDRICH A. VON (1979), *Law, Legislation, and Liberty: The Political Order of a Free People.* Chicago: University of Chicago Press.

HAYNES, JEFF (1999), 'Power, Politics and Environmental Movements in the Third World,' *Environmental Politics*, 8 (1): 222–42.

HAYS, SAMUEL P. (1959), *Conservation and The Gospel of Efficiency: The Progressive Conservation Movement, 1890–1920.* Cambridge, Mass.: Harvard University Press.

—— (1987), *Beauty, Health, and Permanence: Environmental Politics in the United States, 1955–1985.* Cambridge: Cambridge University Press.

HAYWARD, TIM (1995), *Ecological Thought: An Introduction.* Cambridge: Polity.

HEILBRONER, ROBERT (1991), *An Inquiry into the Human Prospect: Looked at Again for the 1990s.* New York: Norton.

HIGGS, ROBERT and CARL B. CLOSE (eds.), (2005), *Re-Thinking Green: Alternatives to Environmental Bureaucracy.* Oakland, Calif.: The Independent Institute.

HOFFMAN, MATTHEW J. (2011), *Climate Governance at the Crossroads: Experimenting with a Global Response.* Oxford: Oxford University Press.

HOLLIDAY, CHARLES O., JR., SCHMIDHEINY, STEPHAN, and WATTS, PHILIP (2002), *Walking the Talk: The Business Case for Sustainable Development.* Sheffield: Greenleaf.

HOMER-DIXON, THOMAS F. (2000), *The Ingenuity Gap: Can We Solve the Problems of the Future?* Toronto: Knopf.

HOPKINS, ROB (2011), *The Transition Companion: Making Your Community More Resilient in Uncertain Times.* Totnes: Transition Books.

HOPWOOD, BILL, MELLOR, MARY, and O'BRIEN, GEOFF (2005), 'Sustainable Development: Mapping Different Perspectives,' *Sustainable Development*, 13: 38–52.

HOWARTH, DAVID (2009), 'Power, Discourse and Policy: Articulating a Hegemonic Approach to Critical Policy Studies,' *Critical Policy Studies*, 3: 309–35.

HUBER, JOSEPH (1982), Die verlorene Unschuld der Okologie. Frankfurt am Main: Fischer Verlag.

INGLEHART, RONALD (1990), *Culture Shift in Advanced Industrial Society.* Princeton, NJ: Princeton University Press.

INNES, JUDITH E., and BOOHER, DAVID E. (2003), 'Collaborative Policymaking: Governance Through Dialogue,' pp. 33–59 in Marten A. Hajer and Hendrik Wagenaar (eds.), *Deliberative Policy Analysis: Understanding Governance in the Network Society.* Cambridge: Cambridge University Press.

International Union for the Conservation of Nature (1980), *World Conservation Strategy.* Gland, Switzerland: International Union for the Conservation of Nature.

JACOBS, MICHAEL (1991), *The Green Economy: Environment, Sustainable Development and the Politics of the Future.* London: Pluto.

—— (1995), 'Financial Incentives: The British Experience,' pp. 113–28 in Robyn Eckersley (ed.), *Markets, the State, and the Environment: Towards Integration.* Melbourne: Macmillan.

—— (1999), *Environmental Modernisation: The New Labour Agenda.* London: Fabian Society.

JACKSON, TIM (2009), *Prosperity Without Growth: Economics for a Finite Planet.* London: Earthscan.

JAGERS, SVERKER C. (2009), 'In Search of the Ecological Citizen,' *Environmental Politics*, 18: 18–36.

JAHN, DETLEF (1998), 'Environmental Performance and Policy Regimes: Explaining Variations in 18 OECD Countries,' *Policy Sciences*, 31: 107–31.

JÄNICKE, MARTIN (1985), *Preventive Environmental Policy as Ecological Modernization and Structural Policy*. Berlin: Wissenschaftszentrum.

—— (1996), 'Democracy as a Condition for Environmental Policy Success: The Importance of Non-institutional Factors,' pp. 71–85 in William M. Lafferty and James Meadowcroft (eds.), *Democracy and the Environment: Problems and Prospects*. Cheltenham: Edward Elgar.

—— and WEIDNER, HELMUT (1997), 'Germany,' pp. 133–55 in Martin Jänicke and Helmut Weidner (eds.), *National Environmental Policies: A Comparative Study of Capacity Building*. Berlin: Springer.

JEVONS, W. STANLEY (1865), *The Coal Question*. London: Macmillan.

JORDAN, ANDREW, WURZEL, RÜDIGER K. W., and ZITO, ANTHONY R. (2003), '"New" Instruments of Environmental Governance: Patterns and Pathways of Change,' *Environmental Politics*, 12 (1): 1–24.

——, HUITEMA, DAVE, VAN ASSELT, HARRO, RAYNER, TIM, and BERKHOUT, FRANS (eds.) (2010), *Climate Change Policy in the European Union: Confronting the Dilemmas of Mitigation and Adaptation*. Cambridge: Cambridge University Press.

KAPLOWITZ, MICHAEL D. (ed.) (2004), *Property, Rights, Economics and the Environment*. London: Routledge.

KAREIVA, PETER, TALLIS, HEATHER, RICKETTS, TAYLOR H., DAILY,

GRETCHEN C., and POLASKY, STEPHEN (2011), *Natural Capital: Theory and Practice of Mapping Ecosystem Services*. Oxford: Oxford University Press.

KEARNS, LAUREL (2011), 'The Role of Religion in Activism,' pp. 414–28 in John S. Dryzek, Richard B. Norgaard, and David Schlosberg (eds.), *The Oxford Handbook of Climate Change and Society*. Oxford: Oxford University Press.

KELMAN, STEVEN (1981), *What Price Incentives? Economists and the Environment*. Boston, Mass.: Auburn House.

—— (1987), *Making Public Policy: A Hopeful View of American Government*. New York: Basic Books.

KEMP, RAY (1985), 'Planning, Public Hearings, and the Politics of Discourse,' pp. 177–201 in John Forester (ed.), *Critical Theory and Public Life*. Cambridge, Mass.: MIT Press.

KERN, FLORIAN and HOWLETT, MICHAEL (2009), 'Implementing Transition Management as Policy Reforms: A Case Study of the Dutch Energy Sector,' *Policy Sciences*, 42: 391–408.

KHEEL, MARTI (2008), *Nature Ethics: An Ecofeminist Perspective*. Lanham, Md: Rowman and Littlefield.

KLEIN, NAOMI (2011), 'Capitalism vs. the Climate,' *The Nation*, Nov. 9.

KNEESE, ALLEN V., and SCHULTZE, CHARLES L. (1975), *Pollution, Prices, and Public Policy*. Washington, DC: Brookings.

KOVEL, JOEL (2007), *The Enemy of Nature: The End of Capitalism or the End of the World*, 2nd edition. London: Zed Books.

—— and LOWY, MICHAEL (2002), 'An Ecosocialist Manifesto,' *Capitalism, Nature, Socialism*, 31 (1): 1–2 and 155–7.

KRUPP, FRED (2007), 'Tapping the Market for a Cleaner Environment,' *Property and Environment Research Center Reports,* 25 (1).

LA CHAPELLE, DOLORES (1978), *Earth Wisdom.* San Diego, Calif.: Guild of Tudors.

LAFFERTY, WILLIAM M. (1996), 'The Politics of Sustainable Development,' *Environmental Politics,* 5 (2): 185–208.

—— and HOVDEN, EIVIND (2003), 'Environmental Policy Integration: Towards an Analytical Framework,' *Environmental Politics,* 12 (3): 1–22.

—— and MEADOWCROFT, JAMES (eds.) (2000), *Implementing Sustainable Development: Strategies and Initiatives in High Consumption Societies.* Oxford: Oxford University Press.

LANGHELLE, OLUF (2000), 'Why Ecological Modernization and Sustainable Development Should Not be Conflated,' *Journal of Environmental Policy and Planning,* 2: 303–22.

LEE, KAI N. (1993), *Compass and Gyroscope: Integrating Science and Politics for the Environment.* Washington, DC: Island Press.

—— (1999), 'Appraising Adaptive Management,' *Conservation Ecology,* 3 (2), online at <**http://www.consecol.org/vol3/iss2/art3/**>.

LEHMBRUCH, GERHARD (1984), 'Concertation and the Structure of Corporatist Networks,' in John H. Goldthorpe (ed.), *Order and Conflict in Contemporary Capitalism.* Oxford: Clarendon.

LEWIS, MARTIN W. (1992), *Green Delusions: An Environmentalist Critique of Radical Environmentalism.* Durham, NC: Duke University Press.

LIGHT, ANDREW, and KATZ, ERIC (1996), *Environmental Pragmatism.* London: Routledge.

LINDBLOM, CHARLES E. (1959), 'The Science of Muddling Through,' *Public Administration Review,* 19: 79–88.

—— (1965), *The Intelligence of Democracy: Decision Making through Mutual Adjustment.* New York: Free Press.

—— (1977), *Politics and Markets: The World's Political-Economic Systems.* New York: Basic Books.

—— (1982), 'The Market as Prison,' *Journal of Politics,* 44: 324–36.

LIPSCHUTZ, RONNIE D. (2009), 'The Sustainability Debate: Déjà Vu All Over Again?' *Global Environmental Politics,* 9: 136–41.

LITFIN, KAREN T. (1994), *Ozone Discourses: Science and Politics in Global Environmental Cooperation.* New York: Columbia University Press.

LOMBORG, BJØRN (2001a), *The Skeptical Environmentalist: Measuring the Real State of the World.* Cambridge: Cambridge University Press.

—— (2001b), 'The Truth About the Environment,' *The Economist,* 360 (August 4): 63.

—— (2007), *Cool It! The Skeptical Environmentalist's Guide to Global Warming.* New York: Knopf.

—— (ed.) (2010), *Smart Solutions to Climate Change: Comparing Costs and Benefits.* Cambridge: Cambridge University Press.

LOVEJOY, THOMAS (2012), 'The Greatest Challenge of Our Species,' *New York Times,* April 5.

LOVELOCK, JAMES E. (1979), *Gaia: A New Look at Life on Earth.* Oxford: Oxford University Press.

LUKE, TIMOTHY (1997), *Ecocritique: Contesting the Politics of Nature, Economy, and Culture.* Minneapolis: University of Minnesota Press.

—— (1999), 'Environmentality as Green Governmentality,' pp. 121–51 in

Eric Darier (ed.), *Discourses of the Environment*. Oxford: Basil Blackwell.

—— (2005), 'Neither Sustainable nor Development: Reconsidering Sustainability in Development,' *Sustainable Development*, 13: 228–38.

LUNDQVIST, LENNART J. (2004), *Sweden and Ecological Governance: Straddling the Fence*. Manchester: Manchester University Press.

MCFAGUE, SALLY (2008), *A New Climate for Theology: God, the World, and Global Warming*. Minneapolis: Fortress.

MCGINNIS, MICHAEL VONCENT (ed.) (1998), *Bioregionalism*. New York: Routledge.

MACGREGOR, SHERILYN (2006), *Beyond Mothering Earth: Ecological Citizenship and the Politics of Care*. Vancouver: University of British Columbia Press.

MCPHEE, JOHN (1970), *Encounters with the Archdruid*. New York: Farrar, Straus, and Giroux.

MANES, CHRISTOPHER (1990), *Green Rage: Radical Environmentalism and the Unmaking of Civilization*. Boston, Mass.: Little, Brown.

MANIATES, MICHAEL F. (2001), 'Individualization: Plant a Tree, Buy a Bike, Save the World,' *Global Environmental Politics*, 1 (3): 31–52.

MEADOWCROFT, JAMES (2000), 'Sustainable Development: A New(ish) Idea for a New Century?' *Political Studies*, 48: 370–87.

MEADOWS, DONELLA H., MEADOWS, DENNIS L., RANDERS, JORGEN, and BEHRENS, WILLIAM H. III (1972), *The Limits to Growth*. New York: Universe Books.

——, MEADOWS, DENNIS L., and RANDERS, JORGEN (1992), *Beyond the Limits: Confronting Global Collapse,*

Envisioning a Sustainable Future. Post Mills, Vt.: Chelsea Green.

MEIDINGER, ERROL E. (2003), 'Forest Certification as a Global Civil Society Regulatory Institution,' pp. 265–89 in Errol E. Meidinger, Chris Elliott, and Gerhard Oesten (eds.), *Social and Political Dimensions of Forest Certification*. Remagen-Oberwinter: Forstbuch Verlag.

MEINERS, ROGER E., and YANDLE, BRUCE (1993), 'Taking the Environment Seriously: What Do We Mean?,' pp. vii–xiv in Roger E. Meiners and BRUCE YANDLE (eds.), *Taking the Environment Seriously*. Lanham, Md.: Rowman and Littlefield.

MERCHANT, CAROLYN (1992), *Radical Ecology*. London: Routledge.

MICHAELS, PATRICK J. (1993), 'Global Warming: Facts vs. The Popular Vision,' pp. 341–62 in David Boaz and Edward H. Crane (eds.), *Market Liberalism: A Paradigm for the 21st Century*. Washington, DC: Cato Institute.

MIKLER, JOHN (2009), *Greening the Car Industry: Varieties of Capitalism and Climate Change*. Cheltenham: Edward Elgar.

MILBRATH, LESTER W. (1989), *Envisioning a Sustainable Society: Learning Our Way Out*. Albany: State University of New York Press.

MITCHELL, WILLIAM C., and SIMMONS, RANDY T. (1994), *Beyond Politics: Markets, Welfare, and the Failure of Bureaucracy*. Boulder, Colo.: Westview.

MOL, ARTHUR P. J. (1996), 'Ecological Modernisation and Institutional Reflexivity: Environmental Reform in the Late Modern Age,' *Environmental Politics*, 5: 302–23.

——, SONNENFELD, DAVID A., and SPAARGAREN, GERT (eds.) (2009), *The Ecological Modernisation Reader:*

Environmental Reform in Theory and Practice. Abingdon: Routledge.

—— and SPAARGAREN, GERT (2000), 'Ecological Modernisation Theory in Debate: A Review,' *Environmental Politics*, 9 (1): 17–49.

MONBIOT, GEORGE (2011), 'Why Fukushima Made Me Stop Worrying and Love Nuclear Power,' *The Guardian*, March 21.

MORAN, ALAN (1995), 'Tools for Environmental Policy: Market Instruments versus Command-and-Control,' pp. 73–85 in Robyn Eckersley (ed.), *Markets, the State, and the Environment: Towards Integration*. Melbourne: Macmillan.

MORTON, KATHERINE (2009), *China and the Global Environment: Learning from the Past, Anticipating the Future*. Sydney: Lowy Institute.

MOSHER, LAWRENCE (1983), 'Distrust of Gorsuch May Stymie EPA Attempt to Integrate Pollution Wars,' *National Journal*, 15: 322–4.

MURPHY, E. F. (1967), *Governing Nature*. Chicago, Ill.: Quadrangle Books.

MYERS, NORMAN, and SIMON, JULIAN L. (1994), *Scarcity or Abundance: A Debate on the Environment*. New York: Norton.

NAESS, ARNE (1973), 'The Shallow and the Deep, Long-Range Ecology Movement: A Summary,' *Inquiry*, 16: 95–100.

—— (1989), *Ecology, Community and Lifestyle*. Cambridge: Cambridge University Press.

NEF, JOHN U. (1977), 'An Early Energy Crisis and its Consequences,' *Scientific American*, 237: 140–51.

NELKIN, DOROTHY, and POLLACK, MICHAEL (1981), *The Atom Besieged*. Cambridge, Mass.: MIT Pess.

NELSON, ROBERT H. (1993), 'How Much is Enough? An Overview of the Benefits and Costs of Environmental Protection,' pp. 1–23 in Roger E. Meiners and Bruce Yandle (eds.), *Taking the Environment Seriously*. Lanham, Md.: Rowman and Littlefield.

NORDHAUS, WILLIAM D. (2007*a*), 'A Review of the Stern Review on the Economics of Climate Change,' *Journal of Economic Literature*, 45: 686–702.

—— (2007*b*), 'To Tax or Not to Tax: Alternative Approaches to Slowing Global Warming,' *Review of Environmental Economics and Policy* 1: 26–44.

NORGAARD, RICHARD B. (2010), 'Ecosystem Services: From Eye-Opening Metaphor to Complexity Blinder,' *Ecological Economics*, 69: 1219–27.

NØRGÅRD, JØRGEN STIG, PEET, JOHN, and RAGNARSDÓTTIR, KRISTIN VALA (2010), 'The History of the Limits to Growth,' *Solutions*, 1: 59–63.

O'CONNOR, JAMES (1988), 'Capitalism, Nature, Socialism: A Theoretical Introduction,' *Capitalism, Nature, Socialism*, 1: 11–38.

OECD (2010), *Taxation, Innovation, and the Environment*. Paris: OECD.

OELOFSE, CATHERINE, SCOTT, DIANNE, OELOFSE, GREGG, and HOUGHTON, JENNIFER (2006), 'Shifts Within Ecological Modernisation in South Africa: Deliberation, Innovation and Institutional Opportunities,' *Local Environment*, 11: 61–78.

OFFE, CLAUS (1985), 'New Social Movements: Challenging the Boundaries of Institutional Politics,' *Social Research*, 52: 817–68

—— (1990), 'Reflections on the Institutional Self-Transformation of Movement Politics: A Tentative Stage Model,' pp. 232–50 in Russell J. Dalton and Manfred Kuechler (eds.), *Challenging the Political Order: New Social and Political Movements in Western Democracies*. New York: Oxford University Press.

OLSON, MANCUR (1965), *The Logic of Collective Action*. Cambridge, Mass.: Harvard University Press.

OPHULS, WILLIAM (1977), *Ecology and the Politics of Scarcity*. San Francisco, Calif.: W. H. Freeman.

—— (2011), *Plato's Revenge: Politics in the Age of Ecology*. Cambridge, Mass.: MIT Press.

—— and STEPHEN BOYAN, A., JR. (1992), *Ecology and the Politics of Scarcity Revisited*. San Francisco, Calif.: W. H. Freeman.

ORESKES, NAOMI and CONWAY, ERIK M. (2010), *Merchants of Doubt: How a Handful of Scientists Obscured the Truth from Tobacco Smoke to Global Warming*. New York: Bloomsbury Press.

OSTROM, ELINOR (2009), 'A Polycentric Approach for Coping with Climate Change,' Washington, DC: World Bank Policy Research Working Paper 595.

PAEHLKE, ROBERT (1988), 'Democracy, Bureaucracy, and Environmentalism,' *Environmental Ethics*, 10: 291–308.

PARR, ADRIAN (2009), *Hijacking Sustainability*. Cambridge, Mass.: MIT Press.

PATERSON, MATTHEW (2011), 'Selling Carbon: From International Climate Regime to Global Market,' 611–24 in John S. Dryzek, Richard B. Norgaard, and David Schlosberg (eds.), *The Oxford Handbook of Climate Change and Society*. Oxford: Oxford University Press.

PEARCE, DAVID, and BARBIER, EDWARD R. (2000), *Blueprint for a Sustainable Economy*. London: Earthscan.

——, David, MARKANDYA, ANIL, and BARBIER, EDWARD R. (1989), *Blueprint for a Green Economy*. London: Earthscan.

PENGRA, BRUCE (2012), 'One Planet, How Many People? A Review of Earth's Carrying Capacity,' United Nations Environment Program. Online at <**http://proclimweb.scnat.ch/portal/ressources/2354.pdf**>.

PEPPER, DAVID (1993), *Ecosocialism: From Deep Ecology to Social Justice*. London: Routledge.

—— (1999), 'Ecological Modernisation or the "Ideal Model" of Sustainable Development? Questions Prompted at Europe's Periphery,' *Environmental Politics*, 8 (4): 1–34.

PICKEL, ANDREAS (1993), 'Authoritarianism or Democracy? Marketization as a Political Problem,' *Policy Sciences*, 26: 139–63.

PLANT, JUDITH (ed.) (1989), *Healing the Wounds: The Promise of Ecofeminism*. Philadelphia, Pa.: New Society Publishers.

PLUMWOOD, VAL (1993), *Feminism and the Mastery of Nature*. London: Routledge.

—— (1995), 'Has Democracy Failed Ecology? An Ecofeminist Perspective,' *Environmental Politics*, 4 (4): 134–68.

—— (2002), *Environmental Culture: The Ecological Crisis of Reason*. London: Routledge.

POGUNTKE, THOMAS (2002), 'Green Parties in National Governments: From Protest to Acquiescence,' *Environmental Politics*, 11 (1): 133–45.

POLONI-STAUDINGER, LORI M. (2008), 'Are Consensus Democracies More Environmentally Effective?' *Environmental Politics*, 17: 410–30.

POPPER, KARL R. (1966), *The Open Society and its Enemies*. London: Routledge and Kegan Paul.

—— (1972), *The Poverty of Historicism*, revised edition. London: Routledge and Kegan Paul.

PORRITT, JONATHAN (2005), *Capitalism as if the World Matters*. London: Earthscan.

PRESS, DANIEL (1994), *Democratic Dilemmas in the Age of Ecology: Trees and Toxics in the American West*. Durham, NC: Duke University Press.

PRESSMAN, JEFFREY, and WILDAVSKY, AARON (1973), *Implementation*. Berkeley, Calif.: University of California Press.

RABE, BARRY G. (1991), 'Beyond the Nimby Syndrome in Hazardous Waste Facility Siting: The Albertan Breakthrough and the Prospects for Cooperation in Canada and the United States,' *Governance*, 4: 184–206.

RASK, MIKKO, WORTHINGTON, TOM, and LAMMI, MINNA (eds.) (2012), *Citizen Participation in Global Environmental Governance*. London: Earthscan.

REISNER, MARC (1993), *Cadillac Desert: The American West and its Disappearing Water*, revised edition. New York: Penguin.

REUVENY, RAFAEL (2002), 'Economic Growth, Environmental Scarcity, and Conflict,' *Global Environmental Politics*, 2 (1): 83–110.

REVELL, ANDREA (2003), 'Is Japan an Ecological Frontrunner Nation?' *Environmental Politics*, 12 (4): 24–48.

RICHARDSON, DICK (1994), 'The Politics of Sustainable Development,' paper presented to the International Conference on the Politics of Sustainable Development within the European Union, University of Crete, Greece.

RIDLEY, MATT (2010), *The Rational Optimist: How Society Evolves*. New York: Harper Collins.

RÖCKSTROM, JOHAN et al (2009), 'A Safe Operating Space for Humanity,' *Nature*, 461: 472–5.

ROCKWOOD, LARRY L., STEWART, RONALD E., and DIETZ, THOMAS (eds.)

(2008), *Foundations of Environmental Sustainability: The Coevolution of Science and Policy*. New York: Oxford University Press.

ROODMAN, DAVID MALIN (1996), 'Harnessing the Market for the Environment,' pp. 168–87 in Lester R. Brown (ed.), *State of the World 1996*. New York: W. W. Norton.

ROOTES, CHRISTOPHER (2003), 'The Transformation of Environmental Activism: An Introduction,' pp. 1–11 in Christopher Rootes (ed.), *Environmental Protest in Western Europe*. Oxford: Oxford University Press.

ROSENBAUM, WALTER A. (1985), *Environmental Politics and Policy*. Washington, DC: Congressional Quarterly Press.

—— (1995), 'The Bureaucracy and Environmental Policy,' pp. 206–41 in James P. Lester (ed.), *Environmental Politics and Policy: Theories and Evidence*, 2nd edition. Durham, NC: Duke University Press.

RÜDIG, WOLFGANG (2012), 'The Perennial Success of the German Greens,' *Environmental Politics*, 21: 108–30.

RUSSELL, JULIA SCOFIELD (1990), 'The Evolution of an Ecofeminist,' pp. 223–30 in Irene Diamond and GLORIA FEMAN ORENSTEIN (eds.), *Reweaving the World: The Emergence of Ecofeminism*. San Francisco, Calif.: Sierra Club Books.

SABEL, CHARLES, FUNG, ARCHON, and KARKKAINEN, BRADLEY (2000), 'Beyond backyard Environmentalism: How Communities are Quietly Refashioning Environmental Regulation,' *Boston Review*, online at <**http://bostonreview.net/BR24.5/sabel.html**>.

SACHS, WOLFGANG (1999), 'Sustainable Development and the Crisis of Nature:

On the Political Anatomy of an Oxymoron,' pp. 23–41 in Frank Fischer and Maarten A. Hajer (eds.), *Living with Nature: Environmental Politics as Cultural Discourse*. Oxford: Oxford University Press.

SAGOFF, MARK (1988), *The Economy of the Earth*. Cambridge: Cambridge University Press.

—— (2008), *The Economy of the Earth Revisited*. Cambridge: Cambridge University Press.

SAIRINEN, RAUNO (2003), 'The Politics of Regulatory Reform: "New" Environmental Policy Instruments in Finland,' *Environmental Politics*, 12 (4): 24–48.

SALE, KIRKPATRICK (1985), *Dwellers in the Land: The Bioregional Vision*. San Francisco, Calif.: Sierra Club Books.

SANDILANDS, CATRIONA (1999), 'Sex at the Limits,' pp. 79–94 in ERIC DARIER (ed.), *Discourses of the Environment*. Oxford: Basil Blackwell.

SAREWITZ, DANIEL (2011), 'Liberalism's Modest Proposals,' in MICHAEL SHELLENBERGER and TED NORDHAUS (eds.), *Love Your Monsters: Postenvironmentalism and the Anthropocene*. Oakland, Calif.: Breakthrough Institute.

SCHEINBERG, ANNE (2003), 'The Proof of the Pudding: Urban Recycling in North America as a Process of Ecological Modernisation,' *Environmental Politics*, 12 (4): 49–75.

SCHLOSBERG, DAVID (1999), *Environmental Justice and the New Pluralism: The Challenge of Difference for Environmentalism*. Oxford: Oxford University Press.

—— (2009), *Defining Environmental Justice: Theories, Movements, and Nature*. Oxford: Oxford University Press.

—— and RINFRET, SARA (2008), 'Ecological Modernisation, American Style,' *Environmental Politics*, 17: 254–75.

SCHMIDHEINY, STEPHAN (1992), *Changing Course: A Global Business Perspective on Development and the Environment*. Cambridge, Mass.: MIT Press.

SCHMIDT, CHARLES W. (2003), 'Subjective Science: Environmental Cost-Benefit Analysis,' *Environmental Health Perspectives*, 110 (10): 530–2.

SCHUMACHER, E. F. (1973), *Small is Beautiful: Economics as if People Mattered*. New York: Harper and Row.

SCRUGGS, LYLE (2001), 'Is There Really a Link Between Neo-Corporatism and Environmental Performance? Updated Evidence and New Data for the 1980s and 1990s,' *British Journal of Political Science*, 31: 686–92.

—— (2003), *Sustaining Abundance: Environmental Performance in Industrial Democracies*. Cambridge: Cambridge University Press.

—— (2009), 'Democracy and Environmental Protection: An Empirical Analysis,' paper presented at the Conference of the Midwest Political Science Association, Chicago.

SEYFANG, GILL (2006), 'Ecological Citizenship and Sustainable Consumption: Examining Local Food Networks,' *Journal of Rural Studies*, 22: 383–95.

SHEARMAN, DAVID, and WAYNE-SMITH, JOSEPH (2007), *The Climate Change Challenge and the Failure of Democracy*. Westport, Conn.: Praeger.

SHELLENBERGER, MICHAEL and TED NORDHAUS (2007), *Break Through: From the Death of Environmentalism to the Politics of Possibility*. New York: Houghton Mifflin.

—— (eds.) (2011), *Love Your Monsters: Postenvironmentalism and the*

Anthropocene. Oakland, Calif.: Breakthrough Institute.

SHIVA, VANDANA (2000). Poverty and Globalisation. BBC Reith Lecture, online at <**http://news.bbc.co.uk/hi/ english/static/events/reith_2000/ lecture5.stm**>.

—— (2005), *Earth Democracy: Justice, Sustainability and Peace*. Cambridge, MA: South End Press.

SHUTKIN, WILLIAM A. (2000), *The Land That Could Be: Environmentalism and Democracy in the Twenty-First Century*. Cambridge, MA: MIT Press.

SIMON, HERBERT A. (1981), *The Sciences of the Artificial*, 2nd edition. Cambridge, Mass.: MIT Press.

SIMON, JULIAN (1981), *The Ultimate Resource*. Princeton, NJ: Princeton University Press.

—— (1996), *The Ultimate Resource 2*. Princeton, NJ: Princeton University Press.

—— and KAHN, HERMAN (eds.) (1984), *The Resourceful Earth: A Response to Global 2000*. New York: Basil Blackwell.

SMITH, GRAHAM (2003), *Deliberative Democracy and the Environment*. London: Routledge.

—— (2009), *Democratic Innovations: Designing Institutions for Citizen Participation*. Cambridge: Cambridge University Press.

SMITH, V. KERRY (ed.) (1979), *Scarcity and Growth Reconsidered*. Baltimore, Md.: Johns Hopkins University Press for Resources for the Future.

SONNENFELD, DAVID A. and ROCK, MICHAEL T. (2009), 'Ecological Modernisation in Asian and Other Emerging Economies,' pp. 359–71 in Arthur P.J. Mol, David A. Sonnenfeld, and Gert Spaargaren (eds.), *The Ecological Modernisation Reader:*

Environmental Reform in Theory and Practice. Abingdon: Routledge.

SOPER, KATE (1995), *What is Nature? Culture, Politics, and the Non-Human*. Oxford: Basil Blackwell.

SPASH, CLIVE L. (2010), 'The Brave New World of Carbon Trading,' *New Political Economy*, 15: 169–95.

SPETH, JAMES GUSTAVE (2008), *The Bridge at the End of the World: Capitalism, the Environment, and Crossing from Crisis to Sustainability*. New Haven: Yale University Press.

SPRETNACK, CHARLENE (1986), *The Spiritual Dimension of Green Politics*. Santa Fe, N. Mex.: Bear and Co.

STARHAWK, (1987), *Truth or Dare: Encounters with Power, Authority and Mystery*. San Francisco, Calif.: Harper and Row.

STAVINS, ROBERT N. (2002). 'Lessons from the American Experience with Market-Based Environmental Instruments,' in John D. Donahue and Joseph S. Nye, Jr. (eds.), *Market-Based Governance*. Washington, DC: Brookings.

—— (2003), 'Taking Fish to Market,' *Forbes*, April 28.

—— (2009), 'Cap and Trade or Carbon Tax?' *Environmental Forum*, 25 (1): 16.

STERN, NICHOLAS (2006), *The Economics of Climate Change: The Stern Review*. Cambridge: Cambridge University Press.

STEVENSON, HAYLEY (2011), 'Representing 'the Peoples'? Post-neoliberal States in the International Climate Negotiations,' Centre for Deliberative Democracy and Global Governance, Australian National University, Working paper 2011/1.

STEWART, JENNY (2009), *The Dilemmas of Engagement: The Role of Consultation in Governance*. Canberra: ANU E-Press.

STROUP, RICHARD L. (2003), *Eco-nomics: What Everyone Should Know About Economics and the Environment*. Washington, DC: Cato Institute.

—— and MEINERS, ROGER E. (2000), *Cutting Green Tape: Toxic Pollutants, Environmental Regulation, and the Law*. Oakland, Calif.: The Independent Institute.

STROUP, RICHARD L., and SHAW, JANE S. (1993), 'Environmental Harms from Federal Government Policy,' pp. 51–72 in Roger E. Meiners and Bruce Yandle (eds.), *Taking the Environment Seriously*. Lanham, Md.: Rowman and Littlefield.

SUSSKIND, LAWRENCE (2009), 'Deliberative Democracy and Dispute Resolution,' *Ohio State Journal on Dispute Resolution*, 24: 395–406.

——, LEVY, PAUL F., and THOMAS, JENNIFER (2000), *Negotiating Environmental Agreements: How to Avoid Escalating Confrontation, Needless Costs, and Unnecessary Litigation*. Washington, DC: Island Press.

SZARKA, JOSEPH (2012), 'Climate Challenges, Ecological Modernization, and Technological Forcing: Policy Lessons from a Comparative US-EU Analysis,' *Global Environmental Politics*, 12: 87–109.

SZASZ, ANDREW (2011), 'Is Green Consumption Part of the Solution?,' 594–608 in John S. Dryzek, Richard B. Norgaard, and David Schlosberg (eds.), *The Oxford Handbook of Climate Change and Society*. Oxford: Oxford University Press.

TAYLOR, BOB PEPPERMAN (1992), *Our Limits Transgressed*. Lawrence, Kan.: University Press of Kansas.

TAYLOR, JERRY (1993), 'The Growing Abundance of Natural Resources,' pp. 363–78 in David Boaz and Edward H. Crane (eds.), *Market Liberalism: A Paradigm for the 21stCentury*. Washington, DC: Cato Institute.

TESH, SYLVIA N. (1993), 'New Social Movements and New Ideas,' paper presented at the Annual Meeting of the American Political Science Association, Washington, DC, September 2–5.

—— (2000), *Uncertain Hazards: Environmental Activists and Scientific Proof*. Ithaca, NY: Cornell University Press.

THALER, RICHARD H. and CASS SUNSTEIN (2008), *Nudge: Improving Decisions About Health, Wealth, and Happiness*. New Haven: Yale University Press.

THIELE, LESLIE PAUL (1999), *Environmentalism for a New Millennium: The Challenge of Coevolution*. New York: Oxford University Press.

THOMPSON, MICHAEL (1993), 'The Meaning of Sustainable Development,' paper presented to the Conference on Global Governability, London School of Economics.

TODD, DOUGLAS (ed.) (208), *Cascadia: The Elusive Utopia*. Vancouver: Ronsdale Press.

TOKE, DAVID (2011), *Ecological Modernisation and Renewable Energy*. Basingstoke: Palgrave Macmillan.

TORGERSON, DOUGLAS (1994), 'Strategy and Ideology in Environmentalism: A Decentered Approach to Sustainability,' *Industrial and Environmental Crisis Quarterly*, 8: 295–321.

—— (1995), 'The Uncertain Quest for Sustainability: Public Discourse and the Politics of Environmentalism,' pp. 3–20 in Frank Fischer and Michael Black (eds.), *Greening Environmental Policy:*

The Politics of a Sustainable Future. Liverpool: Paul Chapman.

—— (1999), *The Promise of Green Politics: Environmentalism and the Public Sphere.* Durham, NC: Duke University Press.

—— (2003), 'Democracy Through Policy Discourse,' pp. 113–38 in Marten A. Hajer and Hendrik Wagenaar (eds.), *Deliberative Policy Analysis: Understanding Governance in the Network Society.* Cambridge: Cambridge University Press.

—— (2005), 'The Ambivalence of Discourse: Beyond the Administrative Mind,' pp. 97–122 in Robert Paehlke and Douglas Torgerson (eds.), *Managing Leviathan: Environmental Politics and the Administrative State,* 2nd edition. Peterborough, Ontario: Broadview.

—— and PAEHLKE, ROBERT (2005), 'Environmental Administration: Revising the Agenda of Inquiry and Practice,' pp. 3–10 in Robert Paehlke and Douglas Torgerson (eds.), *Managing Leviathan: Environmental Politics and the Administrative State,* 2nd edition. Peterborough, Ontario: Broadview.

UN Department of Economic and Social Affairs (2008), *Innovation for Sustainable Development: Local Case Studies from Africa.* New York: United Nations.

VANDERHEIDEN, STEVE (2008), 'Radical Environmentalism in an Age of Terrorism,' *Environmental Politics,* 17: 299–318.

VATN, ARILD (2000), 'The Environment as Commodity,' *Environmental Values,* 94: 493–509.

VOGEL, DAVID (2003), 'Comparing Environmental Governance: Risk Regulation in the EU and US,' paper presented at the Conference on

Environmental Policy Integration and Sustainable Development, National Europe Centre, Australian National University, November 19–20.

VON FRANTZIUS, INA (2004), 'World Summit on Sustainable Development Johannesburg 2002: A Critical Assessment of the Outcomes,' *Environmental Politics,* 13: 467–73.

VON WEIZSÄCKER, ERNST, LOVINS, AMORY B., and LOVINS, L. HUNTER (1997), *Factor Four: Doubling Wealth—Halving Resource Use.* London: Earthscan.

WACKERNAGEL, MATHIS et al. (2002), 'Tracking the Ecological Overshoot of the Human Economy,' *Proceedings of the National Academy of Sciences,* 99 (14): 9266–71.

WANG, HUA (2011), 'Stakeholder Dialogue as an Institutional Strategy for Sustainable Development,' Washington, DC: World Bank Policy Research Working Paper 5759.

WAPNER, PAUL (1996), *Environmental Activism and World Civic Politics.* Albany: State University of New York Press.

—— (2002a), 'Horizontal Politics: Transnational Environmental Activism and Global Cultural Change,' *Global Environmental Politics,* 2 (2): 37–62.

—— (2002b), 'Ecological Displacement and Transnational Environmental Justice,' *Global Dialogue,* 4 (1), online.

—— (2003), 'World Summit on Sustainable Development: Toward a Post-Jo'burg Environmentalism,' *Global Environmental Politics,* 3 (1): 1–10.

WEALE, ALBERT (1992), *The New Politics of Pollution.* Manchester: Manchester University Press.

—— (2001), 'Can we Democratise Decisions on Risk and the Environment? *Government and Opposition,* 36: 355–78.

WHITE, LYNN, JR. (1967), 'The Historical Roots of our Ecologic Crisis,' *Science*, 155:1203–7.

WIDNER, HELMUT and MEZ, LUTZ (2008), 'German Climate Change Policy: A Qualified Success with Some Flaws,' *Journal of Environment and Development*, 17: 356–78.

WHITE, ROB (1994), 'Green Politics and the Question of Population,' *Journal of Australian Studies*, 40: 27–43.

WIESENTHAL, HERBERT (1993), *Realism in Green Politics: Social Movements and Ecological Reform in Germany*. New York: St. Martin's.

WILDAVSKY, AARON (1988), *The New Politics of the Budgetary Process*. Boston, Mass.: Little, Brown.

—— (1995), *But Is It True? A Citizen's Guide to Environmental Health and Safety Issues*. Cambridge, Mass.: Harvard University Press.

WILLIAMS, BRUCE A., and MATHENY, ALBERT R. (1995), *Democracy, Dialogue, and Environmental Disputes: The Contested Languages of Social Regulation*. New Haven, Conn.: Yale University Press.

WISSENBURG, MARCEL (1998), *Green Liberalism: The Free and the Green Society*. London: UCL Press.

WONG, CATHERINE MEI LING (2012), 'The Developmental State in Ecological Modernization and the Politics of Ecological Framings: The Case of Singapore and its Implications for East Asia,' *Nature and Culture*, 7: 95–119.

World Bank (2012), *Inclusive Green Growth: The Pathway to Sustainable Development*. Washington, DC: The World Bank.

World Commission on Environment and Development (1987), *Our Common Future*. Oxford: Oxford University Press.

YANDLE, BRUCE (1993), 'Community Markets to Control Nonpoint Source Pollution,' pp. 185–207 in Roger E. Meiners and Bruce Yandle (eds.), *Taking the Environment Seriously*. Lanham, Md.: Rowman and Littlefield.

ZACCAI, EDWIN (2012), 'Over Two Decades in Pursuit of Sustainable Development: Influence, Transformation, Limits,' *Environmental Development*, 1: 79–90.

ZHANG, LEI, MOL, ARTHUR P.J., and SONNENFELD, DAVID A. (2007), 'The Interpretation of Ecological Modernisation in China,' *Environmental Politics*, 16: 659–68.

INDEX